PEOPLE OF PASSION

PEOPLE OF PASSION

WHAT THE CHURCHES TEACH
ABOUT SEX

ELIZABETH STUART

AND

ADRIAN THATCHER

MOWBRAY

Mowbray
A Cassell imprint
Wellington House, 125 Strand, London WC2R 0BB
PO Box 605, Herndon, VA 20172

First published 1997

British Library Cataloguing-in-Publication Data
A catalogue record for this book is available from the British Library.

ISBN 0-264-67362-X

Acknowledgements

The extract from The Book of Common Prayer of 1662, the rights of which are vested in
the Crown in perpetuity within the United Kingdom, is reproduced by permission of
Cambridge University Press, Her Majesty's Printers.

Biblical quotations not otherwise marked are from the Revised English Bible © 1989 Oxford
and Cambridge University Presses.

A few quotations are taken from the Revised Standard Version (RSV) of the Bible © 1971
and 1952 and from the New Revised Standard Version (NRSV) of the Bible © 1989.

Typeset by York House Typographic Ltd, London
Printed and bound in Great Britain by Biddles Ltd, Guildford and King's Lynn

CONTENTS

1

PEOPLE OF PASSION

1.1 WHO IS THIS BOOK FOR?

People of Passion tells the reader about what Christians have said, and are saying now, about sex.

We have written this book for four broad groups of people. First, clergy, ministers and priests are faced with pastoral situations related to sexuality almost daily. They are the first to recognize the need to be updated, without having to read lengthy reports or technical theology. Lay women and men are also increasingly being asked to contribute to discussion in their churches or denominations about sexuality. Almost every mainstream Christian denomination in Europe, the USA and throughout Christendom is struggling with issues to do with sex and sexuality at the present time.

Second, the study of Christianity and sexuality is regularly appearing on the curriculum in universities, colleges, seminaries and schools throughout the world. Students (and of course their teachers) need a guide book that maps out the terrain, sketches the contours of contemporary controversies, and is easy to read. This book is written as a 'guide' in two senses of that term. It is an introduction to the changes going on in and among the churches in their attitudes to sex and sexuality. And it is a guide in the more personal sense that it offers some tentative pointers through the journey of sexual discovery that each of us inevitably makes in the course of our lives.

Third, millions of people who have abandoned the habit of regular church attendance still entertain respect for what they understand as 'Christian morality' while having also abandoned what they see as outdated and irrelevant aspects of it. Their lives have been touched, perhaps adversely, by Christian influences, and they will be agreeably surprised by the rethinking currently going on in some of the churches. And fourth, professional people outside the churches need an authoritative source which keeps them in touch with contemporary developments in Christian teaching about issues to do with sex and sexuality. Therapists and counsellors may find the book invaluable in discovering new possibilities in Christian teaching which can be seen to promote human well-being. Journalists frequently find themselves having to report on and analyse church documents, pronouncements and debates on various aspects of sexuality. A range of professional people need information about the changes going on at present among the churches with regard to their sexual teaching.

This book then is about the exciting, and sometimes surprising, developments that are taking place in Christian teaching about sex and sexuality. While it is a work of *theology*, we promise to explain all the theological terms we use. It is not a book written principally for other theologians. Indeed it is a theological book for non-theologians, for people who want to explore issues about sex and sexuality from a Christian point of view but feel they may lack knowledge of the historical background and the contemporary developments.

1.2 WHY WAS THIS BOOK WRITTEN?

We have suggested that many people have a need for information about sex and sexuality as Christians understand it. But the need is for more than information. A second reason for writing the book is our belief that the Christian faith is most truly itself when it touches the lives of people who are not conventionally religious at all. We have chosen to place ourselves in the near-impossible position of loyalty to the Christian tradition and loyalty to all those people who have been alienated by it or who think, for whatever reason, it has nothing to offer them. Some people have given up on Christian faith because they feel 'stigmatized' by versions of it that radiate censure instead of love. They may not have lived up to the impossible demands of what they perceive to be Christian teaching in the area of sexuality. They may feel a sense of animosity or reproach directed toward them because of minor deviations from conventional sexual norms. Simply to be divorced, or lesbian, or unmarried but cohabiting, or single and sexually active, or to find oneself bisexual or transsexual, or gay, and also to be a member of a church congregation, may be to risk censure and 'dis-ease'. But what if the churches are entrusted with a message which affirms everyone who feels stigmatized by, and unacceptable to, the churches themselves? Loyalty to Christian faith requires taking sides within the internal struggles of the churches to reconsider their teaching in the light of the contemporary questions, dilemmas, needs and experiences of men and women who are rightly suspicious of, and impatient with, tired reaffirmations of past positions.

A major example of the shifts which will be described in this book is the institution of marriage (see Chapter 3) and the means of entry into it. It is a simple and traditional matter to affirm that all sexual activity is to be confined to marriage. Yet the most common age at which women first marry in Britain is 26, and for men 28.[1] Do the churches seriously assume that women and men will not have sexual intercourse until then? Arguments in the 1960s about whether there could be 'sex before marriage' still assumed that marriage was the sole context for sexual experience. Reliable contraception has enabled millions of people to separate sexual activity from *procreative* activity. Once sexual activity and procreative activity have been separated, then love-making can be valued for its own sake, and the experience of lesbian women and gay men is inevitably seen in a fresh light. The Methodist Church noted in its 1990 Conference Report:

> In recent years, advances in contraception have helped heterosexuals to celebrate sexuality and to engage in sexual activity for itself and not only for its procreative purpose. It is this separation of sexual intercourse from procreation which has brought about a freedom, known already by lesbians and gay men, to value sexual activity for itself.[2]

The point here is merely to illustrate that the later age of first marriages and the widespread availability of contraception are social facts which themselves give rise to new questions and opportunities for re-examining and re-envisioning Christian teaching. There is, of course, a vast difference between acknowledging the sexual practices of contemporary societies and conforming or capitulating to them (some of our Christian friends will of course accuse us of doing precisely that).

A third reason for writing this book is our conviction that secular humanism, or for that matter any other influential world-view or 'value-system', is unable to deal adequately with sexuality. Whatever the internal difficulties to be found in Christian teaching and its evolution, secular alternatives inevitably ignore the vision of sexuality rooted firmly in God's life and love. Attempts to found say, a sexual ethic on 'pragmatism',[3] using the values of respect and responsibility, or on 'democracy' and 'autonomy',[4] omit too much. The first ignores the inevitable link between our sexuality and our spirituality (see Chapter 9); the second ignores our God-given status as persons or beings 'in relation'. And both ignore a heritage of Christian thought which is waiting to be reappropriated.

1.3 HOW TO USE THIS BOOK

There are ten chapters, each on a broad theme, and within each theme particular issues are dealt with. Our approach to each chapter is guided by three objectives derived from our reasons for writing the book. First, each chapter contains reference to biblical, historical and traditional sources. Second, there is reference, as appropriate, to contemporary documents and reports on sexuality currently in use in the churches. Third, assuming the churches' understanding of their teaching about sexuality is not static, we seek to contribute appropriately and overtly to contemporary discussions and controversies.

Much of the literature on theology and sexuality begins with a chapter on the use of the Bible. A feature of the present work is the location of our chapter on the use of the Bible at the end instead of the beginning. This enables us to cite the preceding chapters as examples of how the Bible might be used in handling the issues in the book. A comprehensive bibliography is provided for each chapter and is found at the end of the book. In order to make the book 'user-friendly' for our readers (the majority of whom may *not* have a background in theology), there is a glossary of terms. From this point on, every term shown in bold the first time it appears in the body of each chapter is found in the glossary. Extensive cross-referencing is used (chapter sections being shown in bold), there is a detailed and comprehensive index, and each chapter concludes with summaries.

So there are at least three ways of reading this book. It is written as a narrative with chapters in a sequence. So it can be read like any other book. Or, using it as a reference book, readers may work from the detailed table of contents at the beginning or from the extended subject index, looking up particular subjects of interest. Thirdly, it may be read as a book of essays. Readers interested in a broad theme, e.g. 'the body', may begin with Chapter 4, and then use the cross-references and index to broaden out and pursue particular interests.

1.4 WHAT'S IN THE BOOK

The themes of the book are the themes of the contemporary ferment over **sexuality**. They are described in the next few pages in order to provide readers with an overview of the whole book and help them decide how to read it. The remainder of this chapter sets the scene for what follows. It explains why we call Christians 'people of passion' (**1.5**) and grounds Christian teaching about **sex** firmly in the love of God revealed by Christ. It introduces the important notions of **patriarchy**, **property**, **purity**, **parousia** and procreation (**1.6–1.10**) and indicates how a resolution of the problems posed by each is essential for the 'rekindling of passionate love' (**1.11**).

Chapter 2, 'Passionate **ethics**', sets out the framework of a sexual ethics for the 'people of passion'. We warn against some of the dangers of ethical theorizing (**2.1**), and then consider the range of approaches to ethics within Christian theology. All theologians use the Bible when discussing sexual teaching (**2.2**), but sometimes they use **natural law** ethics as well (**2.3**), or other approaches such as **virtue** ethics (**2.4**), narrative ethics (**2.5**), ecclesial ethics (**2.6**), **situation ethics** (**2.7**) and feminist ethics (**2.8**). These theories and approaches are introduced early in the book both to indicate something of the complexity of the issues and to indicate our own position, that of 'passionate ethics' (**2.12**). The relevance of the theories is demonstrated by contrasting how, when applied to issues such as **masturbation**, abortion and contraception (**2.9–2.11**), they yield different results.

'Relationships' is the theme of Chapter 3. The main biblical symbols for marriage and their entanglement with patriarchy are traced (**3.2**), and the development over the centuries of the churches' understanding of marriage (**3.3**). Analysis of church reports suggests a rethinking of marriage which is described in terms of four trends: from procreation to personal union (**3.4**); from patriarchy to parity (**3.5**); from 'sole relationship' to 'soul-relationship' (**3.6**), and from event to process (**3.7**) The 'goods of marriage' stated by Augustine are reinterpreted and reaffirmed, especially the good of children and the necessity of parental commitment to them (**3.8**).

Unlike the good of children, the goods of 'fidelity' and 'sacrament' are held to be available *outside* marriage (**3.9**). The lives of single people are affirmed without being justified with reference to the married norm (**3.10**).

The 'body' and 'power' are the themes of Chapters 4 and 5. The separation of the human body from the sense of self is blamed on a deep-seated **dualism** (**4.1**). The awareness of the body in the Old and New Testaments is examined, and the question why the 'body-friendliness' of the first Christians did not last is addressed (**4.2**). The growth of dualism, **asceticism** and sexual renunciation is described (**4.3**). An alternative approach to the body is made through 'body theology' (**4.4**), the main emphasis of which is that God became embodied in Jesus Christ (the doctrine of **incarnation**). A renewed theological awareness of the body affirms masturbation (**4.5**), enables a 'body-affirming model' of care for the elderly and disabled (**4.6**), and confronts judgmental **metaphors** associated with **HIV/AIDS** (**4.7**).

The theme of power and its misuse is one of the most neglected issues in sexual ethics. Christian teaching has contributed to and reinforced relationships which are unequal and **hierarchical**, and encouraged submission to the holders of power whether in society, church or family. The difference between authority and force (**5.1**) and between 'power-over' and 'power-with' (**5.2**) is outlined, and church reports from three continents which acknowledge sexual sin as the misuse of power are welcomed (**5.3**). The power of sin over individuals, even when 'consent' is given, is exposed (**5.4**). Harassment and rape are described as the misuse of male power, and we note the disturbing connection between sexual violence and the theological legitimation of female submission and ethics of passive obedience (**5.5–5.6**). The plight of Susanna is considered, a scriptural case study of male malevolence towards women (**5.7**). Other forms of the sexual misuse of power are considered (**5.8–5.10**); the evil of pornography is analysed in the same way (**5.11**). The sheepfold of John 10 becomes the model for the ultimate place of safety from violence, and Christ as the 'door of the sheepfold' (John 10.7) is contrasted with the 'doormat theology' which colludes with violence (**5.12**).

Another major theme of the book is that of **gender**, assessed in Chapter 6. The way we are encouraged to express ourselves as women or men, at home, at work, at leisure or at church, is mediated to us. While gender is a well-trodden theme in sociology, theology is only just beginning to think about it. The male/female binary opposition is located in ancient dualisms which depict women as passive and inferior (**6.1**). The distinction between sex and gender is described (**6.2**) and **androgyny** rejected (**6.3**). Some 'models of masculinity' are criticized; others, especially that of Jesus, are commended (**6.4**). The privileging of men's experience in contemporary theology and church documents is traced (**6.5**) and the recasting of theology on the basis of *women's* experience, i.e., **feminist theology**, is described (**6.6**). A positive assessment of recent theories of gender and their challenge to theology is made (**6.7**).

Nothing could be more central to the credibility of Christian teaching about sex than the account it gives of **homosexuality** and the understanding it shows, or fails to show, of the experience of **lesbian**, **gay** and **bisexual** people. In 1991 the House of Bishops of the Church of England said 'The story of the Church's attitude to homosexuals has too often been one of prejudice, ignorance and oppression. All of us need to acknowledge that, and to repent for any part we may have had in it.'[5] Many publications on the subject have appeared since then, including the new *Catechism of the Catholic Church* which says of 'homosexual acts' that 'under no circumstances can they be approved'.[6] Chapter 7 describes three approaches to homosexuality among the churches. The first is that it is an 'intrinsic moral evil' (**7.2**). The critical response to this position (**7.3**) analyses the connection between sex and pleasure, the alleged 'purpose' of sex, the homosexual 'condition', the distinction between orientation and practice, and the use of scripture. The second approach regards homosexuality as a 'falling short' (**7.4**). The critical response to this position (**7.5**) examines the role of the idea of '**complementarity**' in this approach, the relationship between homosexuality and culture, the fear of bisexuality and the influence of homophobia. The third approach, which is adopted in the book, regards homosexual activity as morally neutral (**7.6**). The lack of influence of **lesbian and gay theology** in church reports (**7.7**), together with the lack of mention of **transvestites** and transsexuals (**7.8**), is noted.

Chapter 8 sets out a theology of **desire**. How can our desires be affirmed and owned, when they are so powerful and dangerous? The chapter looks at how sexual desire became feared as a subversive, destabilizing force (**8.1**). A contrary view, the celebration of desire, is found in the Song of Songs (**8.2**). Contemporary theological writing analyses desire in terms of deep bodily knowledge, the yearning for **mutuality** and right relationship, anger as the passionate desire for justice, embodiment and play (**8.3**). The effect on our desires of living in a late-capitalist and consumerist society which stimulates desire and converts it into greed is noted, together with an analysis of the perversion of desire as **lust**, and the place in our lives of sexual fantasy (**8.4**). The danger associated with sexual desire is illustrated by its absence from church reports (**8.5**). Finally it is suggested that desire, properly ordered, may be the location of our most intense experiences of God (**8.6**).

Chapter 9 links our sexuality with our spirituality. This is by now a common theme in the churches' teaching. The Methodist report referred to earlier acknowledges the 'spiritual elements' of our sexuality;[7] a Church of Scotland report speaks of 'a spiritual dimension' to human sexuality derived from our creation in God's image,[8] and goes on to say it

> **is not an additional adjunct, an 'optional extra'. It is an integral part of being human.** It may or may not be expressed in genital relationships, but it is a basic constituent of our *whole* being, of our personhood. Jesus came to live on earth as fully human as well as fully divine; He was a **whole** person, not only spiritual but with mind and body also, and that necessarily includes sexuality.[9]

Three approaches to spirituality are described (**9.1**) and Christian spirituality anchored in the whole-hearted love of God and neighbour (**9.2**). Church reports are commended for the strong connections they make between spirituality and sexuality (**9.3**). The connections guarantee that there is a powerful sexual dimension to our spiritual life and a powerful spiritual dimension to our sex life. The qualities essential to both are then described (**9.4–9.7**). Possible stages of spiritual growth (normality, reaching out to others, purification, illumination and union) are outlined and extended to a Christian understanding of sexuality and the quest for sexual maturity. This is called *embodied holiness* (**9.8**). The practice of embodied holiness is 'passionate spirituality', and the practical living out of passionate spirituality is explored (**9.9**).

Books and reports about Christianity and sexuality generally have an early chapter on how the authors regard the Bible and how they intend to use it. This is because one of the most sensitive issues among Christians is *how to read it*. What the Bible says and what the Bible means are different questions. Neither question is avoided in the book, but the question of how to read the Bible, unusually in this book, is left to the last chapter, so that all the preceding chapters can

be taken as a case study of a way of reading the Bible which we
commend and which we have ourselves adopted. We will not just be
interrogating the Bible, but letting the Bible interrogate us, agreeing
with Stephen Barton's suggestion that the appropriate attitude of
Christians toward the Bible is like that of an orchestra toward the
score of a symphony,[10] and that it is

> those who know of what just and loving Christian practice consists
> who will be best equipped to read the Bible in a life-giving and
> liberating way. It is those who are themselves transformed and
> being transformed according to the image of Christ who will be best
> able to perform the scriptures in ways which bring life and Christ-
> like transformation to human sexuality.[11]

Christians who believe the Bible to be God's Word, whose authority is
unaffected by the cultural and historical circumstances surrounding
its composition, are criticized. They ignore disagreements about
what the Bible says and treat the Bible as a rule book. But both
conservative and liberal Christians are held to use the Bible in
unhelpful ways when discussing sexuality, one group using it as a
source of proof-texts, the other as a relay race (**10.1**). The use of the
Bible in feminist theology and **liberation theology** is described and
preferred, and a 'strategy' for reading the Bible, involving suspicion,
remembrance, proclamation and imagination, is advocated (**10.2**).
The experience of oppression suffered by lesbian and gay Christians
is built into a 'queer **hermeneutics**' which emphasizes both the
solidarity of Bible-reading Christians with oppression, but also the
Bible as friend, sometimes challenging or confronting us (**10.3**). A
range of problems associated with the liberationist strategy for reading the Bible is examined (**10.4**).

1.5 PEOPLE OF PASSION

This chapter is about 'People of Passion'. The book of that title has
now been described. What about the people? Christians all believe
that Jesus Christ died by crucifixion nearly two thousand years ago,
and that his passion or suffering has a special significance for
everyone everywhere, whether Christians or not. This significance
can be stated in two simple ways. First, his willingness to suffer death
is taken as a **revelation** of the limitless love of God. 'There is no
greater love than this, that someone should lay down his life for his
friends' (John 15.13) And second, Jesus, as a truly human being,
made a response to God with his life and death in which all human

beings can share. His laying down of his life was not for himself: it was *for us*.[12] The passion of Christ is the meeting point and mingling of divine and human loving, and notwithstanding the hi-jacking of the symbol of the cross to fight wars, glorify pain and legitimize humiliation[13] and so on, it roots the Christian faith in the giving and receiving of love. The most sacred act of Christians, that of the eucharist, is a celebration of, and a sharing in, God's love for us, and our love for God. And reflection on the meaning of Christ's death led St John to conclude that God is best understood as 'love', and that the Christian faith is the sharing of it, and the sharing in it (1 John 4.7–21). This is the basis of 'passionate ethics' (see Chapter 2) and Christian spirituality (see **9.2**).

We are entitled to wonder then, why the understanding of the faith as a celebration and sharing of love has not been more prominent in the churches' teaching about sex. The meaning of Christ's 'passion' is not confined to his terrible suffering, for passion is also ardent love, indeed intense emotion, and it is completely appropriate to speak, on the basis of Jesus Christ, of God's passionate love for us. The description of the churches as 'people of passion' draws attention to them as passionate lovers of God, of their neighbours, and of each other. Why then, people may ask, is there little evidence of passionate love in Christian teaching about sexuality?

1.6 PATRIARCHY (*and see* **2.3.5**, **3.5**, **6.6**)

The answer to this vexed question is difficult, and is given here by introducing five themes. The first is 'patriarchy'. 'Patriarchy' literally means the 'rule' (*arche*) of the 'fathers' (*pater* = 'father'). In a strict anthropological sense, a patriarchal society is one in which the father is the head of the family, descent is traced through the father's side of the family, and the social system is governed by men.[14] In contemporary sociological and theological writing the term picks out the social power of men over women. In theology the term is also used to expose the domination of men over women in the Bible, church history, doctrine, liturgy and language, theology, priesthood, ministry and church order. And patriarchy can also mean the 'male-centred' or **androcentric** thinking so deeply established in church and world alike that it passes itself off as something natural, obvious and 'normative'.

Patriarchy is above all male control. Patriarchy wrecks relationships between men and women because it permits them only on male terms, and it thinks and writes about them on the basis of male experience. There are countless examples of patriarchal thought and practice in church and biblical history, but the two which will be discussed here are contemporary. One is a poster, the other a letter. One of the authors of this book, on holiday on the Greek island of Kos, came across a poster affixed to the front door of Kos Cathedral, a Greek Orthodox church, which read, in Greek and English,

> Women!
> Innumerable souls are scandalized
> and perish because of nudism.
> Fear scandals and God
> and be decently dressed.

An ugly cluster of patriarchal attitudes spills out from this poster. It is clearly written by a man. The 'generalized' mode of address, 'Women!', suggests that for this male mind women themselves are the scandal (i.e., 'cause of offence') and not simply women sun-bathers. What settled dispositions towards women are conveyed by these waspish double sentences? There is obvious panic at the sight of partially naked women's bodies. Women are to blame for men's feelings towards them. Women, not men, are responsible for the perishing of men's souls. That men's souls perish because of the exposure of women's bodies represents a massive internalization of guilt within men about finding women desirable. Men's experience is primary. Men have the right to tell generalized 'women' how to behave. Women are expected to listen. Causing offence to men is as bad as not fearing God. Women ought not to have the freedom not to wear what they don't want to wear. Visitors to the church and passers-by cannot but be struck by the message of fear and censure that 'greets' them as they approach the house of God. The author is presumably unaware that his attitudes to women are likely to cause women offence.

This is an extreme example of patriarchy, yet the attitudes which come into view through this poster have been prevalent for much of Christian history. The trivial matter of what not to wear on beaches exposes more than parts of bodies. The flaunted patriarchal mind is revealed in all its frustration and anger. The second example also begins with a generalizing mode of address, this time to 'women throughout the world'. It is the *Letter of Pope John Paul II to Women*.[15] This letter is significant for many reasons beyond the concerns of this book and there is much within it for which all Christians, male and female, can be grateful. But our concern is with patriarchy, and this letter will be used both as an admission of patriarchy, and as evidence for it.

In a remarkable passage the Pope comes very near to an apology for the treatment women have received from the Catholic Church throughout its history. The Pope laments that

> we are heirs to a history which has conditioned us to a remarkable extent. In every time and place, this conditioning has been an obstacle to the progress of women. Women's dignity has often been unacknowledged and their prerogatives misrepresented; they have often been relegated to the margins of society and even reduced to servitude. This has prevented women from truly being themselves and it has resulted in a spiritual impoverishment of humanity.[16]

Many injustices are being recognized here (even if very generally). Men are impoverished too whenever women are demeaned by them. As far as 'personal rights' are concerned, the Pope says 'there is an urgent need to achieve real equality in every area'.[17] How did women's oppression come about? The Pope reflects on this and says:

> Certainly it is no easy task to assign the blame for this, considering the many kinds of **cultural conditioning** which down the centuries have shaped ways of thinking and acting. And if objective blame, especially in particular historical contexts, has belonged to not just a few members of the Church, for this I am truly sorry. May this regret be transformed, on the part of the whole Church, into a renewed commitment of fidelity to the Gospel vision. When it comes to setting women free from every kind of exploitation and domination, the Gospel contains an ever-relevant message which goes back to the attitude of Jesus Christ himself. Transcending the established norms of his own culture, Jesus treated women with openness, respect, acceptance and tenderness. In this way he honoured the dignity which women have always possessed according to God's plan and in his love. As we look to Christ at the end of this second millennium, it is natural to ask ourselves: how much of his message has been heard and acted upon?[18]

The Pope does not use the term 'patriarchy' in his *Letter*, but patriarchy *is* that 'history which has conditioned us to a remarkable extent'. The *Letter* recognizes the evil of patriarchy but without naming it or recognizing its presence throughout the text. Nonetheless the admissions are significant, and there is a vision here of a future time where a rediscovery of the attitudes of Jesus to women will change the Church and the world. Unfortunately the Church has been a principal conveyor of the very attitudes which the Pope now finds objectionable. And women are patronized as much as they are affirmed in this letter. In a list of 'Thank you's to women, what are women to make of 'Thank you, every woman, for the simple fact of being a woman!'?[19] The fact that Christ only chose men to be his disciples is still allowed to be the grounds for excluding women from 'the ministerial priesthood'. There are disturbing 'role distinctions' between men and women which correspond to the different significances accorded to Peter and to Mary in that Church.[20] The Pope seems unaware of the hurt caused to women over centuries by the belief that the purpose of their lives is serving men and children, for he finds 'the genius of women' among 'those ordinary women who reveal the gift of their womanhood by placing themselves at the service of others in their everyday lives. For in giving themselves to others each day women fulfil their deepest vocation.'[21] These papal reflections take us to the heart of issues discussed in Chapters 5 and 6. Our interest in this book is confined to the churches' teaching about sex and sexuality, and unfortunately the *Letter of Pope John Paul II to Women* is as much a reflection, as a refutation, of patriarchy.

1.7 PROPERTY

One of the main features of patriarchy in the area of sexual relations is that women are the property of men. If human relationships are blighted by being carried on between the 'owners' and the 'owned', they can never be fully mutual. Two examples will be taken, one from each Testament of the Bible, to illustrate what is meant by 'sexual property'. We take the position that the gospel of Jesus Christ necessarily confronts every social system, including those taken for granted in biblical and contemporary periods. Patriarchy is no compulsory component of Christian faith, and in this connection the Pope is right to say, 'As we look to Christ at the end of this second millennium, it is natural to ask ourselves: how much of his message has been heard and acted upon?' The more that message is heard, the more superfluous patriarchy becomes.

Here are some of the Ten Commandments of the Old Testament:

> Remember to keep the sabbath day holy. You have six days to labour and do all your work; but the seventh day is a sabbath of the LORD your God; that day you must not do any work, neither you,

nor your son or your daughter, your slave or your slave-girl, your cattle, or the alien residing among you ...
  Do not commit adultery.
  Do not steal.
  Do not give false evidence against your neighbour.
  Do not covet your neighbour's household: you must not covet your neighbour's wife, his slave, his slave-girl, his ox, his donkey, or anything that belongs to him. (Exodus 20.8–10, 14–17)

The Ten Commandments were once very familiar throughout Christendom and with the **Sermon on the Mount** they were regarded as the basis of all Christian morality. They are being used here simply as a clue to unchallenged assumptions about the ownership of human property by male householders. The commandment not to work on the sabbath day has much to say about contemporary patterns of work. According to the Old Testament not even slaves are permitted to work on the sabbath. The commandment assumes the householder has authority over his household, which includes children, slaves, animals and foreign guests. The commandment against adultery is a commandment forbidding the violation of the householder's property, needed to secure a legitimate heir. Intercourse between a married woman and an outsider 'constituted a theft of her husband's right to legitimate offspring'.[22] The moral wrongness of adultery is therefore that it is a form of stealing, which the next commandment expressly forbids. And the commandment forbidding covetousness reinforces the position of householders as owners of human property, wives, male and female slaves, animals and inanimate objects. The Ten Commandments assume that wives and children are owned, and that householders have authority over them.

This understanding of the household is also found in the New Testament and has remained constant for most of Christian history. The household is hierarchically ordered, from the male householder down through to his wife, children, slaves and other property. This hierarchical household is assumed in the New Testament. In the letters of the New Testament there are three '**Household Codes**'[23] which give instructions about how members of a household are to behave towards each other. They concentrate on three pairs of relationships, those between wives and husbands, children and parents, and slaves and masters. One of these states:

Wives, be subject to your husbands; that is your Christian duty.
Husbands, love your wives and do not be harsh with them. Chil-

dren, obey your parents in everything, for that is pleasing to God and is the Christian way. Fathers, do not exasperate your children, in case they lose heart. Slaves, give entire obedience to your earthly masters, ... knowing that there is a master who will give you an inheritance as a reward for your service. Christ is the master you must serve ... Masters, be just and fair to your slaves, knowing that you too have a master in heaven. (Colossians 3.18–4.1)

This passage of scripture, like hundreds of others, shows that morality cannot simply be read off the pages of the Bible, for some moral guidance found in the Bible is, from our different (though not superior) vantage point, plainly immoral. Relations between husbands and wives are locked into a broader hierarchy which raises no questions about the morality of slave-keeping, and borrows language from the master–slave relationships to speak of the relationship between slaves and Christ himself. The subjection of wives to husbands is assumed. The family-head has responsibilities to his household. He must love his wife, not exasperate his children, and be just (!) and fair to his slaves. These relationships are unequal, and they are characterized by hierarchy and property. One commentator writing about the Household Codes says their themes lie in both Jewish and **Hellenistic ethics,**

> where the well-ordered household is the microcosm of the well-ordered state. In a highly hierarchical and patriarchal culture, the fundamental equality of persons is rarely glimpsed, so it is not surprising that social order can be conceived only in terms of the leadership and control of free males over females and of elders over their children.[24]

But such relationships cannot be fully mutual, however well-intentioned the householder may be in 'holding' his house. While vulnerable people need protection, whether old or young, especially in a patriarchal society, it cannot be right to be owned.

1.8 PURITY (*and see* **4.2, 7.3.5**)

Purity is one of the trickiest concepts in ethics. A 'pure' substance is one which has a uniform composition, like pure oxygen, or is free from pollutants like clean air. Purity means 'untainted by pollution and dirt', which are 'impurities'. Soap powder commercials rely on the association, thousands of years old, between dirt and disgust. According to some uses of 'purity' a person who is *racially* pure is one who is of 'unmixed blood'. A person who is *sexually* pure is one who is a virgin, untainted by the stain or dirt of sexual intercourse and the body fluids associated with it. Brides in white wedding dresses emphasize the point, usually with forgotten irony. The charge of impurity is almost certain to offend the people it is laid against because it necessarily associates them or their actions with an instinct of disgust.

Now, in our quest for reasons why the people of passion largely turned away from sexual love, purity is a central idea. The Book of Leviticus in the Old Testament contains rules governing discharges from the body. What is a contemporary reader of the Bible, unfamiliar with the Israelite past, to make of the following passages?

> When a man has emitted semen, he must bathe his whole body in water and be unclean till evening. Every piece of clothing or leather on which there is any semen is to be washed and remain unclean till evening. (Leviticus 15.16–17)

> When a woman has her discharge of blood, her impurity will last for seven days; anyone who touches her will be unclean till evening. Everything on which she lies or sits during her impurity will be unclean, and whoever touches her bedding must wash his clothes, bathe in water, and remain unclean till evening. (Leviticus 15.19–21)

> If a man has intercourse with a man as with a woman, both commit an abomination. They must be put to death; their blood be on their own heads! (Leviticus 20.13)

These, and several other Old Testament passages, read strangely to us, yet we too have our secular equivalents to these purity laws.[25] The practices of homosexual men are generally regarded by **heterosexual** men as an abomination, and in several countries of the world the death penalty for homosexual practice is still in force. TV adverts for tampons in the United Kingdom are absurdly coy and there is scarcely a man alive who would own up to a semen stain on his furniture or trousers. Christians never quite managed to distinguish between the new religion based on the grace of God in Jesus Christ and the older Jewish religion based on Law.

An influential study of the attitudes towards sexuality among New Testament Christians shows conclusively that they rejected Old Testament purity laws. Rather,

> from the New Testament onward, all genuinely Christian ethics had to explain themselves in terms of purity of the heart, which is itself defined primarily as willingness to respect and unwillingness to

harm the neighbor ... The cross represents God's willingness to be least and weakest and creates thereby a model for all Christian behavior characterized by love and humility. It is to this insight that the language of purity, when used positively by New Testament authors, most often refers.[26]

The importance of this conclusion can hardly be over-stressed. Christian faith introduces a basis for sexual morality which renders purity laws redundant and is actually at odds with the strong currents of pagan asceticism in the ancient world which taught that the body was dirty or evil. That is why no purity code can be binding on Christians.[27] 'To be specific', continues Countryman, 'the gospel allows no rule against the following, in and of themselves: masturbation, nonvaginal heterosexual intercourse, bestiality, **polygamy**, homosexual acts, or erotic art and literature.'[28] What happened was that once Christians began to realize that the return of Jesus Christ at the end of time was less imminent than they had supposed, they returned to the Old Testament for moral guidance and the old Levitical rules began to be reimposed. They reinforced a sense of the intrinsic impurity of the sexual organs together with the activities, functions, fluids and pleasures associated with them. The abolition of ritual purity represents not an abandonment of biblical teaching but a necessary recovery of it which will transform conventional attitudes to the body (see **4.2**) whether religious or secular. In this respect the Jesus of the scriptures and the Jesus of contemporary sexual teaching in the churches may not be found to coincide, for, as Countryman says,

> The Jesus who regularly preferred the company of the impure to that of the religious authorities of his day or who predicted that tax collectors and prostitutes would more readily gain entrance into the reign of God than the devout would not have been a popular figure in the church itself in most of the succeeding Christian centuries. He would have been seen as undermining public morality; and, insofar as the church itself adopted a purity ethic from the fourth century onward, that accusation would have been apt.[29]

1.9 PAROUSIA

Mention was made in the previous section of the unexpected delay in the return of Christ, or 'parousia'. The fact that the earliest Christians believed that Christ would return *during their lifetimes* made an enormous contribution to the loss of passion among the 'people of passion'. St Paul had to deal with a group of Christians in Corinth who, because of their expectation of the parousia, were preaching the renunciation of marriage, abstinence from sexual intercourse within marriage and separation from pagan partners. Paul allowed marriage but advocated singleness.

> I should like everyone to be as I myself am ... To the unmarried and to widows I say this: it is a good thing if like me they stay as they are; but if they do not have self-control, they should marry. It is better to be married than burn with desire. (1 Corinthians 7.7–8)[30]

Paul expresses his preference for singleness undogmatically. Unfortunately as the authority of his letters increased, and awareness of the reasons for his preference diminished, he was assumed to be saying that **celibacy** is always better than marriage. This conclusion can even be said to be latent in Paul's own teaching for, as Peter Brown, historian of early Christian attitudes to sexuality, says,

> What was notably lacking, in Paul's letter, was the warm faith shown by contemporary pagans and Jews that the sexual urge, although disorderly, was capable of socialization and of ordered, even warm, expression within marriage. The dangers of *porneia*, of potential immorality brought about by sexual frustration, were allowed to hold the center of the stage. By this essentially negative, even alarmist, strategy, Paul left a fatal legacy to future ages.[31]

This 'fatal legacy' was responsible for the higher valuation of celibacy over marriage, the regulation of sexual intercourse within marriage, the relegation of marriage to a defence against desire, and the reputation for marriage that it was for spiritual failures defeated by carnal lusts.

1.10 PROCREATION (*and see* 3.4)

One more reason for the awkwardness of much of the Christian tradition in the face of sexual desire is the idea that sexual intercourse, in order to be legitimate, must not only be confined to marriage, but must be very strictly controlled. It must have a *purpose*, which must be that of producing children.[32] This gives having sex an earnestness that undermines completely the suggestion that it might be playful and light-hearted (see 8.3.5). By the time of Augustine (354–430) men's desire for women (whether in marriage or not) is thought to arise directly from the '**fall**' (see 8.1). Sex in Eden, speculated Augustine, would have been lust-free and so truly happy even though, as he admitted, we have no knowledge of what it might have been like. Sex after the fall, however, has become contaminated by lust. Proof of the fallen state of men is their inability to stop getting erections, for

> ... if there had been no sin, marriage would have been worthy of the happiness of paradise, and would have given birth to children to be loved, and yet would not have given rise to any lust to be ashamed of; but, as it is, we have no example to show how this could have come about. Yet that does not mean that it should seem incredible that the one part of the body could have been subject to the will, without the familiar lust, seeing that so many other parts are now in subjection to it ... why should we not believe that the sexual organs could have been the obedient servants of mankind, at the bidding of the will, in the same way as the other, if there had been no lust, which came in as the retribution for the sin of disobedience?[33]

These sentiments held sway for a thousand years. Read today they convey a **phallocentric** preoccupation with male sexual desire and a guilt about it which has produced some notorious theology. Even more they introduce a great sense of sadness at the personal consequences of these teachings in the lives of the faithful. Any kind of sexual intimacy which did not end in intercourse was forbidden (because it was not procreative); and any sexual intercourse which proved pleasurable was proof of the fall of the human race which brought about the righteous punishment of God. Augustine's teaching is a strong example of what is meant in this chapter by the extinction of passion. There are better ways of bringing theology and sexuality together.

1.11 RE-KINDLING PASSIONATE LOVE

Christian sexual morality cannot be based on any of the five themes discussed in the five previous sections of this chapter. A patriarchal understanding of relations between the sexes, like the 'missionary position' for making love with which it is connected, will always end up with the woman on the bottom and the man on the top. An ethic based on property is inseparable from ownership, and ownership is ultimately an economic relationship, not a personal one. There are strong reasons within the New Testament itself for avoiding an ethic based on purity, and virtually all Christians wisely ignore the Old

Testament laws about purity with respect to food and sexual activity. Christians still hope for the parousia but at the same time they get themselves educated, embark on careers, take out mortgages and plan extended retirements like everyone else. And while procreation may continue to be high on the agenda of married heterosexual couples at certain times in their lives, a sexual theology based on procreation will never be more than a theology for a minority at any one time.

These negative conclusions may appear disturbing to Christians wishing consciously to affirm the tradition in which they stand. But that would be to ignore alternative and equally biblical sources for Christian sexual morality and to refuse the enormous creative possibilities for rethinking Christian faith and doctrine today. This is a process which is best done in public, and it will be done in public whether or not church theologians wish it, because intense interest is still shown by the secular world and its media in what the churches are saying about sex. The delicious eroticism of the Song of Songs suggests a biblical understanding of human love without any hint of patriarchy, property, purity or procreation (see below, **8.2**). There is no embarrassment here about the amazingly explicit celebrations of love between this unmarried, interracial, passionate couple; no point to their love-making other than their intense desire for each other; no procreative intention justifying their love; no thought of impurity about their bodily organs, smells and fluids; no hierarchy of household here. Love is celebrated with a fervour and a candidness defying any late-night TV chat-show, yet the couple place a value on each other's love which is barely conceivable in contemporary popular Western culture. This is biblical theology, awaiting vibrant rediscovery. By contrast, the theology of sexuality which leads to Augustine's guilt-ridden fear of women's bodies and even of his own penis must be allowed to wither away.

The alternative sources for a sexual theology feature throughout the book, and the Song of Songs is little more than a pointer to these. We have seen how ritual purity became 'purity of heart', characterized by love and humility. Both Testaments of our Bible are about **covenants** between God and God's people which encourage covenant-relationships between people committed to each other. One of us has written of *friendship* as 'the forgotten love', that love which 'can become a sacred space in which people encounter one another, freed from the conscious and unconscious assumptions, prejudices and expectations that we are taught and bring into other relationships'.[34] There are doctrines which are fundamental to Christianity, e.g. Trinity, incarnation, and **sacrament** which have remarkable relevance in the context of sexual experience.[35] They point to a sharing in a passionate divine love which, revealed in the passion of Christ, shows itself through human love, and mingles with it.

1.12 '... THE SAME YESTERDAY, TODAY, AND FOR EVER'?

In this book various changes to the churches' teaching about sex and sexuality will be described, giving rise to the inevitable reaction that Christian doctrines and moral principles can never legitimately change at all. One way of countering this objection is to deploy the popular comparison between living religions and living 'organisms',[36] with the clear implication that there can be no life in either without continuous change. There are other important inferences to be drawn from the comparison between a religion and an organism. In an organism each part crucially depends upon all the other parts in the whole, and the organism itself crucially depends on its wider environment if it is to survive. For religions and organisms alike, there can be no cosy insulation from hostile environments — only the imperative to adapt or die.

Opponents of change within Christianity do not have history on their side, for the churches have had continually to qualify and develop their teaching and have notoriously fallen out with each other about how best to do it. There can be continuity with past traditions without the need to affirm them in all their detail. Just as living organisms cannot be insulated from their life-supporting contexts, so Christians cannot expect to be insulated from the vast social changes which are happening all around them and which inevitably raise new questions, generate new difficulties, and create new demands. Christians will ask different questions of the Bible and the tradition. They are learning that there has always been legitimate diversity among the different Jewish and Christian communities of the period of time covered by the Bible and that diversity can be a sign of dynamism and vigour today. Nonetheless, Christians cannot countenance any and every change proposed by theologians. How can they tell which ones are acceptable?

That question is well beyond the scope of this book, but since it cannot be avoided, some guidelines are needed which enable Christians to begin to distinguish between changes which are legitimate and those which are not. We have no quarrel with the traditional creeds of the churches, as long as every generation including our own has the freedom to interpret them creatively. We have no quarrel with the Bible either, as long as its testimony is allowed to point to Jesus Christ (John 5.39) and is understood in a 'life-giving and liberating way'. We look for Christian sexual teaching which is based less on patriarchy, property, purity and the demand for pro-creation, and more on the reign or 'kingdom' of God inaugurated by Jesus and the love of God which he brought into the world, and which befits the 'people of passion'. We are content for everything in this book to be judged by these criteria. If there is any constant, permanent feature within Christian doctrine, it is Jesus Christ himself: 'Jesus Christ is the same yesterday, today, and for ever' (Hebrews 13.8). One advantage of reserving 'sameness' for Jesus Christ is that change may be expected everywhere else.

1.13 SUMMARY

In this chapter the contents of the book and the reasons for writing it have been described. The question why there has been too little evidence of passionate love in Christian teaching about sexuality has been answered by referring to particular influences, viz., those of patriarchy, property, purity, the imminence of the parousia and the demand for procreation. An alternative and equally biblical approach to Christian sexual teaching has been suggested and reasons for the inevitability of doctrinal and moral change have been given.

Notes

1 *Something to Celebrate: Valuing Families in Church and Society*, Report of a Working Party of the Board for Social Responsibility (of the Church of England) (London: Church House Publishing, 1995), p. 33.

2 The Methodist Church, *Report of Commission on Human Sexuality — as presented to the Methodist Conference 1990*, para. 14, p. 3.

3 See, e.g., Steven Seidman, *Embattled Eros: Sexual Politics and Ethics in Contemporary America* (New York and London: Routledge, 1992), pp. 191–207.

4 Anthony Giddens, *The Transformation of Intimacy: Sexuality, Love and Eroticism in Modern Societies* (Cambridge: Polity Press, 1992), ch. 10.

5 *Issues in Human Sexuality: A Statement by the House of Bishops* (London: Church House Publishing, 1991), p. 48.

6 *Catechism of the Catholic Church* (London: Geoffrey Chapman, 1994), para. 2357, p. 505.

7 *Report of Commission on Human Sexuality*, para. 18, p. 4.

8 Church of Scotland, Report of Board of Social Responsibility, 1994, 7.4.4.1.1, p. 503.

9 *Ibid.*, 7.4.3.1.9, p. 503 (bold and italics in original).

10 Stephen Barton, 'Is the Bible good news for human sexuality? Reflections on method in biblical interpretation', *Theology and Sexuality*, no. 1 (September 1994), p. 45.

11 *Ibid.*, p. 54.

12 *How* the cross of Christ achieves both the divine revelation of the love of God and the loving human response to God on behalf of all humanity, takes us into an area of Christian doctrine, that of **atonement**, which will not be explored here.

13 See Friedrich Nietzsche's fierce attack on the adverse power of the cross in *The Anti-Christ* (1895)

14 On the 'fall into patriarchy' and a thorough examination of the historical evidence, see Rosemary Radford Ruether, *Gaia and God: An Ecofeminist Theology of Earth Healing* (London: SCM Press, 1993), ch. 6. See also Gerda Lerner, *The Creation of Patriarchy* (Oxford: Oxford University Press, 1987).

15 *Letter of Pope John Paul II to Women* (London: Catholic Truth Society, 1995). The text here is taken from *The Tablet*, 249, no. 8084 (15 July 1995), 917–19.

16 *Ibid.*, 3.

17 *Ibid.*, 4.

18 *Ibid.*, 3.

19 *Ibid.*, 2.

20 *Ibid.*, 11.

21 *Ibid.*, 12.

22 William Countryman, *Dirt, Greed and Sex: Sexual Ethics in the New Testament and Their Implications for Today* (London: SCM Press, 1989), p. 157.

23 Ephesians 5.21 – 6.9; Colossians 3.18 – 4.1; 1 Peter 2.18 – 3.7.

24 Carolyn Osiek, 'The New Testament and the family', in Lisa Sowle Cahill and Dietmar Mieth (eds), *The Family, Concilium* (1995/4), p. 7.

25 For the different meanings of ritual purity see Drorah O'Donnell Setel's essay in Bruce M. Metzger and Michael D. Coogan (eds), *The Oxford Companion to the Bible* (New York: Oxford University Press, 1993).

26 *Ibid.*, p. 140.

27 *Ibid.*, p. 35.

28 *Ibid.*, p. 243.

29 *Ibid.*, p. 143.

30 See also 1 Corinthians 7.25–34.

31 Peter Brown, *The Body and Society: Men, Women and Sexual Renunciation in Early Christianity* (London: Faber & Faber, 1989), p. 55.

32 See, e.g., Augustine, *City of God*, Book 14, ch. 18.

33 *Ibid.*, Book 14, ch. 23. Text in *St Augustine: City of God* (Harmondsworth: Penguin Classics, 1972), p. 585.

34 Elizabeth Stuart, *Just Good Friends: Towards a Lesbian and Gay Theology of Relationships* (London: Mowbray, 1995), p. 49. Chapter 2 is entitled 'The forgotten love'.

35 See Adrian Thatcher, *Liberating Sex: A Christian Sexual Theology* (London: SPCK, 1993), ch. 4.

36 See, e.g., Ninian Smart and Steven Konstantine, *Christian Systematic Theology in a World Context* (London: Marshall Pickering, 1991), p. 41.

Suggestions for further reading

Lisa Sowle Cahill, *Between the Sexes: Foundations for a Christian Ethics of Sexuality* (Philadephia: Fortress Press, 1985).

Gerda Lerner, *The Creation of Patriarchy* (Oxford: Oxford University Press, 1987).

House of Bishops, *Issues in Human Sexuality: A Statement* (London: Church House Publishing, 1991).

Uta Ranke-Heinemann, *Eunuchs for the Kingdom of Heaven: The Catholic Church and Sexuality* (Harmondsworth: Penguin Books, 1991).

Report of a Working Party of the Board for Social Responsibility (of the Church of England), *Something to Celebrate: Valuing Families in Church and Society* (London: Church House Publishing), 1995.

2

PASSIONATE ETHICS

2.1 SEXUAL ETHICS AND THE DANGER OF THEORIES

How do Christians know how to do the right thing? How can they tell a good action from a bad one? What has authority for them, in their lives? These questions take us to the heart of '**ethics**', i.e., to the set of principles which govern right conduct. Christians ask such questions in common with everyone else. But Christians also subscribe to a series of beliefs which are not held in common with, say, humanists or Jews. How do they learn 'the will of God' or the 'mind of Christ'? Our *sexual* conduct is only part of a set of wider, more complicated questions about what is involved in living a Christian life. This chapter is in two parts. In the first part we consider some dangers inherent in ethical theories before examining seven of them currently in use in Christian ethics (**2.2–2.8**). This is the largest part of the chapter. In the second part the issues of **masturbation**, abortion and contraception (**2.9–2.11**) are examined in the light of the theories which have been explored in order to make some preliminary judgements about their adequacy. This procedure then enables some positive suggestions to be made about a Christian sexual ethic, provisionally called 'passionate ethics' (**2.12**).

The history of ethics tends to be dominated by *theories*.[1] Theories are the products of the human mind. There is a welcome humility in some contemporary philosophy and theology which recognizes that human reason is prone to exceed its powers in believing it can arrive at a comprehensive account of what we ought to do.[2] Ethical theories have been rightly criticized, generally by feminist scholars, for being the products not just of arrogant human reason, but arrogant human *male* reason. According to this criticism, the theorist assumes too comfortable a distance between himself and what is being theorized.

Too great an emphasis is placed on the abstract powers of thought and on the mistaken belief that ethics somehow can be engaged with in an unembodied way.[3] But ethics, especially sexual ethics, cannot ignore the body, with its sensations, **desires**, ecstasies and pains.[4] We need to be suspicious about theories.

We need also to be suspicious about '**morality**'. While morality is about our relations with other people, these relationships cannot be confined to the personal domain only. There are also social, political, economic and environmental[5] elements to our relationships. If morality is collapsed into our relations with those around us, everyone else is pushed out of sight, and confined to 'the sphere of disattention'.[6] People who are starving because of economic policies which make us rich at their expense, or future generations who receive from us a planet polluted by our short-term rush for prosperity, *are* the people with whom we are in a moral relationship, just because our actions are oppressing them, even if they are unborn. Sexual relations clearly are about the personal domain, about morality in the restricted sense of our relations with those people with whom we are intimate. But a sexual morality cannot be separated from its wider social and political context. Sexual relations are prone to the very distortions of selfishness, domination and exploitation which can be found in the wider world. Our loving must be a manifestation of relationship which, by its quality, is a rejection of the wider distortions of relationships within which we live.

There are yet other problems to do with morality. The original word comes from the Latin adjective *moralis*, which comes from the noun *mos*, meaning 'custom'. But now let us suppose that we live in a society where it is the custom to persecute the people of another faith, or to oppress women, or to pursue economic policies which deliberately make poorer people still poorer. Let us suppose further that all these customs are dressed up and presented as products of Christian morality. Or that what passes as Christian morality is dominated by the customs of a former age. What then are we to do? Another danger confronting Christian ethics is that it has more than a tendency to reflect the interests of rich male Europeans. Or again, let us imagine that some representatives of Christian morality repel us by their unctuousness, by their downright smarmy, smug, serious, self-conscious self-righteousness. We might trust our instincts and reject Christian morality just because some of its spokespeople present themselves as 'anti-life'. This was the root of Nietzsche's criticism of morality. 'If one has grasped the blasphemousness of such a rebellion against life as has, in Christian morality, become virtually sacrosanct, one has fortunately therewith grasped something else as well: the uselessness, illusoriness, absurdity, *falsity* of such a rebellion.'[7]

2.2 BIBLICAL ETHICS (*see also* Chapter 10)

All church reports on **sexuality** aver the centrality of the Bible for their teaching. One such report, renowned for its liberal approach to sexuality, acknowledges that 'it is Scripture that has historically served the **Reformed tradition** as the primary and indispensable resource for theological and ethical reflection'.[8] But we have already seen how the literal reading of the text of the Bible can seriously mislead (see above, **1.7–1.9**). Let us take the practice of **polygamy** as one of dozens of possibly awkward cases for the literalists, and ask whether it can be justified on the basis of scripture. Clearly, on a surface reading of the biblical text it is, for:

> When a man has two wives, one loved and the other unloved, if they both bear him sons, and the son of the unloved wife is the elder, then, when the day comes for him to divide his property among his sons, he must not treat the son of the loved wife as his firstborn in preference to his true firstborn, the son of the unloved wife. (Deuteronomy 21.15–16)

This passage assumes the practice of polygamous marriage and deals only with a (highly **patriarchal**) complication arising from it. The same law provides for the stoning to death of brides who turn out not to be virgins (Deuteronomy 22.13–21), the judicial execution of adulterers (22.22), and even of the victims of rape if they are betrothed to be married and for some reason do not cry for help (22.23–24).

Christians who interpret the whole Bible literally are a danger to themselves and to those who listen to them. They make it harder for other Christians to use the Bible *at all*, because of the wise incredulity of unbelievers who, in the main, are not taken in by the literalists and their simplistic certainties. Fortunately 'biblical ethics' need not be confined to the literalists. J. I. H. McDonald, in an exhaustive survey of what might be meant by biblical ethics, writes:

> The use of biblical material in ethics can be controversial and open to challenge, but it is not thus automatically invalidated. On the

contrary, by virtue of its transcendent horizon or ultimate concern it may well be in a position to present a radical challenge to conventional ethics. The claim of biblical ethics to serious consideration in moral decision-making today rests on its radical openness to the Other — God, neighbour and (at least in Jesus' teaching) enemy, as well as the poor, the needy and the victims of oppression; and on its insistence that one can attain such openness only through the conquest of those powerful forces, operating both internally and externally, which close mind, spirit and will to transformative possibilities.[9]

There are themes here which reclaim the Bible for Christians in their determination to live for God and for their neighbours. But the Bible cannot be used without interpretation, and that is why most of the mainstream churches also advance some guidance about how to do this. The next few sections describe some of the guidance given.[10]

2.3 NATURAL LAW ETHICS

The doctrine of **natural law** is the most influential theory in Christian ethics, in particular in the Roman Catholic Church. It has recently been restated and reaffirmed by Pope John Paul II in an encyclical letter, *Veritatis Splendor*, or *The Splendour of Truth*.[11] Since it is the most comprehensive and influential of all the moral theories it will be described in some detail, using the encyclical as the main source. A good way into natural law theory is through the assertion that Jesus Christ is 'the true light that enlightens everyone'.[12] This is a direct quotation from John 1.9, a text which, together with the whole 'prologue' to this Gospel (John 1.1–18) makes an enormous claim about Jesus Christ. A cursory reading of the verse indicates that the influence of Jesus is confined neither to Christendom nor to the churches. It is universal in its range, transcending religions and cultures. Using **metaphors** of light and life, Jesus or the 'Word' is said to enlighten *everyone*. His life is said to be 'the light of mankind' (John 1.5). Natural law theory is a theory about *how* Christ provides light and life for everyone. We may find that we will be more critical about the theory than about the fundamental assertion which the theory attempts to explain.

Everyone, then, can know the light and life of Christ. This is because there is something called a natural law, or a moral law.[13] Now the existence of a law implies a moral 'order' existing independently of the moral 'citizen', whether she or he is aware of it or not. This is what is meant by an '**objective**' **morality**, one which is written into the order of things, independent of its appreciation by human 'subjects'. Laws of course require obedience, with punishment for law-breakers. However, knowledge of this law is within the grasp of everyone. We discover and apply it through the exercise of something called 'reason'.[14] When we do this, reason 'draws its own truth and authority from the eternal law'. People are '**autonomous**' in that they exercise reason for themselves,[15] yet when they do so, they discover the natural law is also God's law or eternal law and so must be obeyed. Our freedom is exercised, not in interpreting God's law for ourselves, but in seeking it and obeying it. Both 'the light of natural reason' and 'Divine Revelation' combine in our knowing the divine law.[16] 'Natural reason' can be trusted to appropriate the eternal law because the light of reason is itself 'the reflection in man of the splendour of God's countenance'.[17] Because our reason has a 'natural knowledge of God's eternal law', it is 'consequently able to show man the right direction to take in his free actions'.[18]

But how do we know that God's law really *is* divine, as opposed to something we would like to believe is divine, or something we have just been *told* is divine? Clear answers are given to both these questions in the Letter. The moral life has 'an essential "*teleological*" *character*, since it consists in the deliberate ordering of human acts to God, the supreme good and ultimate end (*telos*) of man'.[19] That means that doing the right thing aligns the person directly to God's will. In doing God's will we are thought to fulfil ourselves or our natures. What makes an action right depends '*primarily and fundamentally on the "object" rationally chosen by the deliberate will*'.[20] That means what makes an action right depends on something outside the person. There is an objective moral order which exists independently of our being able to choose it, and in this order there are some actions which can never be good because they are 'intrinsically evil'.[21] Reason 'attests' these intrinsically evil acts. When the Church adds **revelation** to the knowledge acquired by reason it becomes

> fully aware that the true and final answer to the problem of morality lies in him [Christ] alone. In a particular way, it is *in the Crucified Christ* that *the Church finds the answer* to the question troubling so many people today . . . [22]

The content of the objective moral order is comprehensively described. Here the Pope draws on a list of human actions given in a Second Vatican Council document, and much broader than our concern in this book with sexual morality. They include ' "whatever is hostile to life itself, such as any kind of homicide, genocide, abortion, euthanasia and voluntary suicide ... " '.[23] They also include torture, brainwashing and subhuman working and living conditions. Our reason attests that such acts are always and everywhere wrong, and in this encyclical another intrinsically evil act is added to the list — contraception. Pope Paul VI's controversial teaching about contraception in the encyclical *Humanae Vitae* is reaffirmed and given additional weight because 'contraceptive practices whereby the conjugal act is intentionally rendered infertile' now enter the list. They belong in the same class of actions which include torture and all kinds of other practices which the Council called 'a disgrace' and taught that 'so long as they infect human civilization they contaminate those who inflict them more than those who suffer injustice ...'.[24]

Finally, we know God's law is God's law because the Church teaches it, and the **Magisterium** of the Church alone is able to pronounce an authentic interpretation of it.[25]

> The Church's Magisterium intervenes not only in the sphere of faith, but also, and inseparably so, in the sphere of morals ... In proclaiming the commandments of God and the charity of Christ, the Church's Magisterium also teaches the faithful specific particular precepts and requires that they consider them in conscience as morally binding. In addition, the Magisterium carries out an important work of vigilance ...[26]

The highest authority is the Magisterium which cannot err. In relation to 'specific particular precepts' Roman Catholics are given no room for conscientious dissent, and the moral theologians of the Church who teach differently are required 'to give, in the exercise of their ministry, the example of a loyal assent, both internal and external, to the Magisterium's teaching in the areas of both dogma and morality'.

2.3.1 Criticisms of the natural law theory (see also 7.3.2)

Natural law is a comprehensive moral doctrine with many factors to commend it. It is a genuinely universal teaching, and it attempts to make sense of a human knowledge of God which is present in every human consciousness, whatever people's religion or lack of it. Ultimately it rests on the apprehension of Jesus Christ as the whole truth of the moral law. It defends, against the climate of secular moral thinking, a view of morality which is not merely **subjective**, where right actions do not depend on the inclination or choice of the human subject alone. We shall shortly see how natural law handles sexual questions (see below, **2.9–2.11**). Before we get there, however, there are some fairly obvious difficulties with this whole approach.

2.3.2 Arguments from authority

While natural law is an attempt to arrive at a universal morality, there is an obvious lack of agreement about the content and interpretation of it, as acute inside the Roman Catholic Church as anywhere else. The Letter is an attempt to deal firmly with 'an overall and systematic calling into question of traditional moral doctrine' which is happening 'within the Christian community itself'.[27] Yet the Letter gives Catholics no room to think these things through for themselves, since the authority of the Magisterium is supreme (see below, **5.1**). Many Catholics think the Pope can be wrong, as do most non-Catholic Christians. If natural law doctrine has to be shored up by an unquestioning acceptance of the Magisterium's absolute teaching authority, what is now left of the promising beginning which sought to sketch out a human knowledge of Jesus Christ based on the natural light of reason? Natural law has become a dubious article of faith after all.

2.3.3 Law and obedience

A more radical objection to natural law theory concerns the place of moral law, *at all*, in Christian morality. This will be an unwelcome thought for some Christians, but a strong case can be made both from the teaching of Jesus and Paul, and some contemporary observations about the corrupting effects of unquestioning obedience. The gospel writers are said to 'have turned a negative attitude toward the Law ... into the touchstone of Christian identity'.[28] Jesus is reported by Matthew to have said: 'Everything in the law and the prophets hangs on these two commandments [the love of God and neighbour]' (Matthew 22.40). According to Paul 'In Christ Jesus the life-giving law of the Spirit has set you free from the law of sin and death' (Romans 8.2). The 'law of the Spirit' is an interesting metaphor — 'law' retains all the force of written and binding legal precepts while 'Spirit' contrasts the Christian experience of God in Christ with the Jewish experience of God under the law.

The suggestion that 'law', with its inevitable implications of obedience and enforcement, is inessential to Christian morality requires more space than is available here.[29] But the greatest argument against taking obedience too far has been put by the most famous Roman Catholic moral theologian of the present century, Bernard Häring. Häring was a chaplain in the German army in the Second World War. Writing poignantly of this experience he recalls how he 'experienced the most absurd obedience by Christians — God have mercy — toward a criminal regime'.[30] Obedience can never be unquestioning: indeed the unquestioning obedience of victims of child abuse is now seen to be a major factor in the perpetuation of the abuse and the protection of the abuser (see below, **5.10**). Obedience of wives to abusing husbands has trapped them in the wreckage of their marriages (see below, **5.8**). Obedience always implies **hierarchical** relationships whether in the armed forces, or companies or universities. Does it have a place in the moral life? Obedience to God must certainly be protected from obedience to anything other than God (e.g. Magisterium, Bible, nation-state or local pastor). Even obedience to God can be stated in other terms such as 'following', 'befriending', 'loving', etc. An ethic based on *responsibility* would be better.[31]

2.3.4 *The concept of nature*

Natural law ethics seems immune to a raft of criticisms aimed at the elusive and shifting concept of 'nature' itself. Augustine and Aquinas are invoked in the encyclical as saying that God 'commands us to respect the natural order and forbids us to disturb it', and that God's wisdom does the job of 'moving all things to their due end'. But this is obviously a wholly medieval, pre-scientific view of nature. People are also part of nature and have the (God-given) ability to intervene in it, whether in finding cures for sickness, making steel, building airplanes or breeding seedless grapes.[32] Human intervention is part of nature whether or not it always has a beneficial effect. 'Nature itself develops, and human activity involves participation in nature in such a way that some aspects of it are altered.'[33] A moral theory which derives in part from observation of the natural order ought at least to deploy a contemporary account of that order. Such an account could hardly omit evolution and its cruelties, the minutiae of genetics, and current accounts of the contrast between biological and social accounts of human sexuality and **gender**.[34]

2.3.5 Patriarchy

Finally it must be noted that *Veritatis Splendor*, like the *Letter to Women* (see above, **1.6**), is a patriarchal document. An assessment of it by a moderate Roman Catholic woman theologian finds it wanting with regard to the intensification of sexist language when compared with earlier papal encyclicals.[35] Although the *Letter* speaks of 'human nature', 'the person', the 'end of man', etc., it is male experience, not human experience, which is primary. The ancient doctrine of natural law was formulated in a period where the subordination of women to men was taken for granted; and where the fulfilment of sexuality lay in procreation. The '**universals**' which specify the doctrine (e.g. human nature, the will, freedom, etc.) reflect a dominant and dominating view while pretending to appeal to 'an impartial rationality'. They represent a masculine ordering of experience. So, while **feminist theologians** may welcome the encyclical as a 'resource' because it affirms 'a moral foundation on the basis of which injustice of all kinds can be recognized and eradicated', the question they will bring to it is 'whether its defence of moral objectivity is not fatally wounded by a too visible male point of view, and by a tendency to resolve genuinely difficult questions by resort to authority'.[36]

2.4 VIRTUE ETHICS

Contemporary moral philosophers[37] and theologians from different churches are interested in understanding the moral life as the acquisition of **virtue**. Virtue signals a shift of interest from theories about the rightness of actions to the goodness of a person's character. 'An ethics of character focuses our attention more on the person performing an act than on the acts performed by the person.'[38] Virtue theories go back at least to Aristotle and, through Thomas Aquinas, virtue, along with natural law, became established in Roman Catholic moral theology. Unfortunately the theory is complex, obscure and difficult and nothing more than a bare outline of part of it is attempted here. A gentle introduction to virtue theory will be attempted by imagining a person who lacks endowment in the virtues. This lack will give rise to a description of what is lacked, i.e., the virtues themselves.

Imagine a person whose life drifts along with no apparent meaning or purpose. Such a person may be so immersed in personal concerns that he or she cares about no one else. The general good or the welfare of others is simply irrelevant. Another person wants to be successful in his or her career but is racked with self-doubt about passing exams, being generally assertive and seizing opportunities for advancement. Finally, another person has the means to eat and drink too much, consume too much and indulge too much in various sensual pleasures, and does so. Would there be anything morally wrong with such persons?

According to someone who follows Aquinas' moral thought, such persons would be lacking in the cardinal virtues. Virtues are 'dispositions to act well'.[39] Dispositions 'enable us to act as and when we want'.[40] Aquinas believed that everything that exists has a nature or end,[41] and that by acquiring the right dispositions we achieve the end of a happy or fulfilled life. A 'cardinal' virtue is one which is paramount, presupposed by all the others. There are four — prudence, justice, temperance and fortitude.[42] It will now be obvious that the lives just described lack the cardinal virtues. Prudence is the exercise of sound, rational judgement and common sense, especially in the conduct of practical affairs. Justice 'directs the individual to the common good',[43] and away from selfish concerns. Fortitude is that quality of mind that enables one to face danger, fear or opportunity with confidence, self-affirmation and resolution. Temperance is self-control and has been redescribed as 'a capacity for acting appropriately with respect to the fundamental organic processes of human life: appropriate consumption of food, appropriate use of stimulants and intoxicants, appropriate sexual behavior'.[44]

The cardinal virtues can be achieved in part by human effort,[45] partly with the help of God. As with natural law theories, people are made for communion with God, and God realizes this communion by bestowing on us the theological virtues of faith, hope and charity.[46] 'Charity is the mother and root of all virtue.'[47] The 'truly virtuous person' would be one who 'succeeded in integrating the multitude of desires and aversions into a unified character'.[48]

There are undoubted strengths in an approach to ethics through the virtues. The recovery of virtue in contemporary thought signals a welcome shift from concentration on theories of action to the development of a good character: from individual actions to persons who are the subjects of the action. The attention given to virtue reminds us that our characters are partly formed by our actions.[49]

Along with natural law, this approach maintains an emphasis on an objective moral order. When we act virtuously we are more likely to act in accordance with this order. Since love is the 'mother and root' of all virtue, virtue gives us a knowledge of God, a sharing in God's life, we might say. And we will need to return to the positive identification of justice as a virtue. In the sphere of sexual ethics the churches have maximized self-restraint as the dominant virtue, whereas the virtue of justice in sexual conduct has been almost entirely ignored.[50] But sexual justice would be the conduct of sexual relationships without patriarchy, without selfishness, and with equal regard for one's partner (see below, **2.12**).

Nonetheless it is not possible to be exactly enthusiastic about the virtue approach to ethics. Aristotle and Aquinas regarded women as incapable of attainment of the virtues, and virtue theory is not free from this '**androcentric fallacy**' (see **6.6.1**). A close look at the word 'virtue' reveals the Latin gendered word *vir* ('man'). This defect need not be fatal to the virtue-approach to morality: what would be needed would be a list of virtues which was genuinely inclusive, the attributes of morally mature human beings, and not the exclusive prerogative of pious, privileged, white, Christian gentle*men*. But this is a task which should not be underestimated, for it turns out that, as we might expect, the virtues are based entirely on men's experience. Fortitude cannot conceal its militaristic, heroic origin.[51] Christians, especially evangelicals, are rightly suspicious of the influence of philosophy over theology, and any suspicion that philosophy calls the tune here is likely to be justified. Why not remain instead with 'the harvest of the Spirit' which is 'love, joy, peace, patience, kindness, goodness, fidelity, gentleness and self-control. Against such things there is no law' (Galatians 5.22–23)? One contemporary critic of the virtues sees them as part of the attempt to define and separate the public realm or *polis* from the private, domestic realm or *oikos*, and to confine women to the latter. With women thus assigned to the home, the public realm became 'a kind of cultural bypass operation to disassociate continuity and succession from wombs and domestic nurture'.[52]

Suppose we were to set out *the experience of mother-love* as 'an excellent model for the content of agape'.[53] The experiencing of mothering, says a contemporary Christian feminist, is inclusive, other-regarding and unconditional — its 'caring intensity' makes it the best available example of divine love. This kind of love would not find its way into the cardinal virtues. This leads us to a damning criticism of virtue theory. According to one extensive treatment of the virtues in Aquinas, the saint

> treats the virtue of chastity as if it were primarily a capacity to moderate one's desire and enjoyment of physical pleasure, rather than seeing it as a capacity for appropriate feeling and action with respect to other *people* ... As a result, the centrally important personal dimensions of sexual desire and pleasure, the complex ways in which sexuality mediates relations between persons, are almost entirely hidden from his view.[54]

This observation introduces a tragic dimension into his account of the virtues, and leaves the agent shut up in himself,[55] acquiring moral status at the expense of the warmth of real human relationships. For Aquinas,

> the warmer ... capacities for care and responsiveness do not have a central role to play either in the agent's pursuit of her own aims, or in her life in society ... It is not essential ... that the person attain some capacities for empathy and felt concern for others ... the virtuous individual must attain some degree of self-restraint and courage, but a capacity to care for others is not essential to this process.[56]

2.5 NARRATIVE ETHICS

Virtue is also a central theme of 'narrative ethics', an approach to Christian ethics led by the Texan Methodist Stanley Hauerwas. 'Narrative' is a broad term embracing several meanings. First, a narrative is a story which involves people. So the Gospels, the accounts of God's interventions in history in the Old and New Testaments, the Church's profession of its faith through the ages — these are all capable of being called narratives. Second, 'narrative' is also the art or process of narrating, so the Church may be said to be engaging in narrative as it proclaims and lives its message. Third, narrative has been used to describe what it means to be a human being or a self. The meaning of narrative here captures the insight that the individual human being is continually interacting with other people, through whom she or he becomes a person, forms a character, or develops an identity. The point of speaking this way about a person is twofold: first, 'I am the *subject* of a history that is my own and no one else's, that has its own peculiar meaning'; and second, that 'the narrative of any one life is part of an interlocking set of narratives'. So 'I am part of their story, as they are part of mine'.[57]

The life of the individual Christian, then, is a narrative which interlocks with others in the Christian community or church. The Church is 'a community of character',[58] and central to its life are the virtues. The Church does not *have* a social ethic. Its task is to *be* a social ethic, that is, to be 'the servant community... where the stories of Israel and Jesus are told, enacted, and heard'.[59] The virtues do not coincide in every respect with those in Aquinas' thought. Rather they are 'specific skills required to live faithful to a tradition's understanding of the moral project in which its adherents participate'.[60] And we can acquire them only by sharing in 'the embodiment of the story in the communities in which we are born'.[61] High among the virtues is that of peace.[62]

As with the earlier approaches to ethics which we have considered, we have to consider a balance of strengths and weaknesses. Narrative ethics (along with feminist ethics) is perhaps at its most valuable in providing a view of the human self as being fundamentally in relation with other selves in community. It re-envisages the life of the Christian community in an unbelieving world as qualitatively different, being infused with the Christian virtues. But a danger in this approach lies in a disinclination of people outside the churches to believe that the churches are, or ever were, what Hauerwas understands them to be. 'Narrative' as we have seen, has overlapping meanings and probably cannot bear the weight of meaning put upon it. Finally, as we shall see with 'ecclesial ethics' (see below **2.6**), an ethic which emphasizes the historical tradition of the churches is one which may find the handling of doctrinal and moral change difficult.[63]

2.6 ECCLESIAL ETHICS

So far we have been considering Catholic and Protestant approaches to ethics. Ecclesial ethics brings an Armenian **Orthodox** approach into our survey. Vigen Guroian is an Armenian Orthodox priest who is a professor of theology and ethics in Baltimore, and who brings an overt Orthodox perspective into the debate about Christian ethics in the USA. This perspective has no time at all for liberalism in ethics, whether in its Protestant or secular forms. The churches are in 'an especially advanced state of spiritual rigor mortis'.[64] 'Only vestiges of Christendom remain in America.'[65] What contemporary Catholic and Protestant approaches to ethics equally lack is any awareness that the Church's liturgy is the 'nexus of tradition and ethics'.[66] There is a 'liturgical location of Christian tradition and ethics'.[67] The church's moral and doctrinal teaching, like its very life, is expressed in the celebration of its liturgies. Liturgy is central to the Christian tradition. Against Catholic and Protestant, and liberal and biblical theories of ethics, Guroian holds that 'Christian tradition is not merely a selective form of historiography, historical reasoning, or historical memory; it is a eucharistic and eschatological science, a eucharistic and eschatological way of knowing'.[68] The 'continuity' of tradition is 'not located in theological texts, creeds, liturgical forms, or ecclesiastical offices'. Rather 'the collective remembrance of this community, in the power of the Holy Spirit, makes Christ and his sacrifice present . . .'[69]

Ecclesial ethics, then, is the proclamation of the gospel as it is experienced in the rites and liturgies of the Church. The more extensive the available liturgies, the wider the implications for the world. The 'eucharistic and eschatological way of knowing' means that at the eucharist Christians prefigure a future time when the entire world becomes the body of Jesus, i.e., becomes united with God and an expression of divine love. From the celebration of the eucharist Christians derive hope and anticipate this future time while living amidst the abandonment of religious belief.

The method adopted by an ecclesial ethics, intentionally typical of an Orthodox approach, relies on the three key ideas of dialogue, icon and transformation. There must first be a dialogue between all the 'legitimate voices' in the Christian community as they listen to each other and reflect on their experience. 'The lesson here is that the church's authority is dialogic rather than autocratic.'[70] The icon of Orthodox theology is then contrasted with the rationalism of Western attempts to argue to moral conclusions. The icon has 'a remarkable capacity to *attract* people into the reality of which it is an image', whereas liberal ethical theories which emphasize the agent and rational action

> almost never speak of attraction but rather of argument, persuasion, and power in their efforts to describe the nature of the church and its mission. This agency theory emphasizes reason and will, whereas the theology of the icon emphasizes imagination, perception, and interpretation.[71]

The icon is not confined to material figures to be found inside or outside churches, but extends to any 'material representation' of the kingdom of God in the world. Wherever there are conflicting moral voices the Church should seek to 'transform perception' by 'drawing people outside the church into a dialogue that engages their imagination so that they will experience the capacity of Christian truth to illumine the nature of the problems they face and the moral decisions they must make'.

There are great insights here that may have eluded the Western churches. The worship of the Church has seldom been linked with the practice of ethics. The aim of listening to all the voices within the Church is akin to the similar demand within feminist ethics, and the refusal of autocratic models of authority is a riposte for popes and moral theologians alike. The 'pulling power' of the icon, if we may so put it, is a riposte against much elaborate moral philosophy which overvalues reason and undervalues intuition and imagination. Again, though, caution is due. Ecclesial ethics seems to evade critical readings of the Bible,[72] and also of the tradition. What if some of the tradition, e.g. its patriarchal and divisive denominational elements, are a dead weight? Can dialogue dispense with them? Again we might need further assurances that all the legitimate voices in the Church will be heard (see below, **10.2**) and that a non-autocratic model of authority is really in place. We might wonder too which liturgies are to provide us with moral guidance, since liturgy is also a contested area within the churches, and some liturgies from the past are best left unperformed. And are there reasons why an unbelieving world which the Church seeks to transform should be prepared to focus upon the liturgies of a church which it is almost certain to find inscrutable? Once again, we are left with an attractive, but only partial, picture.

2.7 SITUATION ETHICS

The theories so far considered may be said to be conservative in orientation. The best-known liberal theory in Christian ethics is known as '**situation ethics**'. It was popularized by the Anglican bishop John Robinson in *Honest to God*,[73] and was developed in two books by the Episcopalian Joseph Fletcher.[74] '*Christian* situation ethics', says Fletcher,

> has only one norm or principle or law (call it what you will) that is binding and unexceptionable, always good and right regardless of the circumstances. That is 'love' — the *agape* of the summary commandment to love God and the neighbor. Everything else without exception, all laws and rules and principles and ideals and

norms, are only *contingent*, only valid *if they happen* to serve love in
any situation.[75]

The individual Christian herself must decide in the situation how
love must best be served.

> The situationist enters into every decision-making situation fully
> armed with the ethical maxims of his [*sic*] community and its
> heritage, and he treats them with respect as illuminators of his
> problems. Just the same he is prepared in any situation to com-
> promise them or set them aside *in the situation* if love seems better
> served by doing so.[76]

Almost no one is prepared to defend situation ethics today. It is
generally regarded as a symptom of the decadence of the so-called
swinging sixties which capitulated to the spirit of that liberal and
permissive age. This verdict is over-hasty, and is as much influenced
by political developments since the 1960s as ever situation ethics was
influenced by the wider political and social situation in its heyday.
Situation ethics was prepared to take issue with biblical literalism and
'legalism', to encourage a critical reading of tradition, to summon
people to a strong sense of responsibility for their actions, and to
elevate to a position of ultimate importance the commandment of
Jesus to love God and one's neighbour. These are undoubted
strengths which a harsher, more recent, political and theological
climate cannot dilute.

On the other hand its serious weaknesses have to be admitted.
Situation ethics perpetuates the myth of the individual autonomous
agent who freely makes independent decisions. It is a theory that
overloads the individual with more responsibility than he or she can
bear. That is because any situation has to be read in the light of what
best serves 'love', whether or not the agent has the necessary information or whether her power to make the required judgement is
impaired. In any case the injunction to serve love requires much
qualification. Morality is considered as a kind of forum for personal
relationships, yet ethical questions increasingly operate on the social
and political level, not merely on the level of individual choice.
There have been gains in Christian ethics since the 1960s, and we
have been considering some of them. Where, for example, is there
any emphasis on Christian character? Or virtue? Or the sense of
belonging to a moral community? There is a sense (unremarked by
Fletcher) in which a 'situationist' necessarily exhibits the virtue of
fortitude in making brave decisions and living with them. But, as we

have seen, the virtue of fortitude may merely emphasize the loneliness of the moral agent and render the forging of relationships
optional. We may need to be even more on our guard here than
when dealing with rival theories.

2.8 FEMINIST ETHICS

So far the theories we have been considering belong to the so-called
'mainstream' of Christian ethical thought. They are influenced by
the denominational traditions of Christendom. If, as Vigen Guroian
and others have asserted, Christendom is on its last legs, we ought not
to pay too much attention to its divisions but (again with Guroian)
look to God's future where such divisions will count for nothing at
all. Feminist theology and **liberation theology** regard the divisions of
Christendom as irrelevant. They take their agenda from the experience of oppression, that of colonial powers, economic systems and
men. There is time only to consider the first of these.

Feminist theology (see **6.6**) 'takes as its first agenda the criticism of
the masculinist bias of Christian theology'. Its second agenda 'aims at
the discovery of alternative historical traditions supportive of the full
personhood of woman and her inclusion in leadership roles in
church and society'.[77] This masculinist bias is very much broader
than the Christian tradition.[78] It is pervasive in most, if not all,
religions and cultures. It pervades even the discussion of ethics itself,
with its fondness for theories, abstract generalizations,[79] the priority
given to reason, and the suppression of feeling as an element in
ethical decision-making. As we have seen when considering the
virtues, male experience is primary and this primacy has marginalized and devalued women.

A core example of the deep-seated masculinist bias within Christian theology is the concept of *agape*, or self-giving love. This is one of
many which could be given. Nothing is more central to Christian
theology than the statement that 'God is love' (1 John 4.8, 16). Yet in
a patriarchal society or church, *agape* easily becomes an oppressive
male ideology where women do all the giving (and men the taking).
Women who have to cope directly with patriarchy are likely to be
attuned to the demand for obedience, service and unquestioning
devotion to male forms of authority. The last thing they need to hear
in these circumstances is that sacrificial self-giving is what is required
of them. This is not to say that self-giving is *not* required of them, but
that, if it is required, it is required equally of women and men in the

joyful service of God. Most if not all of theology's core concepts come with patriarchal undertones lurking in their depths. That is why Jennifer Rike abandons the concept of *agape* altogether, replacing it instead with a new 'model of feminist Christian love as care'.[80]

A Christian feminist ethic is one which, in 'supporting the full personhood of women', will seek not simply to eliminate male bias from theological language, but to strive for justice and equality for women in all areas of life. These values will be derived, not from **Enlightenment** philosophy, but from the equality of women and men in the image and reign of God.[81] It will lead to a suspicion of the gender roles ascribed to women in a patriarchal social order (see Chapter 6). With regard to sexuality, feminist ethics will confront the pervasive construction of women as sexual objects. It will refuse sexual activity which exists primarily for maximizing male sexual pleasure. It will be suspicious of the institution of **heterosexual** marriage, at least in so far as it manoeuvres women into domestic and nurturing roles without appropriate support from husbands. And it will be ever wary of male violence.

A diversity of approaches to sexual ethics current in the Christian churches has now been briefly considered. While they have much in common, they differ considerably in the treatment given to issues within sexual ethics. Three of these are described next (**2.9–2.11**). These will help us in framing a 'passionate ethics' in **2.12**.

2.9 MASTURBATION (*see also* **4.5**)

This clinical-sounding, Latin-derived word gives no hint of the pleasure associated with the activities it names, viz., the stimulation of one's own or another's genital organs, usually to orgasm, by manual contact or means other than sexual intercourse. When contrasted with the graver moral issues, masturbation hardly seems to warrant a mention. *The Catechism of the Catholic Church*, however, leaves us in no doubt that it is 'an intrinsically and gravely disordered action'. This is because ' "the deliberate use of the sexual faculty, for whatever reason, outside of marriage is essentially contrary to its purpose." For here sexual pleasure is sought outside of "the sexual relationship which is demanded by the moral order and in which the total meaning of mutual self-giving and human procreation in the context of true love is achieved" '.[82]

Masturbation is an 'offence against **chastity**'. It is 'disordered' because the natural law teaches that all sexual activity should be open to the creation of life. There should be no ejaculation of semen anywhere but inside a vagina, and no sexual intercourse except between married heterosexual couples. This is the 'purpose' of the 'sexual faculty'. Neither married party should expect any sexual pleasure except that which is shared between them, and 'those who are *engaged to marry* are called to live chastity in **continence** ... They should reserve for marriage the expressions of affection that belong to married love.'[83] Masturbation is clearly also a failure in the virtue of chastity. 'The virtue of chastity comes under the cardinal virtue of *temperance*, which seeks to permeate the passions and appetites of the senses with reason.'[84] Does one assume that clerical embarrassment precludes any acknowledgement of it?

These conclusions must rank as amazing, whether considered theologically or pastorally. Does *anyone* believe them? Other approaches to ethics do not arrive at this extreme position. Biblical ethics, for example, is noncommittal on the subject, since masturbation is not mentioned in the Bible.[85] The Church of England bishops felt no need to mention the subject in their influential *Issues in Human Sexuality*.[86] The strong influence of natural law, the strong imposition of authority, a strong fear of the body and sexual pleasure, a strong feeling of guilt all combine here with bad biology[87] to produce pastoral chaos. Another Roman Catholic approach to masturbation, unofficial yet deeply devout, acknowledges the goodness and value of what it called 'self-pleasuring', whether for women discovering the mystery of their bodies and the pleasure available to them; for adolescents anticipating full sexual experience; for married couples whose 'mutual caresses' at times 'lead to orgasm without intercourse'; for married people whose partners are temporarily unavailable; for lonely people acknowledging their sexual needs; even women who have been abused, and who 're-learn the loveliness of their bodies, the goodness of sexual pleasure' with a loving female partner.[88] Only when a positive account of self-pleasuring has been given is there then a very proper warning given about 'the possibility of disorder in the solitary exercise of a social arousal'.[89] The contrast between these two evaluations is striking, and the pastoral sensitivity of the second is only one of the grounds for preferring it.

2.10 ABORTION

Official Roman Catholic teaching on abortion converges with the general conviction among Protestant fundamentalist Christians that abortion is always wrong. In the *Catechism*, the wrongness of abortion is situated in the treatment of the fifth commandment, 'You shall not kill' (Exodus 20.13),[90] and derived from it.

> Human life must be respected and protected absolutely from the moment of conception. From the first moment of his existence, a human being must be recognized as having the rights of a person — among which is the inviolable right of every innocent being to life.[91]

'Formal co-operation in an abortion constitutes a grave offence.'[92] And: 'Since it must be treated from conception as a person, the embryo must be defended in its integrity, cared for, and healed, as far as possible, like any other human being.'[93]

This teaching is very clear, definite and simple, but for those prepared to question the authority of the church whose teaching it is, the arguments supporting an absolute prohibition of abortion can be readily criticized. Three obvious criticisms are put by a moderate Roman Catholic commentator on the *Catechism*.[94] The fifth commandment forbids 'murder', not general 'killing' (which might equally apply to animals). There has been rather a lot of killing in the Old Testament and throughout Christendom which the fifth commandment has failed to prevent, and it soon becomes clear in the *Catechism* 'that there are occasions when (morally relevant) circumstances may have to allow for killing to take place'.[95] May there not be morally relevant circumstances here? For the abortion of a foetus to count as murder, the foetus would need to be counted as a human person from the moment of conception. But this is a notorious philosophical problem which until recently was recognized as such even within Catholic teaching about abortion.[96] The arguments are considerably weaker than the prohibitions.

A recent Anglican document on abortion strikes a different tone. Summarizing all recent Church of England statements on abortion up to 1993, it says the Church of England:

> 1. believes that all human life, including life developing in the womb, is to be protected.
> 2. views with great concern the large number of abortions being carried out under the current legislation.
> 3. recognizes that there are situations in which abortion can be justified.[97]

While there is grave concern about the number of abortions carried out, arguments 'from authority' are rejected. They 'only succeed if the legitimacy of the authority' (e.g. 'the Bible, tradition, or the *sensus fidelium*') is recognized, and 'there is agreement about what that authority actually teaches about abortion'.[98] This report is pro-child, not pro-abortion. 'The moral health of a society is to be judged partly by its treatment of its most vulnerable members.'[99] Yet 'honest disagreement' among Christians about the Church's 'stand for life' has to be recognized. In particular the report is to be commended for listening to 'those many women today' who 'are not persuaded that they are morally obliged to give birth to an unwanted child even though it could be assured of a good home'.[100] And there is a warning that 'those who argue for the sanctity of all life' should not be found lacking in pastoral understanding. They should ensure that the burden of carrying the consequences of such a belief is fairly shared. Insistence on the sanctity of life will not be heard as part of the Good News of Jesus Christ if in practice it is associated with a lack of sensitivity towards women and their medical advisers who face agonizing choices.[101]

2.11 CONTRACEPTION

Contraception is now regarded by the Magisterium of the Roman Catholic Church as not merely wrong, but an 'intrinsic evil' (see above, **2.3**). It is hard to see how the gulf between Protestant and Catholic treatments of the subject can now be bridged. Indeed for non-Catholic Christians, contraception is not an issue at all, although sex outside marriage, with or without contraception, clearly is. The reliance of papal arguments on natural law (see above, **2.3**) merely underscores the reliance on authority required of supporters of this position. Can the view that unprotected and uncontracepted heterosexual intercourse is the sole legitimate context for sexual expression really be found in nature or taught by the natural law? If it can, then a similar argument can be found for masturbation and sexual love between **lesbian** and **gay** partners. People who masturbate and people who, because of their **orientation**, are drawn to members of the same sex, find this natural. Married persons who cannot have children find the desire for sexual intercourse natural. The ambiguities in the concept 'nature' are, of course, notorious, yet it is hard to see why, given human diversity, only one version of what is naturally human should be allowed.

The *availability* of contraception, however, contributes greatly to the freedom of users of contraceptives to have sexual intercourse with a much reduced risk of pregnancy and therefore with greater frequency, inside or outside marriage. An argument therefore exists, for Christians convinced that sexual intercourse should only take place within heterosexual marriage, that the availability of contraception, like the availability of abortion and divorce, clearly leads to an increase in the use of each. From this perspective, to call them 'intrinsic evils' has a certain plausibility. The language of absolute and unwavering prohibition has its undoubted attractions. It gives clear teaching. It provides security to people ill at ease with change (generally the teachers rather than the taught). It enables a counter-cultural stance to be taken, which firms up Christian identity in a time when it has become blurred. Those Christians who are unpersuaded by absolute language and arguments from authority will look instead for responsible use of the opportunities afforded by reliable contraception and safe abortion. They will be drawn to different theories.

2.12 PASSIONATE ETHICS

We are now in a more informed position to specify what is meant by a 'passionate ethics', promised in **1.5**. Christians, it was suggested, are 'people of passion', and their loving is a sharing in the passion of Christ. 'Passionate ethics' is not the unveiling of yet another theory of sexual ethics. It is just a simple way of describing some of the resources provided by Christian theology and faith for followers of Jesus as they rejoice in their sexuality before God.

All Christians seek to love God and their neighbour as their response to the summons of Jesus Christ himself (see **9.2**). In this at least there is unanimity. Passionate ethics also has the love of God and neighbour at its root, but discovers in the treatment of the three issues of masturbation, abortion and contraception a certain harshness which does not obviously assist faithful Christians to fulfil either commandment. Natural law arguments supported by ecclesiastical authority proclaim certainties which seem to be achieved at the cost of a lack of empathic identification with the pastoral realities of the lives of sexually active Christian women and men. Such people are entitled to expect a greater understanding of the complexities of their lives. They should not expect to be the victims of a theology which achieves dogmatic certitude at the expense of sensitivity. Natural law theory unfortunately justifies the warnings against theories in **2.1** above. Arguments from authority need the authority of the whole people of God, and there is little evidence that the experience of all the people has been taken into account. The experience which shapes these teachings is that of compulsorily celibate male priests whose unfulfilled sexuality is a constant distraction for them.

There is a fear of pleasure (see **7.3.1**) in the strictures against masturbation (see **4.5**). Are there really no exceptions to be allowed in the case of abortion, when the command to refrain from killing permits so many exceptions elsewhere? Does a pregnant woman whose life is endangered by her pregnancy, or who is a victim of rape, or who knows she will give birth to a seriously deformed (e.g. anencephalic) child, have no freedom over whether or not to have an abortion? Only the freedom to obey an absolute teaching framed historically and exclusively by men? And are not the pastoral consequences of the ban on contraception obvious? Here the testimony of unwanted children, or exhausted mothers, or desperately poor parents, cannot be silenced by the stigmatization of contraceptive use as a crime: yes, a crime comparable with homicide, genocide and torture.

Passionate ethics draws from all the approaches considered in this chapter (**2.1**). No ethics can claim to be Christian which is not grounded in Jesus Christ, and so in the biblical witness to him. But 'the poor, the needy and the victims of oppression' who figure in the teaching of Jesus are represented in our time by unwanted and neglected children, by the bodies of exploited women, by victims of 'those powerful forces, operating both internally and externally' (**2.2**) which conspire to produce an obsession with sex, to posit it as a commodity, and to divorce it from mutual love. If we have had good cause to take issue with natural law theories, we may still affirm what natural law strives to protect: an objective moral order; an ordinary knowledge open to all women and men of the light and life of Christ; and the conviction that the answer to the problem of morality is the Crucified Christ (see above, **2.3**).

Passionate ethics describes the ingredients of this knowledge differently. A beginning might be made by replacing the individual human agent who stands over against the world, other people and God, with the person-in-relation who derives his or her identity in relation with the world, other people and God. Involvement, not detachment, is the fundamental posture. Starting here places us fundamentally 'with others', one of whom is our brother, Jesus Christ. Relatedness is not primarily an intellectual experience, but a personal one involving, like the love of God commanded by Jesus, all

our heart, soul, mind and strength. Being in relation enables empathic identification to take place between ourselves and others as we
begin to discern, from this relational perspective, what Jesus Christ
may have meant when he identified himself with the hungry, the
thirsty, the stranger, the naked, ill and imprisoned (Matthew 25.31–
46). 'Where the victims of the countless massacres, slaveries, ex-
ploitations and petty domestic cruelties of history have left almost no
voice within history, the victims of more recent times have left a
stronger trace.'[102] It is a simple and sustaining Christian belief that
Christ suffers along with victims. That is his continuing passion.
Some of the cries of victims in a Christian sexual ethic come from the
suffering bodies of abused women and children; from the anguish of
partners who have been betrayed or who have never known **mutuality**
and equality in relationship; even from priests whose compulsory
celibacy drives them to seek sexual compensation and isolates them
still further.

Passionate ethics is the practice of neighbour-love which always
affirms the other and never makes him or her a victim of one's own
pursuit of pleasure or quest for dominance. But an objective sexual
ethic does not and need not confine itself to those who are victims of
personal or sexual misconduct, for 'the true light that gives light to
everyone' illumines us to see his face and body in the face and body
of our loved ones and to experience in our cherished relationships
the fruits of the Spirit. What has begun to be sketched here is a
theology which, while critical of some elements of natural law,
emphatically retains both a knowledge of Christ through ordinary
relational experience and an objective moral order.

Passionate ethics is wary of a traditional virtue ethic because of the
latter's preference for starting with the cardinal virtue of temperance
rather than justice. We have seen how, in sexual relations, virtue
begins with chastity, and is seen as negative, consisting primarily in
the ability to moderate desire, rather than as 'a capacity for appropriate feeling and action with respect to other people' (see above,
2.4). Restraint in sexual relations is undoubtedly needed, and coun-
selled in the scriptures. But the shift from an individual view to a
relational view of the human person makes relationships primary,
and a sexual ethic which was based less on temperance, more on
justice, would produce a different result. A sexual ethic based on the
pursuit of the common good would not place the interests of one
individual over another, since the achievement of just relationships,
recognizable by their mutual and non-exploitative character, would

be the aim of a justice ethic. A justice ethic would hold in equal regard the children who might be the possible outcome of uncontracepted sexual intercourse. In this respect, temperance acquires a different meaning. It is moderation neither of desire nor of pleasure, but a holy determination to refrain from procreative sexual activity for the sake of justice to the not yet born. If we are in just relationships with our partners, we may hope to strive better for justice in an unjust world. The theological virtues of faith, hope and love belong to the whole people of God which does not require hierarchical ministry to receive them.

Passionate ethics welcomes renewed emphasis on the Church as a 'community of character' because it is community-orientated and inevitably leads to a relational view of people. An unresolved issue here is how malleable the virtues are. If they can be flexibly regarded as the skills required for a community to live faithful to its tradition (see above, **2.5**) then some of those who currently stretch the normal sexual conventions operating within church life may already be regarded as well endowed with the virtues. One thinks of the virtue of patience possessed by lesbian and gay Christians who remain in the churches despite the likely hostile environment in which they are set. The virtue of hope is severely tested in these oppressive conditions. Those unmarried sexually active couples who remain faithful to each other, to Christ and to their particular churches may be seen to be endowed with the virtue of fortitude, for sticking with their convictions and encouraging the churches to rethink their sexual theology. Creative possibilities for a virtue ethic remain largely unexplored.

Passionate ethics is bound to welcome the emphases on dialogue, icon and transformation, associated with ecclesial ethics (see above, **2.6**). Christian feminism will permeate passionate ethics throughout. We have seen enough of **androcentrism** and the exclusion of women's experience to realize that anything less than an inclusive ethic of equal regard will be distorting and oppressive. Passionate ethics revalues the passions, and like the virtues in narrative ethics, it sees them as *social*, rather than individual, qualities. According to the *Catechism*, 'The term "passions" refers to the affections or the feelings. By his emotions man intuits the good and suspects evil.'[103] 'The principal passions are love and hate, desire and fear, joy, sadness and anger.'[104] The account of the passions given here assumes too readily a medieval and individualistic view of the human person. But relatedness makes the passions primary in our understanding of ourselves. A more relational assessment of the passions sees them treated in

Western thought as passive forces, private feelings, or unwelcome disturbances, all of which elicit the response of suspicion or control.[105] A return to a more biblical understanding of the passions sees them instead as the summons to respond to other people.

> Our passions link us with other persons — in grievance, in sorrow, in delight. These powerful forces are not private, but social . . . our passions are meant to connect us to others. These stirrings are social signals, alerting us and prodding us to respond. We are more likely to react responsibly to our passions if we acknowledge that these personal arousals are not private.[106]

The God of the Old Testament and the life of Jesus testify to divine passion and arousal.[107] Our sexual loving is thus able to mirror the passionate love of God.

2.13 SUMMARY

This chapter has prepared for the examination of the churches' sexual teaching in Chapters 3 to 10 by considering a range of theories in Christian ethics. We shall shortly see how these theories find their way, implicitly or explicitly, into this teaching. Biblical, natural law, virtue, narrative, ecclesial, situation and feminist ethics have been introduced with sufficient detail for them to be recognized in subsequent chapters. No theory by itself has been found wholly adequate, and some difficulties in the attempt to posit ethical theories have been noted. Some criticisms of each have been offered. The attempt has been made, not to reconcile differences, but rather to use the diversity of the approaches considered as a resource for a 'passionate ethics'. Supporters of passionate ethics may justifiably claim that their approach is rooted in Bible and tradition, yet able to make better sense of human sexuality than some of the absolute positions considered. By the end of the book, readers will be able to assess this claim for themselves.

Notes

1 Deontological, emotivist, naturalist, non-naturalist, intuitionist, utilitarian, descriptivist, prescriptivist: these are some of the labels currently in use in philosophical ethics. These are described in W. D. Hudson, *Modern Moral Philosophy*, 2nd edn (London and Basingstoke: Macmillan, 1983). Since they play no part in *People of Passion*, they will not be defined here.

2 This suspicion of theory, or of 'grand narratives', is associated with 'post-modernism'. See, e.g., Zygmunt Bauman, *Postmodern Ethics* (Oxford: Blackwell, 1993), p. 2.

3 See Susan Parsons, 'Feminist reflections on embodiment and sexuality', *Studies in Christian Ethics*, 4.2 (1991), p. 17.

4 Philip Goodchild expresses this well: 'There is a radical difference in nature between any theory, fictional world, tradition, community, character, value, practice, experience, or imperative which we can construct, and the real workings and characteristics of life which are concerned with the encounters and relations between these instances. The messenger of this bad news is always the body, and the physical events which happen to us and those we influence.' See his 'Christian ethics in the 'postmodern condition', *Studies in Christian Ethics*, 8.1 (1995), p. 25.

5 See, e.g., James A. Nash, *Loving Nature: Ecological Integrity and Christian Responsibility* (Nashville: Abingdon Press/Churches' Center for Theology and Public Policy, 1991), especially chs 8–9.

6 Bauman, *Postmodern Ethics*, p. 154.

7 Friedrich Nietzsche, *Twilight of the Idols* (Baltimore: Penguin Books, 1968), p. 45.

8 General Assembly Special Committee on Human Sexuality, Presbyterian Church (USA), *Keeping Body and Soul Together: Sexuality, Spirituality, and Social Justice* (1991), p. 22. The report goes on to make a series of very proper qualifications. It should be noted that the report was received, but not endorsed by the Presbyterian Church.

9 J. I. H. McDonald, *Biblical Interpretation and Christian Ethics* (Cambridge: Cambridge University Press, 1993), pp. 6–7.

10 A more detailed account of the use of the Bible in Christian ethics is attempted in ch. 10.

11 *Encyclical Letter Veritatis Splendor addressed by the Supreme Pontiff Pope John Paul II to all the Bishops of the Catholic Church Regarding Certain Fundamental Questions of the Church's Moral Teaching* (1993).

12 *Ibid.*, para. 1.

13 *Ibid.*, paras 35–53. There is a bewildering number of names for this law in the text, e.g. moral, eternal, natural, natural moral, divine, new, common, interior and perfect.

14 *Ibid.*, para. 40.

15 *Ibid.*, paras 38, 40.

16 *Ibid.*, para. 41.

17 *Ibid.*, para. 42.

18 *Ibid.*, para. 43.

19 *Ibid.*, para. 73 (original emphasis).

20 *Ibid.*, para. 78 (original emphasis).

21 *Ibid.*, paras 79–80.

22 *Ibid.*, para. 85 (original emphases).

23 *Ibid.*, para. 80, drawing on the Pastoral Constitution on the Church in the Modern World, *Gaudium et Spes*, 27.

24 See Nicholas Lash, 'Teaching in crisis', in John Wilkins (ed.), *Understanding Veritatis Splendor* (London: SPCK, 1994), p. 30. But Pope Paul VI did not speak of the use of contraceptives as an intrinsically evil act. The word he used was not *malum* but *inhonestum*, and he used that word deliberately to avoid saying their use was intrinsically evil. The *Catechism of the Catholic Church* (London: Geoffrey Chapman, 1994) describes contraception as 'intrinsically evil' (para. 2370, p. 508).

25 *Catechism of the Catholic Church*, para. 27.

26 *Ibid.*, para. 110.

27 *Ibid.*, para. 4.

28 Paula Fredriksen, in Bruce M. Metzger and Michael D. Coogan (eds), *The Oxford Companion to the Bible* (New York: Oxford University Press, 1993), p. 424.

29 And opinion is divided. Michael Keeling seeks to re-establish the concept of 'law' in Christian ethics in his *The Mandate of Heaven: The Divine Command and*

the Natural Order (Edinburgh: T. & T. Clark, 1996). See also Richard Mouw, *The God Who Commands* (Notre Dame: University of Notre Dame Press, 1990). But moral obligation and moral responsibility is capable of being expressed in other ways. See, e.g., McDonald, *Biblical Interpretation*, p. 140.

30 Bernard Häring, *My Witness for the Church* (New York, 1992), p. 23: cited in Charles Yeats, 'Economic life', in Charles Yeats (ed.), *Veritatis Splendor: A Response* (Norwich: Canterbury Press, 1994), ch. 6, p. 53.

31 Yeats, 'Economic life', p. 54.

32 John Stuart Mill's acerbic essay 'Nature', in his *Nature, the Utility of Religion, and Theism* (1850–58), contains devastating arguments against the credibility of concepts of nature which set 'natural' and 'artificial' against each other.

33 James M. Gustafson, 'Nature: its status in theological ethics', *Logos*, 3 (1982), p. 9.

34 See, e.g., Edward Stein (ed.), *Forms of Desire: Sexual Orientation and the Social Constructionist Controversy* (Routledge: New York and London, 1990).

35 Lisa Sowle Cahill, 'Accent on the masculine', in Wilkins, *Understanding Veritatis Splendor*, p. 54.

36 *Ibid.*, p. 55.

37 Notable in the literature for its pervasive influence is Alasdair McIntyre's *After Virtue: A Study in Moral Theory* (London: Duckworth, 1981).

38 Richard McBrien, *Catholicism* (London: Geoffrey Chapman, 3rd edn, 1994), p. 925.

39 Thomas Aquinas, *Summa Theologiae*, vol. 23, 56.3. See, e.g., Timothy McDermott (ed.), *Summa Theologiae: A Concise Translation* (London: Methuen, 1991), p. 233.

40 Aquinas, *Summa Theologiae*, vol. 22, 49.3: McDermott, p. 225.

41 *Ibid.*

42 *Ibid.*, vol. 23, 60–61: McDermott, pp. 238–40.

43 Jean Porter, *Moral Action and Christian Ethics* (Cambridge: Cambridge University Press, 1995), p. 155.

44 *Ibid.*, p. 170.

45 *Ibid.*, p. 147.

46 Aquinas, *Summa Theologiae*, vol. 23, 61.2: McDermott, p. 240. St Paul mentions these in 1 Corinthians 13.13, but he does not call them virtues.

47 *Ibid.*

48 Porter, *Moral Action*, p. 173.

49 John Stuart Mill was importantly right about this. A person has the 'power to alter his character', he wrote, because 'its being ... formed for him, is not inconsistent with its being, in part, formed *by* him ... His character is formed by his circumstances ... but his own desire to mould it in a particular way is one of those circumstances ... '. See his *A System of Logic* (1843), book 6, ch. 2.

50 For an exception, see *Keeping Body and Soul Together*, 19–20, *et passim.*

51 John Milbank, *Theology and Social Theory: Beyond Secular Reason* (Oxford: Blackwell, 1990), p. 33, and see pp. 332–51. The *Catechism of the Catholic Church* upholds prudence as 'the charioteer of the virtues' (para. 1806, p. 400) and so leaves no doubt about the milieu of militarism and combat.

52 Milbank, *Theology and Social Theory*, p. 364.

53 Sally Purvis, 'Mothers, neighbors and strangers: another look at agape', in A. Thatcher and E. Stuart (eds), *Christian Perspectives on Sexuality and Gender* (Leominster: Gracewing/Fowler Wright, 1996), ch. 6.1.

54 Porter, *Moral Action*, p. 182.

55 Since we are dealing with highly androcentric thought, the male pronoun is ironically retained.

56 Porter, *Moral Action*, p. 183.

57 McIntyre, *After Virtue*, pp. 202–3.

58 The title of one of Hauerwas' works, viz., *A Community of Character: Toward a Constructive Christian Social Ethic* (Notre Dame: University of Notre Dame Press, 1981).

59 Stanley Hauerwas, *The Peaceable Kingdom: A Primer in Christian Ethics* (Notre Dame: University of Notre Dame Press, 1983; London: SCM Press, 1984), pp. 100–1.

60 Hauerwas, *A Community of Character*, p. 115.

61 *Ibid.*, p. 148.

62 Hauerwas, *The Peaceable Kingdom*, ch.5.

63 For a different set of criticisms of Hauerwas' work, see Jean Porter, *The Recovery of Virtue: The Relevance of Aquinas for Christian Ethics* (London: SPCK, 1994), pp. 30–1.

64 Vigen Guroian, *Ethics After Christendom: Toward an Ecclesial Christian Ethic* (Grand Rapids, MI: Eerdmans, 1994), p. 32.

65 *Ibid.*, p. 2.

66 *Ibid.*, p. 32.

67 *Ibid.*, p. 39.

68 *Ibid.*, p. 47.

69 *Ibid.*

70 *Ibid.*, p. 49.

71 *Ibid.*, p. 50.

72 *Ibid.*, p. 66.

73 John A. T. Robinson, *Honest to God* (London: SCM Press, 1963), ch. 6. See also his *Christian Freedom in a Permissive Society* (London: SCM Press, 1970).

74 Joseph Fletcher, *Situation Ethics: The New Morality* (London: SCM Press, 1966), and *Moral Responsibility* (London: SCM Press, 1967).

75 Fletcher, *Situation Ethics*, p. 30 (italics in original). The biblical passages cited are Matthew 5.43–48, 22.34–40; Luke 6.27–28, 10.25–28, 10.29–37; Mark 12.28–34; Galatians 5.14; Romans 13.8–10.

76 *Ibid.*, p. 26 (italics in original).

77 Rosemary Radford Ruether, 'Feminist theology', in Alan Richardson and John Bowden (eds), *A New Dictionary of Christian Theology* (London: SCM Press, 1983), pp. 210–11.

78 See, e.g., Ann Loades, 'Introduction', in Ann Loades (ed.), *Feminist Theology: A Reader* (London: SPCK, 1990), pp. 1–11.

79 This is not to say that feminist ethics is against *all* generalizations. On this, see Susan Parsons, 'Feminist ethics after modernity', *Studies in Christian Ethics*, 8.1 (1995), pp. 77–94.

80 Jennifer Rike, 'The lion and the unicorn: feminist perspectives on Christian love as care', in Thatcher and Stuart, *Christian Perspectives*, ch. 6.2.

81 Genesis 1.26–27. While 'equality' is not found in the teaching of Jesus, women are revalued in his teaching and attitude towards them.

82 *Catechism of the Catholic Church*, para. 2352, p. 503. The quotations are from Congregation for the Doctrine of the Faith, *Persona Humana* 9.

83 *Ibid.*, para. 2350, p. 503.

84 *Ibid.*, para. 2341, p. 501.

85 Onan's sin of spilling his seed on the ground (Genesis 38.9) was his practice of sleeping with his dead brother's wife but ejaculating outside of her, thereby failing to 'do his duty as the husband's brother and raise up offspring for his brother'.

86 *Issues in Human Sexuality: A Statement by the House of Bishops* (London: Church House Publishing, 1991).

87 Aquinas believed an offspring was the completed, male seed, unchanged, and fulfilled. On this view wasting seed is wasting potential babies.

88 Evelyn Eaton Whitehead and James D. Whitehead, *A Sense of Sexuality: Christian Love and Intimacy* (New York: Crossroad, 1994), ch. 8, pp. 133–7.

89 *Ibid.*, p. 137.

90 This is the translation used in the *Catechism of the Catholic Church*, para. 2258, p.486. The Revised English Bible has 'Do not commit murder', which is of course very different.

91 *Ibid.*, para. 2270, p. 489, drawing on *Donum Vitae* I, 1.

92 *Ibid.*, para. 2272, p. 489.

93 *Ibid.*, para. 2274, p. 490.

94 Joseph Selling, 'You shall love your neighbour: commandments 4–10', in Michael J. Walsh (ed.), *Commentary on the Cathechism of the Catholic Church* (London: Geoffrey Chapman, 1994), p. 371.

95 *Ibid.*, p. 372.

96 Earlier texts have been more careful about assigning the status of person to the fertilized ovum. See Selling, 'You shall love', p. 392, n. 13.

97 Board of Social Responsibility (of the Church of England), *Abortion and the Church: What Are the Issues?* [GS Misc 408] (London: Church House Publishing, 1993), pp. 16–17.

98 *Ibid.*, p. 15.

99 *Ibid.*, p. 18.

100 *Ibid.*, p. 19.

101 *Ibid.*, p. 20.

102 Goodchild, 'Christian ethics', p. 22.

103 *Catechism of the Catholic Church*, para. 1771, p. 395.

104 *Ibid.*, para. 1772, p. 395.

105 Whitehead and Whitehead, *A Sense of Sexuality*, pp. 112–15.

106 *Ibid.*, p. 113.

107 *Ibid.*, pp. 115–19.

Suggestions for further reading

Vigen Guroian, *Ethics after Christendom: Toward an Ecclesial Christian Ethic* (Grand Rapids, MI: Eerdmans, 1994).

Stanley Hauerwas, *A Community of Character: Toward a Constructive Christian Social Ethic* (Notre Dame: University of Notre Dame Press, 1981).

J. I. H. McDonald, *Biblical Interpretation and Christian Ethics* (Cambridge: Cambridge University Press, 1993).

Jean Porter, *Moral Action and Christian Ethics* (Cambridge: Cambridge University Press, 1995).

Evelyn Eaton Whitehead and James D. Whitehead, *A Sense of Sexuality: Christian Love and Intimacy* (New York: Crossroad, 1994).

3

MARRIAGE

3.1 RELATIONSHIPS

The traditional teaching of all the churches is that marriage is the sole relationship within which sexual intercourse is legitimate or acceptable to God. However in 1994, in the United Kingdom, fewer than 1 per cent of women born between 1966 and 1975 delayed their first sexual experience until marriage.[1] Since this book is 'about the exciting, and sometimes surprising, developments that are taking place in Christian teaching' (see **1.1**), much of the chapter is about the rethinking which is currently going on in the churches about marriage. This rethinking is untidy, controversial, divisive and incomplete. The re-examination currently in progress cannot but take into account the relationships other than marriage where, as a matter of fact, complete sexual intimacy occurs. These relationships include **cohabitations**, the partnerships of **lesbian** women and **gay** men, and sexual relations involving single and post-married people. The preoccupation of the churches with marriage is often a source of irritation and marginalization among these groups. While this chapter is also preoccupied with marriage, it traces the changes currently going on in the churches' understanding, and shows how these changes themselves contribute to a revaluing of some (but not all) sexual relationships which are non-matrimonial.

3.2 THE BIBLICAL ROOTS OF MARRIAGE

Marriage is a human institution, older and broader than the Christian understanding of it. An issue which has arisen for the Church of England is whether it should continue to honour its legal obligation to provide Christian marriage services for couples who are not

Christians. A 1988 Church of England report argues strongly for the retention of the *status quo*. The theological reason given for this position is based on the assumption that 'the institution of marriage is given by God in the creation of human life'.[2] This report warns against a narrow understanding of marriage, and generously affirms it to be

> particularly unsuitable for the claiming of a Christian monopoly, when the union of husband and wife, as it has been known to human beings since before the dawn of history, is (at its best) a living parable in which human grace gives people a glimpse of what divine grace is like.[3]

There is no detailed teaching about marriage in the Gospels, although when Jesus is drawn into theological controversy about divorce (see **3.2.1**), his opposition to it shows him both to approve of marriage as an institution embedded in the story of creation, and to disapprove of the imbalance of power between the partners which allowed husbands to divorce their wives with ease.[4] The expectation of an early **parousia** led Paul to advocate marriage as second best to singleness (see **1.9**). The '**Household Codes**' (see **1.7**) of the New Testament teach the submission of wives to husbands,[5] and as the Church of Scotland Panel on Doctrine forcibly reminds us, 'the question must be faced of whether such words as "fornication" and "adultery" actually mean the same in a context where women were legally and socially seen as the *property* of the responsible males — e.g. a father, husband, brother'.[6] There is no guidance whatever in the Bible about the marriageable age of intending partners, about the form of the vows or the content of any ceremony, and despite centuries of insistence to the contrary, the Bible does not forbid sexual intercourse before marriage. The Song of Songs presupposes it (see **8.2**).[7]

The meanings assigned to marriage in the Bible may be grouped around three central motifs. They are: a man and a woman becoming *one flesh*; a **covenant** between a man and a woman; and a sharing of the bridal pair in the mystical *union* between Christ and his Church. None of them however is free from **patriarchal** assumptions about male superiority, headship and domination (see **1.6**), however disguised and qualified. It remains a vexed question whether these motifs can continue to inform Christian marriage without at the same time loading the marriage bond with the baggage of male domination.

3.2.1 One flesh

When Jesus was asked about the legality of divorce, his questioners referred to the practice of Jewish husbands issuing a 'certificate of dismissal' (Mark 10.4) to their wives. This practice was based on the Deuteronomic law which allowed a husband to do this 'if . . . she does not win his favour because he finds something offensive in her' (Deuteronomy 24.1). Commenting on this practice, Jesus says:

> It was because of your stubbornness that he [Moses] made this rule for you. But in the beginning, at the creation, 'God made them male and female.' 'That is why a man leaves his father and mother, and is united to his wife, and the two become one flesh.' It follows that they are no longer two individuals: they are one-flesh. Therefore what God has joined together, man must not separate. (Mark 10.5–9)

Jesus quotes from two verses of Genesis which appear in the Christian Bible as 1.27 and 2.24. The second of these is 'Therefore a man leaves his father and mother and cleaves to his wife, and they become one flesh.'[8] He reaffirms the Jewish understanding of marriage as the becoming 'one flesh' of a man and a woman. He teaches that their subsequent union is a state of affairs willed by God and so unbreakable.

The understanding of marriage as a 'one-flesh union' is therefore central to Jews and Christians alike. But there is still legitimate doubt about what 'one flesh' means. In the context of the creation narrative of which it is a part, 'the LORD God' has just taken 'one of the man's ribs' and 'built' it up into a woman (Genesis 2.21–22). Citing Genesis 2.24, Paul clearly thought that a one-flesh relationship need not be confined to marriage — Christians using prostitutes established one-flesh relationships with them (1 Corinthians 6.16). 'One flesh' may mean the restoration of 'the original pattern of human unity' which existed before the rib was taken from the sleeping man.[9] The mythical nature of such thinking will be obvious to everyone. While the one-flesh union is obviously achieved in sexual intercourse in a literal sense, it came to be understood as a lifelong partnership. It is 'the joining of two lives in one', 'a real union of two lives which is both physical and spiritual'.[10]

3.2.2 Covenant

Biblical religion is a religion of 'covenant'. In human affairs a covenant is a binding agreement, a compact, or a legal contract between two parties. In biblical religion the two parties are God and God's people. For Christians the two 'Testaments' of the Bible are the two covenants. On God's side of the covenant, steadfast love, faithfulness and mercy are essential properties of the covenant, but on the human side, selfishness and faithlessness can be expected. The most notorious example of this is found in the book of Hosea where the broken covenant between God and his people is symbolized by Hosea's unfaithful wife Gomer, while the long-suffering husband stands for the ever-faithful God (Hosea 1.2–3). The depiction of Gomer, and the patriarchal attitude of her husband Hosea toward her, contain awkward and unwelcome assumptions about the **gender** relations between them.[11]

When a human covenant and a divine covenant are compared, there will be similarities and dissimilarities between them. It is essential to be clear where the line between them is drawn. A covenant between God and any group of people is not a relationship of equals. Given the unequal distribution of power between the parties, we might say, it is small wonder that, in the Bible, Israel, or humanity, or the world, is in breach of covenant. We are not equal to God. It is possible however to draw out similarities instead of dissimilarities between covenants. The faithful, steadfast love exercised by God towards God's people, in spite of their haphazard and half-hearted response, is a firm conviction of both Christians and Jews. Partners who are committed to each other may well be prompted to regard their relationship also as a sharing of steadfast human love through which something of divine love may be glimpsed and experienced. But the dangers are obvious. An unequal divine–human power relationship may readily replicate itself in an unequal husband–wife relationship, and one will be appealed to as the certain legitimation of the other.

3.2.3 Mystical union

The author of the letter to the Ephesians devotes much of it to the topic of appropriate behaviour in the newly established community of Christians at Ephesus. With regard to relationships within Christian households, he follows conventional **morality** but reflects deeply upon them from the resources of the new faith, providing readers with a heady mix of convention and transformation. There is to be mutual subjection to one another 'out of reverence for Christ' (Ephesians 5.21). However, this potential defusing of the subordinate relationship of husbands to wives is short-lived. Wives are to be 'subject to your husbands as though to the Lord; for the man is the head of the woman, just as Christ is the head of the church' (Ephesians 5.23–24). While husbands are 'to love their wives, as they love their own bodies', the basic domination–submission relationship between husbands and wives receives further reinforcement in an argument from **analogy**. As it is between husband and wife, so it is between Christ and the Church. The union between husband and wife has its more profound parallel in the union between Christ and the Church. The Church is frequently called 'the body of Christ' and the union between the husband and his wife's body is paralleled by the relationship between Christ and his body, the Church.

The author makes specific use of the 'one flesh' passage from Genesis, and says it is a 'great truth' which applies both 'to Christ and to the church' and 'also to each one of you'. There lies here a profound mystical theology of marriage which is to influence every century of Christian thought including the present. Sadly however, the legacy of interpretation it has produced is also deeply ambiguous, since the mystical theology which elevates the marital relationship to a new level of understanding and experience also reinforces the husband's domination over the wife. The ambiguity of the passage is best summed up in a comment on it by Carolyn Osiek who calls it 'one of the most dangerous texts in the New Testament'. Why? Because

> Here the submission of the wife to the husband and the love of the husband for the wife are assimilated to the relationship of the church to Christ. In the ancient context of patriarchal marriage, this comparison must have been one of the most effective ways of sanctifying the marriage bond and of proposing just as challenging a role for both parties. Because of the ecclesiological comparison, however, the text has too often been seen to render normative the subordinate relationship.[12]

3.3 THE CHANGING PURPOSES OF MARRIAGE

Paul's clear preference for celibacy over marriage continued to be influential in the second and subsequent centuries of the Church.[13]

Augustine wrote in 401 that the 'goods of marriage' (see below, **3.8**) were the procreation of children, fidelity, and the binding obligation (*sacramentum*) that prevented the partners ever dissolving their marriage.[14] For both Augustine and Aquinas **celibacy** is preferred to marriage and sexual intercourse is allowed to the married only for the sake of procreation, or, following Paul (1 Corinthians 7.5–6), to prevent the fornication of either partner which the withholding of intercourse might precipitate.[15] There is little if any thought of mutual love in these highly regulated authorized couplings; indeed uninhibited love-making was equated with adultery.[16]

The Protestant churches of the Reformation retained the three 'goods of marriage'. However they abolished the rule of compulsory celibacy for priests, and refused to regard celibacy as superior. According to the Book of Common Prayer holy matrimony was

> First, ... ordained for the procreation of children, to be brought up in the fear and nurture of the Lord, and to the praise of his holy Name.
>
> Secondly, It was ordained for a remedy against sin, and to avoid fornication; that such persons as have not the gift of **continency** might marry, and keep themselves undefiled members of Christ's body.
>
> Thirdly, It was ordained for the mutual society, help, and comfort, that the one ought to have of the other, both in prosperity and adversity.

There was disagreement about whether this numerical order of causes also represented an order of importance of each.[17] The second cause clearly bears the continued influence of the tradition that celibacy is preferable to marriage, and so confers only a negative benefit. The third should be read in conjunction with the newly established presence within the Reformed churches of married theologians and ministers whose married state was held to produce significant benefits, not least 'in an increasingly profound theological understanding of the relational aspects of sex and marriage, such as could come only from reflection upon the inner meaning of an experience hitherto denied to the clergy'.[18] By the seventeenth century a majority of Protestant theologians held that the 'mutual society' of husband and wife was the most significant of the three causes.[19] This change of balance in the understanding of the purposes of marriage, whereby the personal union of the couple and the mutual enriching of their lives becomes its primary meaning, is profound, and was consolidated later, especially in nonconformist Protestant churches.

There is a further difficulty in specifying the purpose of marriage. In **natural law** theories (see **2.3**) everything has a purpose. In such a scheme of things a basic question to be asked is 'What it is *for*?' But this **teleological** way of understanding the world is nothing like as obvious to us today as it was in the past to the followers of Aristotle and Aquinas. We might be happier to accept that something just is, without pressing purposive or functional questions about it. Marriage might just be (more of this shortly). One of the contributors to a notable collection of essays on marriage published by the United Reformed Church has reminded us that the very quest for a suitable description of the purpose of marriage took place in a period of the Church's life when celibacy was regarded as better, and so a theological justification for the inferior state of married life had to be found.[20] But perhaps justifications do not need to be found for the diversity of relationships and statuses that occur among us. This is not to say that marriage ought not to be clearly defined, for otherwise partners would not know what they were committing themselves to, or why. It is to say that descriptions and justifications are different. And descriptions are never fixed or final.

Those people in the churches who affirm the churches' 'traditional doctrine' of marriage will therefore have a problem specifying what that doctrine is. The value of marriage in relation to celibacy has changed, like the value of the respective internal goods of marriage in relation to each other. For most of the Church's history, marriage has not been regarded as a **sacrament**. In the twentieth century the arrival of reliable contraceptives has weakened the procreative justification for marriage still further. The essential point to grasp is that the churches' understanding of marriage is a dynamic one. It has never been finally formulated, and it is open to further changes. It may be possible to discern some of the changes which are happening now, even though, because one is in the middle of them, a clear vantage point is unreachable. However, the next four sections suggest other transitions in the understanding of marriage which may be recognizable in the available literature. They are certainly evident in the wider culture.

3.4 FROM PROCREATION TO PERSONAL UNION?

We have seen (see **1.10**) how the main purpose of sexual activity was regarded as that of having children. From Augustine to the Second Vatican Council the Roman Catholic Church has taught that 'the primary end of marriage is the procreation and nurture of children; its secondary end is mutual help and the remedying of **concupiscence**'.[21] The Council ended the distinction between primary and secondary ends. Faced with pressure to restate the traditional view, the Council refused. It taught explicitly that procreation 'does not make the other ends of marriage of less account' and that marriage 'is not instituted solely for procreation'.[22] In fresh, positive (but still sexist) language, the Council taught:

> The biblical Word of God several times urges the betrothed and the married to nourish and develop their wedlock by pure conjugal love and undivided affection. Many men of our new age also highly regard true love between husband and wife as it manifests itself in a variety of ways depending on the worthy customs of various peoples and times. This love is an eminently human one since it is directed from one person to another through an affection of the will ... Thus the Christian family, which springs from marriage as a reflection of the loving covenant uniting Christ and the Church, and as a participation in that covenant, will manifest to all men the Saviour's living presence in the world, and the genuine nature of the Church.[23]

One wonders why, if the fostering of pure conjugal love is so biblically obvious, emphasis on it prior to the Council is so slight. The 1983 revised *Code of Canon Law* clearly re-emphasizes the theological significance of the love between partners. It says that

> The matrimonial covenant, by which a man and a woman establish between themselves a partnership of the whole of life, is by its nature ordered toward the good of the spouses and the procreation and education of offspring; this covenant between baptized persons has been raised by Christ the Lord to the dignity of a sacrament.[24]

In summary, there are now two equal purposes of marriage in Catholic doctrine, the 'procreative' and the 'unitive', and neither is more important than the other. The transition 'from procreation to personal union' means nothing more or less than this. In this respect Catholicism catches up with the churches of the Reformation. The 'marital love' between spouses *and* the procreation and nurture of children are equally important.

There are undoubted changes here in Catholic doctrine. One well-known Catholic writer, delighted at the changes, says, 'For those who see the Roman Catholic Church as a monolithic, unchanging institution they need to read the treatment of marriage within that Church in the last fifty years. They will be amazed at the changes that have occurred.'[25] Others point out that that Church arrives at this position very late, and that it is overshadowed by still later teaching on contraception and women which dispels any gain the Council made. However, it is certain that a change occurred at Vatican II, and it is therefore difficult for those who are opposed to developments in that Church's teaching about **sexuality** and marriage to maintain that traditional doctrine is unchanging. The point to be made, and pushed, is that changes in the churches' teaching have occurred continually and some are occurring now.

3.5 FROM PATRIARCHY TO PARITY?

It might be thought that the stress on mutual help and society which marked the Reformed churches on marriage paved the way for an understanding of the relationship between the partners based on parity of esteem. Such a view would be gravely mistaken. Derrick Sherwin Bailey, a pioneering exponent of Christian teaching about sexuality in a previous generation of theologians, recalls how the very seventeenth-century Anglican divines who affirmed the mutual society of marriage were uncompromising about the subordinate relationship of wives to husbands which was ordained by God. They taught that:

> The basic principle of sexual relationship is that of male headship; men in general are credited with superior understanding and a prerogative of reason and government, while women are alleged to be so constituted as to require guidance, control, and protection. They are intrinsically inferior in excellence, imbecile by sex and nature, weak in body, inconstant in mind, and imperfect and infirm in character.[26]

By contrast, most recent formularies stress the mutual joy and partnership which is to be found in marriage. La Fédération Protestante de France stated in 1975 that:

> By the free marital engagement in which they affirm their love, a man and a woman unite in accordance with the plan of the Creator and the vocation given to most people whether Christian or not ...

Marriage establishes a mutual relation of complete and unselfish love, integrating sexuality and fertility. It includes the decision and the hope of lifelong fidelity and mutual respect, and openness to other people and society . . . [27]

In 1978, the Anglican report *Marriage and the Church's Task* proclaimed marriage to be 'a relational bond of personal love, a compound of commitment, experience and response, in which the commitment clothes itself in the flesh and blood of a living union. The commitment looks forward to this deeper union of love . . . '[28] The 1988 Lambeth Conference of Anglican Bishops, continuing the emphasis away from procreation and towards the personal union of the couple, stated:

> Anglican formularies have traditionally taught that the union of husband and wife in heart, body and mind is intended of God for their mutual joy; for help and comfort of one another in both prosperity and adversity; and, when it is God's will, for the procreation of children and their nurture in the knowledge and love of the Lord.[29]

The *Catechism* also affirms the equality of the men and women and bases it on Genesis 2.24.

> Holy Scripture affirms that man and woman were created for one another: 'It is not good that the man should be alone.' The woman, 'flesh of his flesh', i.e. his counterpart, *his equal*, his nearest in all things, is given to him by God as a 'helpmate'; she thus represents God from whom comes our help.[30]

These recent trends indicate a transition away from patriarchy and towards parity in the theological understanding of the marital relationship. The South African Anglican Theological Commission could hardly be more emphatic that male domination in marriage is as bad as racial domination in society. That Church's ministers are told to teach their congregations regularly and frankly about sexuality, and such teaching

> must refer especially to ways of sexual intimacy as expressions of love and of self-discovery in discovering the other. Above all else, it must stress the *mutual* commitment of both partners to each other and the need to avoid any sense of domination of one partner by the other. Ethical judgements about sexual behaviour must be consistent with those about racism, sexism and other sins.[31]

It is possible to view these, and many more, similar, contemporary statements about marriage as welcome developments in the over-coming of biological and patriarchal views about its purpose. They are. Even the *Catechism* bemoans the fact that marriage was 'changed into a relationship of domination and lust' as a result of human sinfulness, thereby affirming that domination has no place in Chris-tian marriage at all.[32] But some of these statements also provide evidence of an immense gap between the world of theology (of all varieties) and the actual experience of marriages, particularly the experiences of wives. That is why one of us has spoken of 'the idolatry of the ideal',[33] and why we want to know whether 'an institution conceived on the premiss of unequal power relations' can 'ever fulfil the purposes of marriage'[34] which these documents prescribe. One such report which does overtly acknowledge the lived experience of some women in patriarchal marriages is that of the Presbyterian Church of the USA. This report acknowledges the pointlessness of lofty pronouncements which fail to connect with the actual experi-ence of married life. With a rare honesty, coupled with a delicate subtlety, the Presbyterians seek to commend marriages as 'cour-ageous experiments in risking **mutuality**'[35] while at the same time admitting the destructive effects of patriarchy. They say:

> As moral teacher and advocate, the church, on the one hand, must insist that patriarchal marriages, based on male dominance and female submission, are morally unacceptable. Such marriages offer little more than distorted power dynamics between two unequal partners. The church has a primary obligation also to break painful silences surrounding marriage in our culture, including the fact that wife-battering is rampant and almost 40 percent of rapes happen inside **heterosexual** marriages. For many women, the tradi-tional male-dominant marriage is simply not a safe place. Control and violation through sexualized terror hardly gladden the heart or lift the spirit.
>
> On the other hand, the church must enthusiastically promote egalitarian marriage relations, ones in which 'friendship [is] sealed by commitment'. In such relations persons do not 'lose' themselves as much as relocate themselves within a new center of gravity, the in-betweenness of self and other as they receive and give, give and receive affection, passion, energy, investment and time. Such mar-riages are grounded in mutual trust, affection, and high regard for the spiritual and bodily integrity of both parties.[36]

3.6 FROM 'SOLE RELATIONSHIP' TO 'SOUL-RELATIONSHIP'?

The third transition in Christian attitudes to marriage is between that which regards it as the *only*, the sole relationship, within which sexual intimacy and intercourse may take place, and that which regards it as one, or the principal, relationship within which sexual intimacy and intercourse may be appropriate. The Church of Scotland report, while affirming that 'the marriage relationship is of unique importance',[37] 're-affirm[s] that marriage is *one of the patterns of relationship* offered by God for our human well-being because it is not good for us to be alone'.[38] The inference cannot be avoided that other patterns of relationship are also offered by God for our well-being, a factor which doubtless led to a strident dissenting appendage to the report from 6 of the 14 members of the Panel that produced it. Among its errors, according to this minority, is that

> the Report in its recommendations concerning same-sex relationships and pre-marital sex, weakens the Church's ability to speak prophetically by implying that these forms of sexual relationships are *morally equivalent to marriage,* thereby weakening the normative status of marriage and diminishing the significance of the two-parent family.[39]

Those churches who allow their theology to be influenced by the pastoral realities which are daily faced by their clergy and ministers may find themselves speaking more charitably, if less prophetically, about same-sex relationships (see Chapter 7) and 'pre-marital' sex. The Anglican Bishops' report *Issues in Human Sexuality* recognizes that the traditional teaching about **chastity** is simply not being observed and is unclear what to do about it. Without defining chastity it says that chastity is 'God's will for married people' before marriage. This is an 'ideal' but (this is where pastoral honesty influences the theology):

> We recognise that it is increasingly hard today for the unmarried generally, and for young people facing peer group pressure in particular, to hold to this ideal, and therefore both the Church and its individual members need to be clearer and stronger in supporting those who are struggling against the tide of changing sexual standards.[40]

This puts pastoral carers in a dilemma. On the one hand, for the sake of that diminishing number of very faithful Christians who uphold the traditional teaching such teaching is to be asserted more clearly and strongly. On the other hand, this teaching is pastorally (and as it will turn out, theologically) unrealistic, and so the more it is affirmed, the more it will alienate Christians who do not live by it and add to the incredulity of those outside the churches.

To their credit, the bishops recognize this and go halfway towards resolving it. For they argue:

> If we believe in a Gospel of grace and restoration freely offered to all, we need to give this support in such a way that those who may eventually go with the tide will not feel that in the Church's eyes they are from then on simply failures for whom there is neither place nor love in the Christian community.

This is a godly, typically Anglican, muddle. The bishops are sufficiently in tune with the gospel to recognize that it is for sinners, and those who sinfully deviate from the Church's teaching do not place themselves outside of the Church's care. On the other hand the *Statement* is clear that swimmers with the tide will have fallen short of an 'ideal' and been swept along by the swirling currents of changing, i.e. falling, sexual standards. Dissent from the traditional teaching is allowed, indeed expected, but characterized as a 'falling short'.

The more recent Anglican report *Something to Celebrate* gives us important information about the tide of changing standards. The marriage rate for first marriages in England and Wales fell from 82 per thousand bachelors aged 16 and over in 1971 to 37 per thousand in 1992. The most common age for first marriages is 26 for women and 28 for men.[41] The report expects 'about 80 per cent of all women marrying in the 1990s to have cohabited before their first marriage'.[42] Behind these statistics lie massive social changes. There is now regularly a 15-year gap between the age of puberty and marriage. Higher education, training for jobs, the cost of housing, all contribute to the gap. More importantly there are many criticisms to be made of the institution of marriage as it has been historically practised (see below, **3.9**). A greater openness about sexuality has allowed sexual minorities to become heard. A growing number of people will not choose marriage at all. And above all the availability of a range of reliable contraceptives has fundamentally changed the meanings of sexual activity.

The authors of *Something to Celebrate* have not yet received the credit due to them both for addressing the world as it is and for making some courageous proposals for dealing with it. With regard to cohabitation it suggests:

> The wisest and most practical way forward . . . may be for Christians
> both to hold fast to the centrality of marriage and at the same to
> accept that cohabitation is, for many people, a step along the way
> towards that fuller and more complete commitment.[43]

Here at any rate is a constructive proposal for dealing with what some
theologians are still calling 'pre-marital sex'. 'The first step the
Church should take is to abandon the phrase "living in sin".'[44] But
the report also acknowledges the presence in the churches and in
society of large numbers of sexually active single people whom a
marriage-centred Christian sexual ethic will never reach (see below,
3.10). 'We are aware', they say,

> of the many mature single people in contemporary society who do
> not feel called to be celibate and yet seek to to live creatively and
> ethically in right relationships with others, with themselves and with
> God. We believe that one of the tasks facing the Church in the years
> ahead will be to develop a sexual **ethic** which embraces a dynamic
> view of sexual development, which acknowledges the profound
> cultural changes of the last decades and supports people in their
> search for commitment, faithfulness and constancy.[45]

This extract of the report is clear evidence of the trend away from
regarding marriage as the sole relationship for the sexually active.
There is little theology in the report, although there is a call for
theological work to be done. The sexual ethic envisaged remains in
the future, and given the rough ride the document was given at the
meeting of the General Synod of the Church of England which
received it, the task of producing it may not be undertaken by the
Church of England at all.[46]

3.7 FROM EVENT TO PROCESS?

The widespread practice of cohabitation does not make it right.
Nothing can be inferred from the extent of a practice to its moral
propriety. So why not speak prophetically to cohabitees, as the
Scottish dissenting minority wants, instead of watering down the
churches' teaching? There are in fact good historical and theological
reasons (as well as pastoral ones) why the churches should *not* do this
but should rethink cohabitation instead. We think there is almost a
collective amnesia among the denominations about the practice of

cohabitation in previous centuries, and that if the authors of *Something to Celebrate* had been more historically aware of the earlier practice of **betrothal** and the phased entry into the married state which such a practice provided, their proposal to abandon the phrase 'living in sin' would have been undergirded with additional and weighty support.

Christians do not generally have a service of official betrothal available to them to mark the beginning of intended (but not irrevocable) lifelong commitment prior to marriage. This is a pity. Such an arrangement was common in earlier periods. Parts of the marriage ceremony which are now taken for granted, like the joining of hands and exchanging of rings, 'are deep within our culture, but the roots of them are in domestic betrothal rituals that have been incorporated into the service, rather than the outworking of reflection on biblical concepts of marriage'.[47] Betrothal was the beginning, not the end, of the entry into marriage. Betrothal, says the historian John Gillis, writing of sixteenth-century practice in Britain,

> constituted the recognized rite of transition from friends to lovers, conferring on the couple the right to sexual as well as social intimacy ... Betrothal granted freedom to explore for any personal faults or incompatibilities that had remained hidden during the earlier, more inhibited phases of courtship and could be disastrous if carried into the indissoluble status of marriage.[48]

The Anglican report *An Honourable Estate* frankly states that:

> The espousal or betrothal followed by consummation was as much a marriage in the eyes of the courts as any subsequent church ceremony. In many areas a binding agreement between the parties in the face of witnesses sufficed for a marriage recognised by all concerned, including, in practice, the local church, provided no ecclesiastical offence was alleged.[49]

The Marriage Act of 1753 required all marriages in England and Wales to be registered. The report notes that in some places 10 to 15 per cent of the population was illegitimate at the end of the eighteenth century, and says:

> It is possible to interpret such trends as a continuation of the distinction between public and private marriage, with the difference that the 1753 Act deterred some of those entering into more private relationships from seeking ministrations of the Church.[50]

Many marrieds could not afford a public wedding and so lived together anyway. In Scotland, such 'irregular' or 'common law' marriages are still recognized by the courts provided there has been 'cohabitation with habit and repute "for a considerable time" (usually at least three years)'.[51]

Why have the churches forgotten about betrothal — a practice which has persisted since before the birth of Jesus and was observed by his parents (Matthew 1.18)? It is tempting to suggest the answer lies in the attempt to make a direct appeal to the scriptures without regard for the intervening history between biblical times and our own. Any group of theologians wishing to respond to the call of the authors of *Something to Celebrate* 'to develop a sexual ethic ... which acknowledges the profound cultural changes of the last decades' will want to draw a range of parallels between ancient traditions of betrothal and private marriage and the 'growing practice of betrothal'.[52]

The transition from event to process signals a new realization that marriages are not necessarily begun by weddings. The gradual entry into marriage may be fruitfully compared with the gradual entry of persons into the monastic life. When becoming married 'is compared with the analogous process of becoming a monk or nun, the temporal events of exclusivity, betrothal and marriage in a couple's relationship, might have their parallels in the stages of aspirant, postulant and novice'.[53] The transition from event to process makes it much harder for theologians to speak prophetically about sex before marriage because the married state and the event of a wedding may not coincide. Should any think this is a heretical and subversive suggestion, they should consult the title of the marriage service in the Book of Common Prayer. It is called 'the Form of Solemnization of Matrimony'. The service confirms, makes public, commemorates, a state of affairs *that already exists.*

3.8 THE 'GOODS' OF MARRIAGE

Let us return to the traditional view of marriage which has as its 'primary end' the procreation of children. Its 'goods' are children, fidelity and sacrament (see above, **3.4**). There can be no doubt that Augustine and Aquinas would have trouble with some of the accounts of marriage being developed by the churches, yet it may be remarkable and insufficiently recognized that the transitions which have just been described (see above, **3.4–3.7**) are actually congruent with the much older understanding. A strong case can be made for

reaffirming each of Augustine's three 'goods' within the wider framework of the churches' emerging understanding of marriage and
sexuality at the very end of the second millennium.

3.8.1 Children

All the churches insist that marriage is the proper context for having
and bringing up children. Of the transitions considered in this
chapter, the one relevant here is the move from regarding procreation as the sole or main purpose of marriage to regarding it as *one* of
the purposes of marriage (see above, **3.6**). Most people think it is the
main purpose of marriage.[54] The *Book of Common Order* of the Church
of Scotland is representative of this conviction. Marriage is 'a gift and
calling of God', but it is linked with 'the ordering of family life, where
children — who are also God's gifts to us — may enjoy the security of
love and the heritage of faith'.[55] Aquinas, despite the **androcentrism**
of the thirteenth century which leaps out at us from his writings with
a disabling force, only on one occasion linked the indissolubility of
marriage to the commitment of spouses to each *other*. Rather was it
'more centrally related to the needs of the species for the raising of
offspring'.[56] Sex outside marriage, he thought, was wrong because it
was 'disadvantageous to the care of children, and for this reason a
fatal sin ... One act of intercourse can beget a child, so any disorder
in that act which disadvantages a child that could be born of it is a
fatal disorder as such ...'[57]

A distinguished group of ethical socialists has recently drawn
attention to the plight of children who are victims of their parents'
promiscuity or lack of commitment to each other. A. H. Halsey
bluntly writes:

> No one can deny that divorce, separation, birth outside marriage
> and one-parent families as well as cohabitation and extra-marital
> sexual intercourse have increased rapidly. Many applaud these
> freedoms. But what should be universally acknowledged is that the
> children of parents who do not follow the traditional norm (i.e.
> taking on personal, active and long-term responsibility for the
> social upbringing of the children they generate) are thereby dis-
> advantaged in many major aspects of their chances of living a
> successful life. On the evidence available such children tend to die
> earlier, to have more illness, to do less well at school, to exist at a
> lower level of nutrition, comfort and conviviality, to suffer more
> unemployment, to be more prone to deviance and crime, and

finally to repeat the cycle of unstable parenting from which they themselves have suffered.[58]

This depressing and disturbing picture is confirmed by extensive studies in Britain and the United States.[59] It is of course deeply unwelcome, and powerful ammunition for conservative politicians and Christians who want to advocate a particular view of family life or to conjure up a former golden age of the family which, since the 1960s, has allegedly been spurned. Much of the failure to thrive is the result of poverty. The presence of two parents in a home itself guarantees nothing and may result in unbearable suffering. Men (in some cases impeded by their employers) show few signs of willingness to share their co-responsibility for child care, and without fundamental changes here there will always be an unequal burden of child care on mothers. Nonetheless children with parents whose commitments to them and to each other are unquestioned are generally more advantaged than those without. The sketch of passionate ethics (see **2.12**) included unwanted and neglected children among victims of oppression who call forth passionate love. A reason why sexual restraint was said there to be necessary was out of regard for children who might be the unwelcome consequences of love-making. Fathers most of all cannot dodge an ethic of relationality. Their children are their neighbours in the most obvious, direct, dependent and vulnerable sense, and any refusal of fatherly neighbourly love even to their own children diminishes both them and their offspring.

3.8.2 Fidelity

Faithfulness is also a good of marriage. We have seen that one of the biblical roots of marriage is the ancient idea of covenant (see above, **3.2**). The *Catechism* says the 'nuptial covenant'[60] is itself thought to be a participation in that wider, eternal covenant between God and God's people. This means that in their awareness of their commitment to one another Christian partners may experience their commitment to each other as a sharing in the 'new covenant' that all Christians affirm.

But now that the contours of marriage are being more widely drawn among many of the churches, the question insistently returns: if faithfulness between spouses is an experiential sharing in the faithfulness of God, what compelling reason could there be to confine this sharing just to marriage? The only compelling reason might be: children. Children must be encompassed by the fidelity which exists (assuming it does) between their parents. But there are friends who are committed to each other; lesbian and gay couples who remain committed to each other; cohabiting couples who are fiercely and monogamously faithful to each other. If the experience of faithfulness is itself a means, or even the principal means, of experiencing the faithfulness of God, then its exclusive concentration in marital faithfulness cannot be sustained. Children remain the reason why the faithfulness of married couples may be more demanding, but they are not the reason why only married couples are able to share in the faithfulness of God.

3.8.3 Sacrament

According to the Canon Law of the Catholic Church,

> The matrimonial covenant, by which a man and a woman establish between themselves a partnership of the whole of life, is by its nature ordered toward the good of the spouses and the procreation and education of offspring; this covenant between baptized persons has been raised by Christ the Lord to the dignity of a sacrament.[61]
> (see above, **3.4**)

The themes of the covenant and the twofold purpose of marriage are by now familiar. While marriage is a divinely appointed institution for the good of everyone, only baptized Christians are able to receive it as a sacrament. Immediately we are in difficulties. Marriage was not declared to be a sacrament until the second Council of Lyons in 1274, so the unqualified assertion that it has been 'raised by Christ the Lord' to sacramental status seems an astonishing claim. Add to this the difficulty that celibacy continued to be regarded as a superior state, and one can see why, at the time of the Reformation, the 'sacramentality' of marriage was denied. There is no need to resurrect bitter squabbles over whether marriage is or is not a sacrament. Attention to the meaning of the term together with a broader interpretation of it will make it an appropriate one to use of committed partnerships generally.

At the time of Augustine, the Latin *sacramentum* meant an oath, a promise of allegiance. A Roman soldier was required to swear a *sacramentum* when he enlisted. The term also translated the Greek *musterion* or 'mystery'. This term is used in the Letter to the Ephesians of the becoming one flesh of a man and his wife, and of the unity between Christ and his church[62] (see above, **3.2**). So Augustine may have thought that a good of marriage lay in the promises of the partners to each other. This vowed state may be seen as a means of strengthening the bond between partners by its public proclamation and the sense of obligation instilled by its being a promise as well as a sharing in the 'great mystery' which is the indwelling of Christ in his church. Augustine did not, and could not, have meant that marriage was a sacrament in the much later sense of a liturgical ritual, administered by a priest, delivering spiritual benefits on account of their proper performance.

If a sacrament is a sign of, or means of receiving, the grace of God, it is hard to avoid pressing toward the conclusion that all of life is, potentially at least, a sacrament. This view is affirmed by a recent Quaker statement on sexuality.[63] That is why, among others, the Church of Scotland makes the appropriate distinction between

> a looser and wider sense of sacramentality in which we may appro-
> priately speak of marriage: the sense in which the Church of
> Scotland has been happy to speak of 'holy matrimony', believing
> that marriage at its best is transparent of the goodness of God,
> offering glimpses of the joy, fidelity and communion which mark
> the life of the Kingdom, and enjoying the benediction of God's
> lovingkindness. This sense of marriage as a sacramental mystery is
> confirmed by the widespread human experience of the marriage
> relationship as the most precious and deep exploration people
> make in their life history.[64]

This statement marks what might even be deemed a fifth transition in addition to the four we have already considered in this chapter. Seen this way it *marks a transition from a formal to an experiential assessment of the meaning of marriage.* Partners discover the grace of God through their ongoing relationship as well as through the initial declarations, promises, pronouncements and public celebrations which constitute their relationship as a marriage in the first place. Marriage 'at its best' is said to be a sacramental mystery. Marriage which is not at its best is, at least by implication, something else. The experiential quality of a marriage is what may lead some people to speak of its sacramental depth. But that would be something realized by the couple themselves, not something which had been automati-cally or externally conferred upon them.

The transition from a formal to an experiential emphasis on the sacrament of marriage also gives rise to the question why there might not be a sacramental element in committed partnerships other than marriage. We might wonder just how far there is a 'widespread human experience of the marriage relationship as the most precious and deep exploration people make'. While this is undeniably true for some married people, this text assumes it cannot be true at all for people who have not engaged in nuptial 'exploration'. But even the term 'exploration' expresses something risky, unpredictable and adventurous about marriage. While the procreative purpose of some marriages provides an additional dimension to the promises married people make, there seem to be no convincing grounds for reserving the 'looser sense of sacramentality' to married people alone.

3.9 SO WHY MARRIAGE?

John Gillis' influential study of courtship and marriage in Britain from the sixteenth century to the present helps in the comparison between women's experience of marriage now with the experience of it in previous centuries. The staged procedures of courtship which included betrothal and a big wedding (at least in the earlier part of the period) enabled both parties to negotiate the transition from becoming lovers to becoming spouses. This process was a public one and its publicness enabled the lovers' community, as well as the lovers themselves, to adapt to the changed pattern of relationships that a marriage would bring among parents, relations and friends. But, says Gillis, previous generations were under no illusion that marriage was an equal partnership, and he accuses the present generation of something called the 'conjugal myth':

> In the sixteenth and seventeenth centuries people took the incompatibility of love and marriage for granted and, through various ritual means, put aside intimacy and equality when they founded a household and family. The conjugal myth is so dominant today that many would deny there is anything fundamentally irreconcilable between the egalitarian assumption of conjugal love and the roles women and men assume when they set up home and have children.[65]

The conjugal myth is the unfounded expectation that romantic love which grows in courtship and betrothal can be sustained undiminished when children arrive. This historian holds that the present generation has duped itself into thinking that marriage is a relationship of equality. Rather, we have deployed the rhetoric of equality, perhaps sincerely, but with the result that the actual experience of being a wife and mother is overladen with a false idealism.

'Today, both men and women *say* they believe in equal relationships, and the language of the official ceremony may be more egalitarian ... '[66] 'Ideologically, the society is committed to an egalitarian conjugal ideal, but in practice it is very far from achieving it.'[67] When children arrive 'many couples face their first marital crisis because their relationship, however egalitarian, is overwhelmed by a stereotyped division of parental roles'. 'Young fathers mean to be more helpful, but studies show that in reality the woman's burden in homemaking and childbearing has not been substantially alleviated', and it may even have become more onerous.[68] For many mothers, motherhood is said to be 'a major crisis'. 'Children diminish marital happiness, more so for women than men. Sexual relations deteriorate and couples draw apart. Mothers are more subject to poor health and mental depression, conditions that necessarily affect the marriage.'[69]

These observations from an historical perspective support the criticisms of the experiences of some wives already made by one of us in *Just Good Friends*.[70] It is necessary to add that 'overall, the mental health of women deteriorates significantly when they get married, whilst the mental health of men improves'.[71] The terrifying degree of violence and abuse committed by husbands and fathers (see Chapter 5) underscores the warning (see above, **3.5**) that 'for many women, the traditional male-dominant marriage is simply not a safe place'. Despite the cumulative case against marriage in *Just Good Friends* it is acknowledged there that 'it would be foolish and dishonest to ignore the fact that many heterosexual marriages do work', for 'commitment, hard work and a great deal of struggle can produce relationships which clearly manifest the presence of God within them'. The quality of *these* relationships raises the question: 'If marriage as an institution does not automatically guarantee this kind of relationship, is there a relationship which is in operation among those couples who do have successful marriages?'[72] The answer to that question, and the contribution of lesbian women and gay men to it, is developed below (see Chapter 7).

The view that friendship might be the common substance of committed relationships inside and outside marriage receives support from Thomas Aquinas' description of the married relationship as a form of friendship. Once again, startling medieval insights are available to us. One of his arguments against **polygamy** is that in a polygamous marriage 'the friendship will not be equal on both sides'. There is 'the greatest friendship between husband and wife'.[73] Lisa

Sowle Cahill thinks Aquinas' 'most valuable and original contribution to a Christian theology and ethics of sexuality is his insight that marital commitment is a profound form of friendship, intensified by physical expression'.[74] Further theological work remains to be done in order to explore all committed relationships, including marriage, as forms of friendship.[75] Yet in the light of the various difficulties, theological and experiential, has marriage a future?

The biblical understandings of marriage will not be cast aside. Neither should they. The churches however, may yet need to search the scriptures a good deal more intensively, in the light of the real, pastoral needs of children, women and men, to enable them to be read authoritatively as good news. Many theologians will support Gillis' historical judgement that 'for most of the twentieth century both sexes have been torn between the potent force of modern individualism and the equally strong desire to have a home and family'.[76] Individualism is an all-pervasive influence in late-capitalist societies, sometimes referred to as 'The Myth of Me'.[77] In seeking to encourage faithfulness among partners, the churches need to make available the resources of deep commitment which derive ultimately from God who is committed to everyone in the gift of Christ. Since it appears to be universally true that marriages are considerably harder for women than for men, the uncritical affirmation of marriage and the family without regard for the evidence is a breach of faith, even if the rhetoric is fashionable.

It may also be necessary to recover the biblical teaching that marriage is a 'vocation' (see below, **3.10**). We have seen that Paul discouraged it, and as far as we know, Jesus avoided it. When the disciples challenged Jesus' teaching on divorce and remarriage, they said to him, ' "If that is how things stand for a man with a wife, it is better not to marry" ' (Matthew 19.9–10). The disciples' line was 'simply a male chauvinist protest'[78] equivalent to the rejoinder 'Better not to marry at all if you can't get divorced'. But Jesus agreed with them, albeit for very different reasons. It is a warning that without deep commitment it is better not to take the plunge at all. The strangeness of his teaching is a reminder that marriage does not have to be inevitable. There are large pastoral responsibilities here which are beyond the scope of this book. Several factors have to be balanced. The vulnerability and dependence of children cannot be overemphasized. Theologies and liturgies of marriage have mainly reflected the experience of men. Women's experience of marriage is likely to be different, and unlikely to improve without further social changes and 'a radical reorganization of both housekeeping and child care'.[79] The transitions which have been described in this chapter are incomplete, and much further work on the theology of marriage needs to be done.

3.10 Singleness and celibacy

The bishops who wrote the 1991 Statement, *Issues in Human Sexuality*, ask: 'What is God's will for the single person?'[80] and say,

> The first thing the Christian will want to say to the single is that Jesus himself was single. Any idea that to be unmarried is to fall short as a human being is totally false. On the contrary, the heart of what it is to be human was shown to us in one who never married.[81]

Some guilt is expressed about the Church's failure to 'give prayerful attention to the human and spiritual needs of single people'.[82] Friendship is said to be a 'special gift' especially appropriate to singles.[83] And singles are to be 'chaste' rather than celibate in all their relationships. The three 'ways of life', marriage, singleness and celibacy, are 'ones by which the grace of God can help to transform our fallen human nature'.[84]

There is just one paragraph about singles in *The Catechism of the Catholic Church*, tacked on to the section on 'the sacrament of matrimony'. It says:

> We must also remember the great number of *single persons* who, because of the particular circumstances in which they have to live — often not of their choosing — are especially close to Jesus' heart and therefore deserve the special affection and active solicitude of the Church, especially of pastors ... The doors of homes, the '**domestic churches**', and of the great family which is the Church must be open to all of them.[85]

Borrowing from the earlier *Familiaris Consortio*, singles are reminded that 'No one is without a family in this world: the Church is a home and family for everyone, especially those who "labour and are heavy laden".' The placing of singles at the end of the section on the sacrament of marriage signifies the awkwardness which *the very existence of singles* presents to a theological understanding of people dominated by the categories of celibacy and marriage. The depiction of the attitude of Jesus to all single people is based, not on his teaching but on the assumption of his special solidarity with singles, being one of, and one with, them. Pastors, also being single (as well as celibate), have a special understanding of, and responsibility for, single people. But, we might ask, why should singles be closer to the heart of Jesus than, say, people who are hungry, thirsty, strangers, naked or prisoners (Matthew 25.35–36), quite irrespective of their marital status? Is marital status, or rather its absence, the key to human solidarity, whether with each other or with Christ?

A different account of singleness is offered in *Something to Celebrate* which goes a considerable way towards a full and equal recognition of singles inside and outside the churches. The definition of 'family' is left to singles themselves and 'singleness' and 'family' are said to be not 'mutually exclusive'. There is a welcome denial that singleness is to be seen as 'an incomplete state on its way to becoming something else'.[87] Single people are to be affirmed, and 'one sure sign of an inadequate set of social and moral values is the tendency to see singleness as a problem ... '.[88] 'The single life is as valid as the married life.' 'The Christian tradition of singleness has rich resources of practical wisdom in this area which need to be rediscovered and creatively reaffirmed.'[89]

This report is less worried than the House of Bishops about preserving the difference between celibacy and singleness. Singleness appears to be a term which includes celibate and non-celibate people, and the phrase 'Christian tradition of singleness' is used in this inclusive sense. The discussion of singleness is linked in the report with cohabitation (which is a state of singleness only for those working with ecclesiastical and legal categories!). There are clear signs of parity in *Something to Celebrate* between married and unmarried people within the Church and a recognition that the lofty theological purposes of marriage and celibacy have devalued singleness. A difference between marrieds and singles is that marrieds have commitments to each other and to the dependent strangers (if any) who are their offspring. This difference resides in commitments undertaken, not on hierarchy or status (social or ontological). This is a view close to St Paul's teaching. With regard to the difference between the single and married states, he remarked, 'I should like everyone to be as I myself am; but each person has the gift God has granted him, one this gift and another that' (1 Corinthians 7.7). Each of these two states is called a 'charisma' and is from God. There is little hint that Paul understands his singleness as a celibate calling (at least as the term came later to be understood). The full recognition of singleness, a long time coming in the churches, is a recovery of biblical teaching. The charisma of singleness, then, does not have to be assigned a meaning, or given a purpose. It is a charisma. Being a gift, it requires no further justification. It should be received and lived as singles themselves choose. The faithfulness of partners which is a sign of the faithfulness of God need not be confined to heterosexual marriage (see above, **3.8**), and the existence of a sacramental depth to marriage cannot be maintained without allowing such depth elsewhere.

3.11 SUMMARY

Passionate ethics is neighbour-love which shares in the passion of Christ (see **2.12**). This chapter is an outworking of passionate ethics. In particular it is an ethic of justice for children. We have examined the biblical roots of Christian marriage and the theology presupposed by them. We have noted that there is no final agreement about the purpose of marriage, and some difficulty in even speaking of marriage in this teleological way. The recognition in Catholic thought of both the unitive and procreative purposes of marriage as equally important is evidence of the development of the traditional view of marriage.

Further evidence of development was found in trends, grounded in contemporary reports, which we have called 'from patriarchy to parity', from 'sole relationship to soul-relationship', and 'from event to process'. An examination of ancient teaching about the goods of marriage has revealed that the commitments and demands of married people are unique mostly because of any children they might have, while the other 'goods of marriage' cannot be confined to married people alone. Singleness remains a genuine alternative to marriage. Criticisms of marriage have reinforced the view that sacramental grace cannot be assumed without the openness of each party to receive it, and with no automatic conferral of sacramentality, other relationships than marriage are found to have a sacramental quality.

Notes

1 For this, and a mass of detail about the sex lives of contemporary British people, see Kaye Wellings *et al.*, *Sexual Behaviour in Britain* (Harmondsworth: Penguin Books, 1994).

2 *An Honourable Estate* (London: Church House Publishing, 1988), para. 30, p. 10.

3 *Ibid.*, para. 41, p. 13.

4 See Adrian Thatcher, *Liberating Sex: A Christian Sexual Theology* (London: SPCK, 1993), p. 86.

5 Ephesians 5.22; Colossians 3.18; 1 Peter 3.1–6.

6 Church of Scotland, *Report on the Theology of Marriage*, 3.10(ii), p. 264.

7 See, e.g., A. E. Harvey, *Promise or Pretence? A Christian's Guide to Sexual Morals* (London: SCM Press, 1994), p. 62. See in particular the comment that 'Modern versions, e.g. the Revised English Bible, which ascribe parts to "bride" and "bridegroom" are pulling the wool over our eyes ... '.

8 Revised Standard Version. The Revised English Bible has '... and the two become one', thereby omitting 'flesh'.

9 Derrick Sherwin Bailey, *The Mystery of Love and Marriage: A Study in the Theology of Sexual Relation* (London: SCM Press, 1952), p. 44.

10 Helen Oppenheimer, *Marriage* (London: Mowbray, 1990), pp. 35, 111.

11 Elizabeth Stuart, *Just Good Friends — Towards a Lesbian and Gay Theology of Relationships* (London: Mowbray, 1995), p. 122.

12 Carolyn Osiek, 'The New Testament and the family', in Lisa Sowle Cahill and Dietmar Mieth (eds), *The Family, Concilium* (1995/4), p. 8.

13 For the details of this complex story, see Peter Brown, *The Body and Society: Men, Women and Sexual Renunciation in Early Christianity* (London and Boston: Faber & Faber, 1988).

14 *On the Goods of Marriage.* The teaching of this book is well summarized by Henry Chadwick in his *Augustine* (Oxford: Oxford University Press, 1986), pp. 112–15.

15 Uta Ranke-Heinemann, *Eunuchs for the Kingdom of Heaven: The Catholic Church and Sexuality* (Harmondsworth: Penguin Books, 1991), p. 195.

16 From Ambrose (d. 397) on. See Brown, *The Body and Society*, p. 362.

17 Derrick Sherwin Bailey, *The Man–Woman Relation in Christian Thought* (London: Longmans, 1959), pp. 197–9.

18 *Ibid.*, p. 180.

19 *Ibid.*, p. 199.

20 David Hilborn, 'For the procreation of children', in Susan Durber (ed.), *As Man and Woman Made: Theological Reflections on Marriage* (London: United Reformed Church, 1994), p. 23.

21 Canon 1013,1, in 1917 *Code of Canon Law*, quoted in Michael G. Lawler, *Marriage and Sacrament: A Theology of Christian Marriage* (Collegeville, MN: Liturgical Press, 1993), p. 11.

22 *Gaudium et Spes: Pastoral Constitution on the Church in the Modern World*, 50.

23 *Ibid.*, part 2, Ch. 1.

24 *Codex Iuris Canonici* (1983), canon 1055.1. See also *Catechism of the Catholic Church*, para. 1604, p. 359.

25 Jack Dominian, *Passionate and Compassionate Love: A Vision for Christian Marriage* (London: Darton, Longman & Todd, 1991), p. 28.

26 Bailey, *The Man–Woman Relationship*, p. 202.

27 See Robin Smith, *Living in Covenant with God and One Another* (Geneva: World Council of Churches, 1990), p. 55.

28 *Marriage and the Church's Task* (The Lichfield Report) (London: Church Information Office, 1978), section 99.

29 Smith, *Living in Covenant*, p. 55.

30 *Catechism of the Catholic Church*, para. 1605, pp. 359–60 (emphasis added).

31 South African Anglican Theological Commission, *The Church and Human Sexuality* (Marshalltown, South Africa, 1995), E10, p. 17.

32 *Catechism of the Catholic Church*, para. 1607, p. 360.

33 Stuart, *Just Good Friends*, ch.4, especially pp. 116–17.

34 *Ibid.*, p. 117.

35 General Assembly Special Committee on Human Sexuality, Presbyterian Church (USA), *Keeping Body and Soul Together: Sexuality, Spirituality, and Social Justice* (1991), p. 54.

36 *Ibid.*, p. 53.

37 Church of Scotland Panel on Doctrine, *Report on the Theology of Marriage* (1994), section 4.2, p. 265.

38 *Ibid.*, section 4.1, p. 265 (added emphasis).

39 *Ibid.*, p. 285 (original emphasis).

40 *Issues in Human Sexuality: A Statement by the House of Bishops* (London: Church House Publishing, 1991), para. 3.8.

41 *Something to Celebrate: Valuing Families in Church and Society* (London: Church House Publishing, 1995), p. 33.

42 *Ibid.*, p. 34.

43 *Ibid.*, p. 115.

44 *Ibid.*, p. 117.

45 *Ibid.*, p. 109.

46 There was substantial opposition even to a motion to 'take note' of it. For a report of the unhappy meeting of the Synod, see the *Church Times*, 8 December 1995.

47 Phillip Tovey, 'Matrimony: an excellent mystery', *Theology*, 97, no.777 (May/June 1994), p. 165.

48 John R. Gillis, *For Better, for Worse: British Marriages, 1600 to the Present* (New York: Oxford University Press, 1985), p. 47.

49 *An Honourable Estate*, para. 60, p. 20.

50 *Ibid.*, para. 60, p. 22.

51 *Ibid.*, para. 75, p. 25.

52 This will be attempted in Adrian Thatcher, *Marriage after Modernity*, forthcoming.

53 Thatcher, *Liberating Sex*, p. 106.

54 Gillis, *For Better, for Worse*, pp. 314–15.

55 *Book of Common Order* (1979), p. 73: *cit.*, Church of Scotland, *Report*, p. 265.

56 Lisa Sowle Cahill, *Between the Sexes: Foundations for a Christian Ethics of Sexuality* (Philadelphia: Fortress Press, 1985), p. 113.

57 *Summa Theologiae*, vol. 43, 154.3. See Timothy McDermott (ed.), *St Thomas Aquinas, Summa Theologiae: A Concise Translation* (London: Methuen, 1989), p. 432.

58 A. H. Halsey, 'Foreword', in Norman Dennis and George Erdos, *Families without Fatherhood* (London: IEA Health and Welfare Unit, 1993), p. xii.

59 *Ibid.*

60 *Catechism of the Catholic Church*, para. 1612, p. 361.

61 *Codex Iuris Canonici*, can.1055.1, cited in *Catechism*, para. 1601, p. 358.

62 Ephesians 5.32. Unfortunately the Revised English Bible translates the words 'This is a great mystery' by 'There is hidden here a great truth', thereby giving no direct clue that the term *musterion* lies behind the English.

63 'For Quakers the whole of life is sacred, to be lived in the Spirit. We cannot separate our religion from our life if it is to be authentic, and so we cannot separate our sexual experiences from our religious experiences.' *This We Can Say: Talking Honestly about Sex* (Reading: Nine Friends Press, 1995), p. 12.

64 Church of Scotland, *Report* 4.7, p. 266.

65 Gillis, *For Better, for Worse*, p. 313.

66 *Ibid.*, pp. 308, 311 (emphasis added).

67 *Ibid.*, p. 313.

68 *Ibid.*, p. 316.

69 *Ibid.*, p. 318.

70 Stuart, *Just Good Friends*, pp. 107–17.

71 Julian Hafner, *The End of Marriage: Why Monogamy Isn't Working* (London: Century, 1993), p.7, cited in Stuart, *Just Good Friends*, p. 107.

72 *Ibid.*, p. 117.

73 Cahill, *Between the Sexes*, p. 113: citing *Summa contra Gentiles* 3/II.123.6.

74 Cahill, *Between the Sexes*, p. 119.

75 See Thatcher, *Marriage after Modernity*, forthcoming.

76 Gillis, *For Better, for Worse*, p. 319.

77 See Thatcher, *Liberating Sex*, pp. 51–2.

78 Ranke-Heinemann, *Eunuchs for the Kingdom of Heaven*, p. 33.

79 Gillis, *For Better, for Worse*, p. 320.

80 *Issues in Human Sexuality*, 3.9.

81 *Ibid.*, 3.10.

82 *Ibid.*, 3.11.

83 *Ibid.*, 3.12–13.

84 *Ibid.*, 3.16.

85 *Catechism of the Catholic Church*, para. 1658.

86 Singleness is explored in greater depth in Adrian Thatcher, 'Singles and families', *Theology and Sexuality*, no. 4 (March 1996).

87 *Something to Celebrate*, p. 106.

88 *Ibid.*, p. 107.

89 *Ibid.*

Suggestions for further reading

Derrick Sherwin Bailey, *The Man–Woman Relation in Christian Thought* (London: Longmans, 1959).

Susan Dowell, *They Two Shall Be One: Monogamy in History and Religion* (London: Collins, Flame, 1990).

Helen Oppenheimer, *Marriage* (London: Mowbray, 1990).

John Shelby Spong, *Living in Sin: A Bishop Rethinks Human Sexuality* (San Francisco: Harper & Row, 1988).

Adrian Thatcher, *Liberating Sex: A Christian Sexual Theology* (London; SPCK, 1993).

4

THE BODY

4.1 AM I MY BODY?

We do not think of ourselves as being bodies — few of us would feel comfortable saying 'I am my body' — rather we each think of ourselves as *having* a body. We tend to view our bodies as instruments of our essential selves. They are there to serve us. When our body goes wrong we often treat it like a bit of essential machinery that has broken down. We get annoyed with it, we feel let down, we complain that our back, or heart, or digestion, is 'playing up', we take it to someone to get it repaired and we make resolutions to take better care of it in future. But our bodies defy our attempts to turn them into thin, trim, working machines. Our bodies are part of the self-image we project and we do not want to be thought of as being lazy, self-indulgent, weak-willed or stupid, which is how the Western world currently interprets round, full, 'overweight' bodies. Alienation exists between ourselves and our bodies. Often it is only the onset of serious illness that forces us to confront the fact that our bodies are not simply a heavy overcoat covering our real selves but an essential part of who we are. At that point we can no longer isolate one part of our bodies and say that it is sick; we have to admit that '*I* am ill'. They are not a dispensable outer coating — they are us. Alienation can also be traced in the indiscriminate use of the body for the pursuit of personal pleasure. We separate our bodies from our selves. We speak about sex in terms of *acts* and *performance.* This distancing of our true selves from our bodies has had two important repercussions: on the one hand it has led to a failure, particularly amongst men, to take responsibility for sins of the body — the body is blamed for leading the true self into sin. On the other hand, women became associated with the bodily half of the body–soul dualism (see below, **4.2**) and their bodies in particular were viewed as dangerous and in need of taming and controlling. Today many see the ongoing debate over reproductive rights as women's struggle to free their bodies from male control.

There is some evidence that the Christian churches are beginning to realize the problems and dangers of body–soul **dualism** (a dualism which was reinforced by Newtonian understanding of matter as dense, dead stuff), but few have completely transcended dualism. A recent Church of England report on salvation strongly affirms the unity of body and soul, stating that the soul is that which provides continuity and unity as the body changes,

> the vastly complex information-bearing pattern in which that material is organised. That 'pattern' can surely be considered as the carrier of memories and of personality. We are close to the Aristotelian notion of the soul as the 'form' of the body, found also in Aquinas.'[1]

However, this 'pattern' is envisaged as being able to survive without a body.[2] The unity of body and soul is also strongly upheld in the new *Catechism of the Catholic Church*, as is the resurrection from the dead. Yet body and soul are still depicted there as two distinct entities which are parted at death to be reunited at the resurrection[3] and mastery of unruly dangerous passions is still depicted as an essential task: 'Either man [*sic*] governs his passions and finds peace, or he lets himself be dominated by them and becomes unhappy.'[4] This reluctance to drop dualism may have something to do with the fact that people often think that the alternative to dualism is materialistic **monism**, the belief that a human being is merely tissue and bone and nothing else. This is evidently untrue; human beings cannot simply be explained by reference to biology, but there is an alternative theory of personhood which avoids the dissection of the person proposed by dualists and the reductionism of the monists. The double-aspect theory maintains that human personhood is so complicated that to explain it requires two perspectives or aspects — material and spiritual.[5]

4.2 THE BODY AND THE BIBLE

Ancient Hebrew theology lacked any sense of body–soul dualism. The body and **sexuality** were regarded as gifts from God and human beings were unitary. However, ancient Israelite society does appear to have been riddled with another kind of dualism — **gender** dualism (see **6.1**). This gender dualism had an effect upon the way that women's bodies were interpreted — they were the **property** of men (see **1.7**), first fathers and then husbands, as were the bodies of children and slaves. Body–soul dualism did begin to seep into ancient Israel, probably as a result of foreign influences at the time of the Babylonian exile. In her study of primitive societies Mary Douglas noted the way in which the human body, through ritual and other means, is fashioned to represent the social and religious structures it inhabits.[6] In her classic study of **purity** rules surrounding the body she concluded that dirt symbolizes disorder (see **1.8**). Things become labelled as 'dirty' because they jumble and confuse our social classifications. James Nelson has noted that this concern with dirt is not only a facet of primitive societies: 'Food in itself is not dirty, but it is dirty to leave specks of food on one's clothing. Or to leave upstairs equipment downstairs. Or to put underclothing over outerclothing.'[7]

This concern lies behind the book of Leviticus with its **Holiness Code** (17–26). For the ancient Israelites holiness required order, and order rested on the ability to classify those things, animals or humans into distinct and discrete categories. Humans, animals or other things which could not be easily classified and which seemed to blur the divisions were disorderly and therefore dirty. People who wore clothes associated with members of the other **sex**, or a man who had sex with other men, blurred some of the most obvious boundaries and therefore threatened the integrity of the nation. Similarly, bodies in processes of transformation or transition, deviating from their normal state, were regarded as unclean. So the normal state of a woman is to be non-menstrual, and when she does bleed she is therefore unclean. Douglas saw a connection between a nation's concern with keeping itself pure and a sense of threat. When the body of a society is threatened, part of the response is to take great care over the unity, purity and integrity of the human body. The ancient Israelites were certainly under threat a great deal. The Holiness Code, which dates from the period after the exile when Israel was disillusioned and despondent, seeks to unite and rebuild the nation as a distinct and whole entity. The theology of Leviticus is summed up in Leviticus 20:

> I am the Lord your God. I have separated you from the peoples. You shall make a distinction between the clean animal and the unclean, and between the unclean bird and the clean; you shall not bring abomination on yourselves by animal or bird or by anything with which the ground teems, which I have set apart for you to hold

> unclean. You shall be holy to me; for I the Lord am holy, and I have
> separated you from the other peoples to be mine. (24b-26
> NRSV)

Israel is a holy nation and therefore must be kept separate from other
nations and must be distinguishable from other nations in the
boundaries and classifications that it treats as significant. To the
priests who fashioned the Holiness Code the difference between
male and female, with the male being considered to be superior to
the female, was one of the clearest and most important distinctions.
Our bodies therefore become symbols of our wider society and the
meanings that we attach to various bodily gestures are dictated by
wider society. The theological implications of this insight are profound: our bodies have no pre-set or determined meanings but are
dynamic and fluid in their significance.

'The beginnings of the Jesus movement are stamped by a revalua-
tion of the body.'[8] The reassessment was caused by the belief that in
Jesus God had become human, and by the behaviour of Jesus
himself. William Countryman is convinced that Jesus abolished the
two concepts ancient Israelites used to interpret the body — purity
(see **1.8**) and property (see **1.7**). He clearly dispenses with the notion
of purity in Mark 7.18–23 and property in his teaching on divorce
(Mark 10.1–12).[9] Healings, eating and drinking were at the heart of
Jesus' ministry. He addressed people in their totality (not merely in
their souls as later Christianity would have it), and salvation encompassed the totality of human experience, at the heart of which
was the body. And not only individual bodies but the body of a
society. The story of the healing of the woman with the flow of blood
(Mark 5.24–34) is an important one in seeking to establish the
earliest Christian approach to the body in the scheme of salvation. It
is a story told in each of the three **Synoptic Gospels** but both Matthew
and Luke have toned down the vivid physical descriptions of Mark,
perhaps reflecting an increasing discomfort with the body in early
Christian circles. The term 'flow of blood' used by Mark deliberately
reflects the purity laws of the Old Testament (Leviticus 15.25–30).
She is not suffering from her regular menstrual bleeding but from
some other kind of illness which makes herself, her belongings and
all who touch them unclean. It is her need for bodily healing that
makes her reach out to Jesus to touch his physical form, even though
by doing so she knew that she was defying the law. Jesus feels
something happen in his own body but the woman has to explain

exactly what. The message is clear: God's power works in and through bodies, salvation is embodied (see **9.4**) and not only that, this power breaks through the barriers of purity which keep bodies apart — a theme which will be taken up later in the Gospel when Jesus offers up his own body on the cross and that same body is resurrected, breaking the barrier of death. People are not just healed by Jesus — they are then placed into a new set of relationships which will ensure their liberation from social restraints and enable them to be active, fulfilled human beings. Mark also interestingly draws verbal parallels between the woman's suffering and the suffering of Jesus. In both the forces of a healing God are evident.

For a brief time, at least, notions of cleanness and uncleanness were absent from at least parts of the Church, and this explains why women were able to exercise leadership in some ecclesial communities. This was part of a wider revolutionary approach to all social norms rooted in biology which the Jesus movement subverted, most clearly in its rejection of blood kinship as the sociological and theological centre of the world. Why then was this body-friendliness lost? Moltmann-Wendel singles out two causes: St Paul begins to reflect a sexual and gender dualism (see **6.1**), and the radical vision was lost as the imminent **parousia** (see **1.9**) which made it possible receded in likelihood. 'Small, often persecuted, groups turned into communities which were compelled to adapt while retaining many distinctive features, and could not escape the social, ideological and philosophical trends.'[10]

> In Paul's letters, we are presented with the human body as in a photograph taken against the sun: it is a jet-black shape whose edges are suffused with light. Perishable, weak, 'sown in dishonour', 'always carrying the death of Jesus' in its vulnerability to physical risk and to bitter frustration, Paul's body was very much an 'earthen vessel'. Yet it already glowed with a measure of the same spirit that had raised the inert body of Jesus from the grave: 'so that the life of Jesus may be manifested in our mortal flesh'.[11]

Paul was a Jew, he could not be a thorough-going dualist.

> It is from the body of sin and death that we are delivered; it is through the body of Christ on the Cross that we are saved; it is into his body the Church that we are incorporated; it is by his body in the Eucharist that this Community is sustained; it is in our body that its new life has to be manifested; it is to a resurrection of this body to the likeness of his glorious body that we are destined.[12]

When Paul compares and contrasts life in the 'flesh' (*sarx*) with life in the spirit (Galatians 5.17), he is not speaking about the body (*soma*) versus the spirit. For Paul 'flesh' is shorthand for human beings' refusal to recognize their dependence upon God. Paul's understanding of the resurrection emphasizes both discontinuity and continuity with our present bodies. Our present bodies will be transformed into different kinds of bodies, but Paul was quite clear that our future existence would be embodied. Paul was also a Diaspora Jew who had absorbed something of the Hellenistic culture. The body for him was a weak thing liable to sin and to be overcome by the force of the flesh. The body was the temple of the Holy Spirit (1 Corinthians 6.19), and therefore had to mirror the new order or creation of Christ. Indeed, for Paul, what Christians did with their bodies was the most obvious sign of their separateness from the pagan world in which they lived. Absent from Paul's letters was the contemporary Jewish notion that the sexual urges of the body, although capable of wreaking individual and social disarray, were capable of being tamed and ordered for good in marriage. Thus he left a dangerous and unfortunate legacy to Christianity.

Thereafter, according to Moltmann-Wendel, three recurring trends shaped Christianity's approach to the body. Firstly, Christianity adapted to the social expectations of the body of those around them. In particular it exchanged its radical vision for **Stoic** sexual **ethics** which were dualistic and anti-passion. Secondly, the male body became the norm of bodiliness and remains so today — women, if they are to achieve equality, can only do so by adapting to the male norm. Thirdly, a tendency for the radical, body-friendly tradition to be preserved on the margins of Christianity, from the medieval Franciscan movement to today's **creation-centred spirituality**, is also apparent.

4.3 THE BODY AND THE CHRISTIAN TRADITION

In the ancient world into which Christianity was born, sexuality was perceived as involving the whole body, not just the genitals. Making love brought into play the brain, the blood which boiled, the kidneys, the back and so on.[13] The ancient Romans were not as amoral as most of us were brought up to believe: the public domain was extremely intolerant of lack of sexual restraint, although slaves, who of course were the property of their masters, were considered fair game. Christianity, interestingly, said little about the sexual use of slaves.[14]

The inhabitants of the ancient world espoused what Peter Brown has called a 'benevolent dualism':

> The soul met the body as the inferior 'other' to the self. The body was as different from the soul, and as intractable, as were women, slaves, and the opaque and restless populace of the cities ... It was a clay on which age, disease, and death fastened inexorably. At the end of so much long pain, it was best for the soul to go away — perhaps to the stars — 'clean of a body', the diseased flesh melted at last from the mind.[15]

The body was not to be despised, it had its rightful place, but it needed to be refined and gently controlled. Christians interacting with this philosophy went one stage further. The body was capable of being not just controlled but completely transformed, and just as the individual body could be transformed, so could the social body. This was the position of Clement of Alexandria (*c*.150–*c*.215) who embraced the Stoic ideal of *apatheia*, of freedom from the passions which disturb and disorder the person. Clement took an entirely positive view of marriage. He only wished sexual activity to be conscious, an orderly act undertaken for the procreation of children, devoid of bestial, unthinking, purely pleasure-motivated **desire** (see **8.1**). An extreme view was represented by a number of small Christian groups who believed that:

> By renouncing all sexual activity the human body could join in Christ's victory [over the grave]: it could turn back the inexorable. The body could wrench itself free from the grip of the animal world. By refusing to act upon the youthful stirrings of desire, Christians could bring marriage and childbirth to an end. With marriage at an end, the huge fabric of organized society would crumble like a sandcastle ... [16]

But by the second century CE in the most orthodox and mainstream of Christian circles sexual renunciation had become a central part of the Christian resistance to the society that surrounded them. The virgin, untouched human body became the 'charged joining point of heaven and earth, and, on earth itself, as the symbolic rallying point for a rapidly expanding Church'.[17] What we must always remember, though, is that only a small proportion of the Christian population opted for total sexual renunciation. The married majority, however, became increasingly silent.

For Origen (*c*. 185–*c*. 254) the body was fundamentally fluid. The body, sexuality, and sex difference were not permanent. The spirit simply occupied them for a time on its journey back to a non-embodied, purely spiritual union with the divine. As it progressed back it took on different bodies, each in succession becoming less heavy, thick and material. Sexuality was therefore for Origen not in any way essential to the human person and could be abandoned even in this life; indeed to do so was to declare in one's own flesh where the spirit was heading. Origen had himself castrated, possibly to avoid slanderous gossip about his relationship with women with whom he engaged in conversations about spirituality. Brown points out that in the mind-set of the culture in which Origen lived, the eunuch was believed to have blurred the boundaries between the sexes: 'He was a walking lesson in the basic indeterminacy of the body.'[18] In Origen we see that sexual **continence** had moved from being a matter for widowed middle-aged men and women (as it was in the late first century) to being a matter for the young. Young Christian girls, whose bodies had previously been guarded by their fathers in preparation for marriage, now were expected to take responsibility for their own bodies and choose perpetual continence.

Ambrose of Milan (*c.* 339–397) was a man who thought of the world in terms of dualisms: Christian and pagan, Church and the world, soul and body, Catholic and heretic. Any blurring of these rigid boundaries polluted both the individual body and that of the Church. He therefore understood Paul's dark words about the power of the flesh over the spirit to refer to the body. The body was a 'veil', it was not essential to personhood; but the body was 'slippery': on it the soul could lose its balance and tumble out of control. Every human body bore an ugly scar as a result of the **fall**, the scar of sexuality. The virgin birth of Christ spoke to him of God's intention that the new flesh, the flesh of Christ into which Christians were to be baptized, would be free from this scar. He therefore urged the unmarried to stay celibate, the married to be continent and the clergy to refrain from marriage.

Augustine of Hippo (354–430) believed that human beings were created physical beings and had before the fall enjoyed a unity of body and soul, their bodies completely under the control of the will and the will fixed upon God. Sex had been part of the experience of Adam and Eve but it was very different to that experienced by humans subsequently, since it was under the complete control of human will. That had been lost when humanity subverted the ordered relationship between itself and God and disobeyed. At that point something truly tragic happened — desire and the will ceased to be friends and became enemies struggling for the control of human beings. Human bodies became the battleground for this struggle and nowhere was it more fierce than in the genital region. **Lust** overwhelms the will:

> When it comes to children being generated, the members created for this purpose do not obey the will, but lust has to be waited for to set these members in motion, as having rights over them, and sometimes it will not act when the mind is willing, while sometimes it even acts against the mind's will![19]

This was most clearly evident for Augustine in a man's inability to control his erections. As Gareth Moore has noted, Augustine approaches the whole issue from an unambiguously male perspective; indeed for Augustine the problem is focused on and in men, because 'it is the man who is supposed to be superior, to be in the heights, and to be in control'.[20] Lust overwhelms the will and indeed the entire body so that reason — the distinctive mark of humanity — is flattened and human beings are thereby reduced to the status of an animal (which is an evil); to desire evil, to seek this pleasure is sinful. Only sexual intercourse for the purpose of procreation is justified.

The dualistic attitude to the body, and its desires, represented in various different forms by Clement, Ambrose and Augustine, certainly came to dominate the Christian tradition, although it should be noted that most Christian theologians rigorously opposed the suggestion of some Gnostics that the body and all matter were actually and inherently evil. Belief in God as creator of the world and in the **incarnation** prevented this. However, there were always those who took a non-dualistic attitude to the body. Ironically, some of those Christians who went to live in the wilderness to purify the soul by conquering bodily passions found that life in the desert revealed the interdependence of body and soul. Sexual images of the relation between the ascetic and God pepper the writings of the church fathers. The body became the schoolteacher of the soul and sexuality came to be understood as an essential part of the human person.[21] The Rhineland Mystics (a group of women who were members of various religious orders in the Middle Ages who reflected upon their own mystical experiences) and other women mystics like Teresa of Avila in the sixteenth century defied the view of male theologians that 'all experience of Christ must be immaterial, noncorporeal',[22] by experiencing union with Christ in their own bodies, this union often being manifest in the appearance of the stigmata or in rapture. These women had 'body knowledge' of Christ.

4.4 BODY THEOLOGY (*and see* **6.7**)

For centuries the body has been treated as an object by theologians, something about which they did theology and upon which they imposed theology. The recognition both of the problems caused by dualism and the fact that we are bodies has led to the birth of **body theology**, inspired and initiated by the **feminist** movement which has reclaimed women's bodies from their **objectification** by men.[23] Body theology, like the medieval women mentioned above, uses the body as the subject of God's **revelation** (see Chapter 8). The justification for such an approach lies in the central Christian notion of the incarnation — that God has become human in Christ. Christianity has tended to treat this as a unique event, despite proclaiming that the Church has become the body of Christ on earth, and in the eucharist celebrating Christ's giving of his body again and again in the physical form of bread and wine which we take into our own bodies. But body theologians maintain that the incarnation is a sign and revelation of the way that God works generally — in and through bodies. We therefore have to learn to listen to our bodies, to attend to our feelings and to learn the lessons that bodies teach us. Body theology is in its infancy, but it is possible to grasp something of its nature by looking at the issue of salvation.

We fear death. We fear the unknown. We fear non-being. Dualism does something to salve those fears by postulating the existence of an immortal soul belonging to and of importance to God in a way that the body is not, for it will decay. Salvation does not therefore lie in the body, although the body can imperil the salvation of the soul if it is indulged in ways that are sinful. This theology carries the message that the body is not of God and is therefore at best unimportant, at worst a threat to eternal salvation which lies beyond this world. God is therefore propelled out of this world and the world becomes, in Luce Irigaray's phrase, 'a great deportation camp, where men await celestial redemption'.[24] And the deportation camp as a temporary residence becomes exploitable: we enter into a similar relationship with the body of the earth and the non-human life upon it as we do with our own bodies — it is separate from us, to be used as a machine for our own purpose. The fear of death has not only locked us into a potentially fatal relationship with the planet that sustains and nurtures us. It may also fuel our desire to 'make a mark', by working excessively hard or accumulating material goods, or our desperate desire to have children. Yet earliest Christianity proclaimed that the dead were taken back into the earth from which they had come, to be raised on the last day. The earth is only feared as our final destiny because we do not see God in it.

Some feminist theologians envisage the earth as the body of God (see **6.6.2**). If that **metaphor** rings true, then in death our selves are not lost but taken into the very being of God, to turn into a literal and metaphorical kind of compost that nourishes those who come after us — this is resurrection and it can also be experienced now, because as Moltmann-Wendel has noted, death loses its sting. We can relax and enjoy our bodies now whilst focusing our energies on changing and transforming this world:

> 'Don't be anxious', 'Don't be afraid'. That is the message which stands at the beginning of the incarnation, God's becoming body, and it can also accompany us as we become human beings. It is also the message of the resurrection on Easter Day, the message of hope that all that is cannot be separated from the love of God, whether blade of grass, or human being, or animal.[25]

An embodied theology relocates salvation in and through the body. Our alienation from our bodies is healed and we experience the saving grace of God within them. It is a discovery of ourselves as we are, as bodies. Grace to become enfleshed, this is the message of the incarnation, and it reaches out to us through other fleshy creatures. Becoming bodies, accepting ourselves as embodied, leads to a full appreciation of the sacredness of bodies. We discover what Virginia Ramey Mollenkott has described as a 'shiver of solidarity'[26] with all bodies, including the body of the earth, which leads us to behave in ways that are just. The following three sections are offered as examples of body theology.

4.5 MASTURBATION

We have already had good reason to discuss **masturbation** in the context of the inability of **natural law** theory to provide a convincing reason for its wrongness (see **2.9**). It is discussed here in the context of body theology (see above, **4.4**). Masturbation is probably the most widely practised genital sexual act. Yet it is still regarded as something of a taboo topic both in Western society in general and in the churches. Almost everybody does it or has done it or will be doing it and yet it is not discussed except in the most abstract of terms. There is no biblical condemnation of masturbation, although the story of Onan (Genesis 38.6–10) has been utilized by many generations of Christians in the war against it. However Onan's sin, which was to spill his 'seed upon the ground', was not masturbation but a refusal to inseminate his dead brother's wife, thereby breaking the laws of Levirate marriage (Deuteronomy 25:5–10). He may have engaged in *coitus interruptus*, withdrawing his penis from the woman before ejaculation. Ancient Israelite and early Christian objections to masturbation probably rested upon the belief that male sperm alone contained the ingredients to produce a child. Therefore to spill male seed outside a women's vagina was tantamount to murder. In the medieval period this argument was replaced by arguments based upon natural law (see **2.3**). Aquinas argued that since the purpose of semen was 'obviously' for the generation of new life, it must only be emitted for this purpose. Masturbation was therefore a sin against nature and a graver sin than rape, which was a 'natural' act even though sinful.

In the eighteenth, nineteenth and early twentieth centuries science added its authority, blaming masturbation for all manner of medical and psychological illnesses. Foods were invented which claimed to be able to dampen the drives that led to masturbation, one of which has since become one of the most popular breakfast cereals! We now know that these fears were groundless and yet there is still resistance to the acceptance of masturbation as a normal everyday part of life. Some have suggested that, because Western culture values sexual ignorance, associating it with a carefree almost pre-fall 'innocence', we want to postpone or avoid altogether our children's first experience of sexual pleasure, which will often be through masturbation.

The new *Catechism of the Catholic Church* regards masturbation as an 'offence against **chastity**' and condemns it as 'an intrinsically and gravely disordered action', on the grounds that sexual pleasure outside of marriage is immoral. However, in deciding the degree of guilt attached to the act pastors are instructed to take into account 'the affective immaturity, force of acquired habit, conditions of anxiety or other psychological factors'.[27] The Vatican therefore acknowledges the part that masturbation plays in the development of adolescent sexuality and implies that in such cases the one who masturbates is not guilty of sin. Yet it still appeals to natural law to condemn the act.

From the point of view of body theology (see above, **4.4**) masturbation appears differently. It can help the young learn to love and appreciate their bodies, as long as it is not looked upon as dirty by parents. It is also a way of relieving sexual tension in adults and preventing premature ejaculation in men.

> Since the Christian faith upholds the institution of monogamous marriage, it cannot but consistently uphold the practice of masturbation within it, at least at times, since partners may wish to have sex with different frequency, or be unavailable or parted from each other. Masturbation provides an innocent and innocuous outlet for sexual desire without recourse to promiscuous sex or partner-threatening liaisons.[28]

There is a tendency among some theologians to argue that masturbation, although not sinful, is always an inferior form of sexual activity because it is not relational. Gareth Moore argues that Woody Allen's famous remark about masturbation, 'Don't knock it, it's sex with someone you love', is

> witty, but false. The most obvious fact about masturbation is that it is not sex with anybody, let alone with someone you love; this means that it has limited possibilities for pleasure. Part of the pleasure of sex with someone you love is the pleasure you take in the fact that it is the loved one who is doing this with you and to you. But if Peter masturbates, however much he loves himself, he does not normally delight that it is just *this* hand that is grasping his penis, precisely *he* who is doing it with or to himself.[29]

Passionate ethics (see **2.12** and **9.2**) roots sexual activity in the commandment of Jesus to love God and our neighbour (Mark 12.29–31). However, feminist theologians have drawn attention to the fact that a precondition of neighbour-love is self-love. The Christian tradition's tendency to define sin in terms of self-centredness has been exposed by feminist theologians to be a particularly male perspective. Women's 'sin' has often been to fail to love themselves or their bodies and to allow them to be exploited or abused by others too easily.

> Learning to love yourself is the most difficult and the most important task we have, and masturbation can play an important part in that ... Perhaps for women especially, whose bodies are objectified and despised by society at large, expressing passion for yourself through touch can be a self-saving act. It is worth reminding

ourselves that masturbation is sometimes the only way women can
experience orgasm ... Touching is a sign of friendship; touching
yourself in ways that give you pleasure, that build you up, that
unlock your passion is a good thing to do.[30]

This too is the verdict of body theology. Masturbation need not be
understood as an inferior type of sexual activity to be engaged in only
when sex with another person is not possible. It can be an act of self-
love and of independence, both of which are needed if a person is to
enjoy a mature sexual relationship with another based upon **mutuality** and justice. Like any other sexual 'act' masturbation takes on
different meanings in different contexts. Where it is associated with
pornography and the objectification of women (see **5.11**), it is
disordered because it is not ordered towards friendship. It can be
used as a way of avoiding and escaping from deep-rooted psychological problems, in which case it is potentially dangerous, but by and
large it is at least a harmless, at most a self-affirming, form of
touch.

4.6 THE BODY, DISABILITY AND OLD AGE

When persons are desexualised through silence or rejection concerning their sexuality, their self-esteem is undercut, their sense of
person power diminished, and they are dehumanised. In such
situations, they may experience loneliness, anxiety, anger, depression, and behaviour problems. When these things are caused, there
is an affront to God's inclusive justice.[31]

The Presbyterian Church in the USA is one of the very few churches
ever to address the sexual needs of the disabled and the elderly. The
other is the Church of Scotland in its 1994 *Report on Human Sexuality*.
Western society idolizes youth and 'beauty' (which it defines in very
narrow terms), and a great deal of the attention we pay to our bodies
is designed to keep them looking youthful and whole. Churches,
political parties and other societies give a great deal of attention to
trying to attract the young and virtually none to attracting the old,
despite the fact that the number of elderly people in Western
societies is increasing. In Western societies 'the aged body has
become a spectre, a spectre contrasting with the ideals of these
countries with their self-images of health and success'.[32]
    The disabled body induces a response similar to that induced by
the old body. The elderly and the disabled are a reminder of our

bodiliness and therefore our mortality. And since most of us are likely to reach old age and experience some form of disability during our lifetime, the reminder is particularly apt. However, our aliena-tion from our bodies is such that instead of facing up to this inevitability we run way from it and part of that flight involves depersonalizing and desexualizing the elderly and disabled. The Church of Scotland report makes the important point that the disabled and elderly are not just sexually disenfranchised but also often deprived of any sense of bodily identity. This is particularly applicable to people with learning difficulties and people with severe physical disability.

> Young people [with learning difficulties] also have difficulty learn-ing about their own bodies. This relates not only to sexual develop-ment but also to basic bodily functions. Sensitive education is essential for them to learn about puberty and physical change. To be educated properly about all issues concerning themselves, in-cluding sexual development, is the right of all young people and no less so of those who have learning difficulties.[33]

In our desexualizing of the elderly and disabled we reveal two understandings of sexuality which we may in fact not admit to: a belief that sexuality is actually not essential to our personhood as human beings, and a purely genital definition of what constitutes sexual activity. Many people find the very idea of the elderly and disabled enjoying sexual activity profoundly disturbing, even disgust-ing. Nothing reveals our discomfort with our bodies and sexuality more than this reaction. We only 'tolerate' sexuality among those who are young and perfect, whose bodies do not yet show signs of 'bodiliness' — change and decay. The elderly and disabled absorb this discomfort from the society around them and deny their own sexuality. Here the Bible most certainly challenges our own disgust, to some extent at least. The Hebrew scriptures are littered with stories which acknowledge and honour the sexuality of the old, from Abraham onwards. In Leviticus, however, the disabled body is an unclean body. Disability is perceived to be an affront to holiness. However, by abolishing the Holiness Codes Jesus abolished the notion that disabled people are somehow less made in the image of God than the rest of us.

> All Christians would accept that it is a Christian duty to care for the sick, the old and the disabled, but when we are prepared to recognize that such care involves making sure that they are able to

experience intimate bodily pleasure and relationships if that is
their desire we will know that we have finally conquered two
thousand years of disastrous dualism.[34]

Body theology affirms the body in the midst of its decay and
mortality. A body-affirming model of Christian care for the elderly
and disabled would at least involve providing appropriate sex and
body education for the young disabled, ensuring that disabled and
elderly people have privacy to be intimate with spouses if they are
living or staying in residential homes or hospitals, and by generally
ensuring that the elderly and disabled are affirmed as sexual beings
with sexual needs. Our sexual needs are met in a variety of ways, from
normal everyday touching to intimate genital contact, and the elderly and disabled may be deprived of all or most of these forms of
touch. The Church of Scotland report notes that 'practices may be
indulged in to give comfort and relief and staff must be trained to
understand this and to accept that masturbation or genital touching
are part of the pattern of coping'.[35] The Presbyterian report goes
much further than many Christians would be comfortable with in
arguing that the elderly and disabled challenge the Church to
recognize that confining sexual activity solely to marriage can help to
diminish the life experience of those who are disabled or who are
elderly:

> We must be open to a range of possibilities if we are to secure sexual
> justice for older adults. The traditional norm of 'sex only in
> marriage, celibacy in singleness' is extremely limiting for older
> adults. Remarriage is a near-impossibility for many persons due not
> only to the lack of available partners, but also to welfare and social
> security restrictions that make marriage financially burdensome.
> Thus we must continue to resist restrictions on welfare and Social
> Security benefits to older adults regardless of marital status. In
> addition, we must eliminate ideas of strict age limits for appropriate
> partners of older adults and redefine family in a broader, Christian
> sense.[36]

One of the most exciting developments in contemporary theology
is the emergence of a liberatory theology of disability. Disabled
people themselves have begun to reflect on their Christian faith from
their own perspective. Nancy Eiesland has noted the need to develop
a 'theology of access' which will give persons with disabilities access to
the social and symbolic life of the Church and the other Christians
access to the social and symbolic life of persons with disabilities.[37] She

points out that the resurrection of Christ both indicates that perfection is not about bodily wholeness (Christ still bears the scars of his death) but ability to survive, and that in Christ we have an image of the divine as Disabled God. Disabled theologians remind us that in our concern to restore the body and sexuality to the heart of the Christian vision we should not fall victim to the idealization of the perfect body beautiful which is an oppressive and divisive image.

4.7 HIV/AIDS

'We need to get it right this time. If we as a body fail to meet this challenge I'm not sure that we will get another chance.'[38] So wrote the **HIV/AIDS** worker Sebastian Sandys about the Church's response to AIDS. He along with many Christians of differing viewpoints believes that AIDS presents the churches with an urgent, unique and ultimate opportunity to preach an unambiguous theology and ethic of sexuality. When news of the HIV virus reached the popular media in the mid-1980s there was general panic. This virus that fatally attacked the immune system causing the syndrome AIDS but could lie undetected in the human body for years and was passed on through the exchange of bodily fluids threatened everyone and yet was particularly associated with **gay** men. Some spoke of the virus as God's punishment on **homosexuals**. Some Christians became wary of sharing the communion cup, even though the virus can only be passed on through intimate bodily contact, the sharing of used needles or infected blood transfusions. Some Christians called for the quarantining of all those who carried the virus, and one prominent Catholic cleric even advocated the quarantining of all **lesbians** and gay men. It was common to make a distinction between 'innocent' victims, i.e., children who had been infected by their mother in the womb and those who had received blood transfusions, and the 'guilty' victims: gay men and drug users. AIDS became a disease laden with metaphorical meaning.[39] It stood for death, punishment and plague. Nelson points out that 'plague' carries connotations of invasion from outside and people were very quick to look for 'foreign' origins — Haiti or Russia were the two chief suspects. It has been argued that the metaphor of the plague encouraged much of the panic.

> The plague metaphor ... encourages us to fear all things bodily. AIDS teaches us to fear sexuality itself. It teaches us to suspect that modern medicine, contrary to our expectations, has not made our

bodies safer after all. It teaches us to fear bodily polluting fluids —
not only sexual fluids but also contaminated blood and the contaminated Communion cup. Finally, the image of the plague nurtures
apocalyptic thinking . . . Yet all of these are inaccurate perceptions
when applied to AIDS.[40]

The metaphor gives the disease a moral meaning, a meaning that has
led to untold extra suffering among those living with HIV/AIDS.

Why is it then that AIDS has become an illness which bears a
negative metaphorical meaning whereas other lethal illnesses such as
influenza, which has already killed over twenty million people this
century, have not? Certainly the fact that it is incurable is important,
but there are other incurable illnesses. AIDS forces us to face two of
our taboos, sex and death, and our deepest fears about embodiment.
It resurrects (if in fact they ever went away) notions of contamination
and uncleanness emanating from our bodies, particularly during sex.
It confronts us with the uncomfortable fact of mortality and bodily
decay among our peers or those younger than us. And most important of all it taps into the sexual insecurities of Western society.
The very existence of lesbian, gay and **bisexual** people challenges the
dominant understanding of sexuality and much of the social order
built upon it — AIDS has focused and to some extent increased the
sense of these people being the 'enemy within', despite the fact that
more **heterosexual** Africans are affected than gay men and AIDS is
becoming feminized, i.e., the people whom it is affecting most
throughout the world are women.

But AIDS has also at last made gay people much more visible and
in ways that have inspired admiration:

> Many people, even those deeply horrified at any homosexuality,
> probably admire the way in which the gay community has re-
> sponded to AIDS. The qualities that this disease has brought to
> light may have matured under its onslaught but they were always
> present in what it is to be gay. They include: Male tenderness, being
> at ease with the human body, sensitivity to vulnerability, realism
> about sexuality, deep acceptance of other people's weaknesses,
> refusal to dismiss anyone as 'unclean', artistic flair and creativity,
> intuitive grasp on how to engage society's imagination, sense of
> irony, genius for celebration, ability to move from gentle humour
> to well-crafted anger.[41]

The churches' response to AIDS was slow, one of the earliest (1983)
being that of the Universal Fellowship of Metropolitan Community
Churches which was founded in the late 1960s by and for lesbians

and gay men. Its approach was unique because it did not have a problem with homosexuality. It therefore concentrated on the need for appropriate education, pastoral care, political activism and sexual responsibility among gay people. Theirs is one of the very few documents to recognize that AIDS would be an issue in, as well as for, the Church.[42] The World Council of Churches (1987) and a handful of other church bodies acknowledged that the Church itself would have to be changed by AIDS and that, in order to be the healing community it was called to be, it would itself need forgiveness for its 'inactivity and rigid moralisms'.[43]

Other churches responded in one of two ways: some used the fact that AIDS was not confined to gay men to avoid the sexuality issue altogether and concentrate instead on offering non-judgemental, well-informed pastoral care to all. A perfect example of this approach is found in some guidelines issued by the Church of England in 1986.[44] Others waded into the ethical debate. The Greek Orthodox Archdiocese of North and South America in a pamphlet to its members (1988) was clear that 'abstention and monogamous [heterosexual] relationships' promoted by the Church since its inception were the only way to combat the disease. Like the Roman Catholic Church it argued that encouraging people to use condoms to prevent the spread of the virus was not the answer, because it 'distorts the value of responsibility by suggesting that being responsible about one's sexuality simply means taking precautions against pregnancy and AIDS'.[45] Many churches blamed **promiscuity** for the disease and used the opportunity to encourage heterosexuals to be **monogamous** and homosexuals to be celibate. In fact AIDS is not caused by promiscuity, it is passed on through certain sexual acts. It is perfectly possible to live a very promiscuous lifestyle and never put yourself at risk from contracting the virus, by engaging in sexual acts that do not involve the exchange of bodily fluids, e.g. mutual masturbation.

The Evangelical Free Church was one of the very few churches explicitly to link AIDS with God's judgement (1986):

> As Christians we are called to uphold biblical standards of righteousness and godly lifestyle, and part of our task in proclaiming the good news of the gospel is to announce God's judgement upon sin and the penalties which accompany patterns of sinful living.[46]

Most other Churches vigorously denied the connection between illness and divine judgement. Some have questioned whether the liberal Christian response to AIDS — which is to respond with compassion leaving on one side the questions of **morality** — does ultimately work, suggesting that it both reflects and further cements dualistic thinking in the Church:

> By divorcing the sexuality of gay people from their humanity, by treating **sexual orientation** or activity as accidental to that humanity, the church gives the impression of ministering not to actual persons who are suffering *qua* persons, but to bodies separated from psyches . . . Healing demands respect for the human integrity of the patient. If the church cannot minister effectively to gay persons with AIDS because its dualistic theology of human sexuality prevents it from embracing their personhood, then perhaps the AIDS crisis is not so much an occasion for the church to be healer, as to be healed.[47]

James Nelson uses the story of the healing of the blind man (John 9.1–2), first of all to demonstrate that Jesus rejected any notion of a connection between divine punishment and illness, but also to highlight the second part of Jesus' reply, 'he was born blind so that God's works might be revealed in him'. Nelson suggests that in concentrating on the question, 'Is AIDS divine punishment?' the churches have been asking the wrong question. The question that we should be asking is 'What works of God are possibly being revealed through this pain?' If we accept that the incarnation teaches us that God is revealed in and through bodies, what is God revealing to us through the bodies of those living with HIV/AIDS? The **hierarchies** of the churches do not seem to be too interested in that question, though Christians working with people touched by the virus often find their previous understandings of homosexuality, drug abuse, etc. completely changed. Most of the theologizing around HIV/AIDS has been done by people whose lives have been touched by the virus. Carter Heyward, meditating on the AIDS quilt which consists of panels representing the lives of those who have died, believes that it is a sign and sacrament of undying friendship which stretches into eternity and which is part of the divine.[48] Mark Pryce, too, in his observation of the way in which gay men have shared and borne each other's pain and grief during the AIDS crisis, finds a new model of God, a God who is not distant and condemnatory, a remote father personified for him in the church hierarchy, but a God who is near, a friend who supports and stands beside us: 'When we stand together, when we love one another, it is then that we know this God.'[49] Though some people living with the virus have felt a profound disconnection from their bodies and long to escape them, for others AIDS has brought a profound sense of embodiment, a sense which body theology (see above, **4.4**) celebrates. One of the earliest films made about AIDS, *Long-time Companion,* closes with a resurrection sequence. The dead and the living congregate on a beach to have a party, the sun is shining, the emaciated bodies are healthy again, there are hugs and laughter and play. I doubt whether many watching the film would have made a connection between that scene and the resurrected Jesus' encounter with his friends on a beach in John 21, but it must be one of the most moving and powerful modern representations of resurrection. Resurrection, like incarnation, declares that bodies are not outer coatings to be discarded once we enter the warm room of heaven, but are so essential to our personhood that they are taken up into God.

4.8 SUMMARY

This chapter has explored embodiment and the Church's historical discomfort with it. It has introduced the concept of the body as a source rather than simply an object of theology and has engaged in some applied body theology when examining the issues of masturbation, sex and the elderly and disabled, and HIV/AIDS. What is clear is that most of the Christian tradition is built upon anti-body theology and that theological reflection done from the body will result in radically different approaches to Christian doctrine, ethical teaching and practice.

Notes

1 The Doctrine Commission of the Church of England, *The Mystery of Salvation* (London: Church House Publishing, 1995), p. 12.

2 *Ibid.,* p. 191.

3 *Catechism of the Catholic Church* (London: Geoffrey Chapman, 1994), paras 362–368.

4 *Ibid.,* para. 2339.

5 Elizabeth Stuart, *Just Good Friends: Towards a Lesbian and Gay Theology of Relationships* (London: Mowbray, 1995), p. 56.

6 Mary Douglas, *Purity and Danger: An Analysis of Concepts of Pollution and Taboo* (London: Routledge and Kegan Paul, 1966).

7　James B. Nelson, *Embodiment: An Approach to Sexuality and Christian Theology* (Minneapolis: Augsburg Publishing House, 1978), p. 23.

8　Elisabeth Moltmann-Wendel, *I Am My Body: New Ways of Embodiment* (London: SCM Press, 1994), p. 36.

9　William Countryman, *Dirt, Greed and Sex: Sexual Ethics in the New Testament and Their Implications for Today* (London: SCM Press, 1989).

10　Moltmann-Wendel, *I Am My Body*, p. 41.

11　Peter Brown, *The Body and Society: Men, Women and Sexual Renunciation in Early Christianity* (London and Boston: Faber & Faber and Columbia University Press, 1988), p. 47.

12　John A. T. Robinson, *The Body: A Study in Pauline Theology* (London: SCM Press, 1952), p. 9.

13　Brown, *The Body and Society*, p. 17.

14　*Ibid.*, pp. 22–3.

15　*Ibid.*, p. 26.

16　*Ibid.*, p. 32.

17　*Ibid.*, p. 139.

18　*Ibid.*, p. 169.

19　Augustine, *De Nuptiis et Concupiscentia* 1.6.

20　Gareth Moore, *The Body in Context: Sex and Catholicism* (London: SCM Press, 1992), p. 47.

21　Brown, *The Body and Society*, pp. 213–40.

22　J. Giles Milhaven, 'A medieval lesson on bodily knowing: women's experience and men's thought', *Journal of the American Academy of Religion*, vol. 57, no. 2 (Summer 1989), p. 360.

23　The person who has done most work around 'body theology' is James Nelson.

24　Luce Irigaray, *Marine Lover of Friedrich Nietzsche* (New York: Columbia University Press, 1991), p. 174.

25　Moltmann-Wendel, *I Am My Body*, p. 77.

26 Virginia Ramey Mollenkott, *Sensuous Spirituality: Out from Fundamentalism* (New York: Crossroad, 1993), p. 162.

27 *Catechism of the Catholic Church*, para. 2352.

28 Adrian Thatcher, *Liberating Sex: A Christian Sexual Theology* (London: SPCK, 1993), p. 183.

29 Moore, *The Body in Context*, p. 57.

30 Stuart, *Just Good Friends*, pp. 205–6.

31 *Keeping Body and Soul Together*, p. 109.

32 Moltmann-Wendel, *I Am My Body*, p. 27.

33 The Board of Social Responsibility of the Church of Scotland, *Report on Human Sexuality* (Edinburgh: Church of Scotland, 1994), para. 5.4.2.

34 Stuart, *Just Good Friends*, p. 209.

35 *Report on Human Sexuality*, para. 7.1.4.

36 *Ibid.*, p. 118.

37 Nancy L. Eiesland, *The Disabled God: Toward a Liberatory Theology of Disability* (Nashville: Abingdon Press, 1994), p. 20.

38 In James Woodward, *Embracing the Chaos: Theological Responses to AIDS* (London: SPCK, 1990), p. 81.

39 Susan Sontag, *AIDS and Its Metaphors* (New York: Farrar, Strauss and Giroux, 1989).

40 Nelson, *Body Theology* (Louisville: Westminster/John Knox Press, 1992), p. 167.

41 Michael Vasey, *Strangers and Friends: A New Exploration of Homosexuality and the Bible* (London: Hodder and Stoughton, 1995), p. 239.

42 J. Gordon Melton, *The Churches Speak on AIDS* (Detroit: Gale Research Inc., 1989), pp. 154–5. This book contains statements on AIDS from churches in Britain and the USA.

43 *Ibid.*, p. 159.

44 *Ibid.*, pp. 68–73.

45 *Ibid.*, pp. 87–8.

46 *Ibid.*, p. 81.

47 William D. Lindsey, 'The AIDS crisis and the Church: a time to heal', in Adrian Thatcher and Elizabeth Stuart, *Christian Perspectives on Sexuality and Gender* (Leominster: Gracewing/Fowler Wright, 1996), pp. 348–9.

48 Carter Heyward, *Touching Our Strength: The Erotic as Power and the Love of God* (San Francisco: Harper and Row, 1989), pp. 138–9.

49 Mark Pryce, 'New showings: God revealed in friendship', in Woodward, *Embracing the Chaos*, p. 52.

Suggestions for further reading

Peter Brown, *The Body and Society: Men, Women and Sexual Renunciation in Early Christianity* (London and Boston: Faber; Columbia University Press, 1988).

Nancy L. Eiesland, *The Disabled God: Toward a Liberatory Theology of Disability* (Nashville: Abingdon Press, 1994).

Elisabeth Moltmann-Wendel, *I Am My Body: New Ways of Embodiment* (London: SCM Press, 1994).

James Nelson, *Body Theology* (Louisville: Westminster/John Knox Press, 1992).

Ronald Nicholson, *God in AIDS: A Theological Enquiry* (London: SCM Press, 1996)

5

POWER

In every chapter so far it has been necessary to speak of that fundamental dominance of men over women which has come to be known as **patriarchy**. Patriarchy (see **1.6**) is a form of 'power-over' (see below, **5.2**), the individual and social power of men over women. This chapter considers examples of the abusive use of power over women in a sexual context. It recognizes the contribution which Christian theology has made to the support of patriarchy and seeks to contribute to the theological quest for relations between women and men which are free from domination. Elaine Graham has shown how an analysis of power between women and men is more fundamental than an analysis of **sexuality**, since analyses of sexuality and **gender** are themselves likely to be premissed on unequal power relations between women and men.[1] That is why in this book, the chapter on 'Power' precedes the one on 'Gender' (Chapter 6). Both chapters should be taken together.

5.1.POWER IN CHRISTIAN ETHICS: CONSENSUAL FREEDOM

Two contemporary theological analyses of power will provide the introduction to the theme of power in sexual relationships. The first is political. James Mackey, in *Power and Christian Ethics*, calls power 'a phenomenon which brings about states of affairs and which can be located on a continuum between the extremes of force and authority'.[2] Force is 'detected . . . by the sheer efficacy with which the state is secured against external threat and internal disruption', and so may neither require nor respect the rule of law. Authority

> names that factor by which a system of law, any system of law, is itself legitimized or validated, if only because it indicates the common

goals that motivate a social group which takes the law to be obligatory upon itself.[3]

Unjust laws then, can have no authority if they do not promote the common good of all who are subject to them.

> Any rule, even the rule of law, must be such as to facilitate rather than suppress the moral agency of its subjects, their ability and human need to evaluate, that is, to make their own moral assessment of the moral values to which the laws must be directed ... [4]

The kind of power under discussion here is clearly the power of governments and states, but it is relevant to the theme of sexual relationships because Mackey shows that *churches* have behaved like oppressive political states, and so the experience of power which is manifested through them is likely to run counter to the example of power relations taught and lived by Jesus. Mackey's main target is the exercise of power in the Roman Catholic Church and how it vitiates much of that Church's moral teaching. When women and men act freely *moral* considerations come into play because states of affairs are brought about due to the choice of a person as a moral subject.[5] Whenever submission is required to teachings, doctrines, rulings, canon laws and so on, force is used because there is actually no room left for a Christian to dissent, criticize, or even consider the possibility of error. It follows then that

> if the beliefs on which I am to act or the rules of my behaviour are simply revealed to me, if they are put in such a way that I am prevented from judging them, much less arriving at them, then I am once more in the presence of force and not of authority.[6]

It follows from this analysis that punishment or the threat of punishment in the sphere of religious or moral beliefs is immoral because no agent can choose freely in such circumstances. 'Recourse to force and fear'[7] when recommending that particular moral actions might be performed is absurd, since it uses non-moral force in order to bring about moral ends. The simplest definition of **morality** is 'a way of living' and 'a way of knowing our world',[8] which, for Christians, also includes 'something that seems to them to reveal the vision and force of the ultimate source of life and existence' which is 'the ultimate word-spirit' or God.[9] For Christians 'There is a word-spirit ... that can be encountered in the body of the followers of Jesus, and which is to be identified with that embodied or **incarnate** in the life, death, and destiny of the man Jesus himself.'[10] Anyone wishing to compose a pastiche of the life of Jesus which emphasizes his refusal to use force might include details from the Gospels of

> Jesus explicitly forbidding the use of force in order to liberate him from unjust arrest and detention, declaring even in these circum-stances that those who live by such force will die by it; Jesus, though he never decides on the forms of governmental structures which his community of followers will eventually need, being most explicit that those who would be leaders in that community must act always as servants of all the others and never in any way attempt to lord it over them, and himself giving the example of being their slave to the ultimate point of consistency of dying a death reserved for slaves and other non-citizens; and so on, and so on.[11]

This analysis of power in the secular state is illuminating, and represents a plausible foil against which to contrast the subsequent exercise of power among the followers of Jesus. Some churches do, of course, abjure any forms of **hierarchical** authority, to the point of refusing to invest any power at all in their central organizations except that of advice and service. However the Roman Catholic Church (of which Mackey is a member) is said to be concentrating and exercising its power in immoral ways; indeed the arrangement of human ecclesiastical power to look like divinely ordained super-natural power is itself a naked act of enforcement. Its method of disseminating its teaching (which in any case belongs to all its members) relies on domination and submission (and thereby by-passes positive assent); it is small wonder that the actual teaching itself cannot be dissociated from the forms of power through which it is proclaimed. The worst example of the misuse of power, both with regard to the content of the teaching and the coercive attempts to ensure its acceptance, is identified by Mackey as the promulgation of the encyclical *Humanae Vitae*. 'Widely seen to be mistaken', and 'ignored by virtually all married Roman Catholics in the world' (see **2.11**), it stands

> as the most significant example of the most characteristic abuse of what has been called **natural law** moralizing [see **2.3**] to this day. It brought a very great deal of unnecessary suffering on the few faithful ones who did try to live by it during their reproductive years, as on many others who suffered the painful wrench of **conscience** in risking, in this instance, the rejection of their spiritual leaders. The sighs of these suffering ones were too often met by celibates, sometimes in very high places indeed, explaining that, if it were up to them, if it was their law, they could do something about it, but

since it was the law of God there was nothing they could do except to urge its victims to pray to God for strength and the grace to endure. This response, in addition to showing its maker more compassionate than God, confirmed the view that human morality was reduced to simple conformity, in this simple conformity to natural processes. But that, of course, is not morality at all.[12]

5.2. POWER IN CHRISTIAN ETHICS: 'POWER-OVER' OR 'POWER-WITH'?

Mackey's warning about the misuse of power in an ecclesial and doctrinal setting is complemented next by the analysis, made by Pamela Cooper-White, an Episcopalian priest, of personal male power over women, in her book *The Cry of Tamar*. Cooper-White contrasts 'power-over' with 'power-within' and 'power-with'. 'Power-over' is domination, 'the normative understanding of power in Judeo-Christian civilizations for approximately four thousand years'.[13] 'Power in this world-view is associated with virility, potency, masculinity, and even biological male sexuality, as revealed in our language: "the thrust of his argument", "a penetrating analysis" '[14] (see **6.3**). 'Power-within' and 'power-with' are the feminist alternatives to the masculinist 'power-over'. The first of these is

> the power of one's own inner wisdom, intuition, self-esteem, even the spark of the divine. Theology that values power-within is joyfully incarnational, celebrating the inherent goodness or 'original blessing' implanted, in the human being, not preoccupied with human sinfulness but rather with human goodness and inspiration.[15]

Power-with 'carries the dignity of power-within into relationship'. It 'is the power of an individual to reach out in a manner that negates neither self nor other. It prizes **mutuality** over control and operates by negotiation and consensus.'[16] When power-with extends to groups, it becomes 'power-in-community'. Power-in-community

> recognizes the power that is *beyond* the individual and the relationship. This power enters the realm of the prophetic, which holds both individuality and relationality and transforms them into something much larger — something that finally approaches what Jesus referred to as the 'Kingdom of God'.[17]

Power-in-community, like Mackey's account of power among the followers of Jesus, derives theological support from St Paul's metaphor of Christians being members of a body, the body of Christ

(1 Corinthians 12.13–31). The need for a 'head' or leader(s) is acknowledged,

> but leadership in this model, unlike a patriarchal power-over model of hierarchy, is authorized by those who are served by that leadership and is accountable to them. Compassion and justice are embraced as the goals of the community together with its leadership, rather than competition for dominance.[18]

People in the community with 'power-over' roles 'must be authorized by the community as a whole'. They 'do not *have* the power; it is on loan from the community'.[19]

Have we become so accustomed to power as control that 'power-with' seems unfamiliar and unrealistic? Organizations with which we are familiar like police forces, schools and commercial companies need line-managers and structures which make clear how accountability happens at every level. Even here there is usually far more room for 'power-with' than those with 'power-over' will admit. 'Power-in-community' confronts 'power-over' in transformative versions of Christian faith, and nowhere ought transformation to be more obvious than in sexual relationships. These provide a forum where alternative relations of power, based on equal participation of women and men in the image of God, are able to be played out. Since the community of believers is committed to such alternative non-linear relations of power, sexual love should be a good guide to the love which Christians are enjoined to have for one another in the Spirit (1 John 4.7–21).

No pastiche of power relations in Christianity could afford to omit Jesus' refusal to assure two of his disciples that they would be granted prestige and status at the end of the world. Their failure to understand that the reign of God in the teaching of Jesus meant the reversal of worldly power led Jesus to amplify his refusal to them in these words:

> 'You know that among the Gentiles the recognized rulers lord it over their subjects, and the great make their authority felt. It shall not be so with you; among you, whoever wants to be great must be your servant, and whoever wants to be first must be the slave of all.' (Mark 10.42–44)

Now women have good reason to fear exhortations from anyone to become servants or slaves, because patriarchy can convert even this most radical teaching of Jesus into a compassionless expectation of human devotion. Another reading of the text sees in it precisely the refusal of what Mackey calls 'force' and Cooper-White calls 'power-over'. In the reign of God mutual service is the only power that counts. Power-with and power-in-community are how relations in the reign of God are to be conducted. This is why John Milbank redescribes Christian theology as 'the discourse of non-mastery',[20] the one and only approach to reality which offers peace instead of violence.

5.3. POWER IN CHURCH REPORTS

The issue of relations between the sexes being distorted by the misuse or abuse of power between them is not yet generally taken up by the churches. There are several reasons for this. The churches have generally regarded sexual sins as the transgressions of individuals. This understanding colludes alarmingly with modern notions of the human person as first and foremost an individual whose being-with-others is something derivative and secondary. A more social (and so biblical) understanding of the person would examine the social practices of societies and examine how these already influence the self-understanding of individuals and their alleged free choices. Secondly, there is still a suspicion within academic theology about the value of sociology to theological study. This is partly because some sociological theory, while methodologically neutral, has tended to be atheistic. This ought not however to call into question the theological use of sociology. Thirdly, those branches of theology which have best utilized sociological insights are **liberation theology** and **feminist theology**. Both of these types of theology are generally unwelcome in the mainstream churches of the First World, largely because those churches are accused by those theologies of colluding with the oppression of women and of the poor. Liberation and feminist theologies are essential to any attempt to speak meaningfully about human sexuality as Christians.

There is mention of the misuse of power in recent reports from Scotland, South Africa and the United States (this is not to say it cannot be found elsewhere). The Church of Scotland acknowledges that the Church

> has, in much of its traditional utterance and practice, accepted and reinforced a patriarchal account [see **1.6**] of family structures which makes women subservient to men [see **1.7**]. This account has treated women, informally if not officially, as domestic servants or

possessions, whose time and energy are at the disposal of husband and family with or without consent.[21]

This Church wisely counsels against accepting accounts of promiscuous or irresponsible sexual activity solely as 'individual sin or moral failure'. Instead a wider social or structural view of sin is commended, for any 'diminished or trivialized view of sex' is

> almost always ... a consequence of the systematic exploitation of sexual **desire** and aspiration by the powers of advertising and commerce. Vulnerable young people are made to feel furtive, inadequate and ashamed of sexual inexperience, and are constantly bombarded with images of **sex** as immediate self-gratification. For the Churches to reinforce the conviction that sexuality is rightly expressed within committed, long term relationship, we need not just to challenge individual moral responses and behaviour; we need also to resist the commercialization of sex at the macro level, in the market place. When we call for personal standards so at odds with the dominant cultural messages associated with power, money and success, we must also tackle the commercial and almost systematic exploitation of people's desire for attractiveness and well-being.[22]

This Report deploys a social explanation for the trivialization of sex. It relies, that is, on what liberation theology calls '**structural sin**'[23] but without using the term. The term 'power' is enlarged to include the power of commerce and advertising, the power of peer pressure and the power of sexual role models which reinforce male self-gratification and female submission. These manifestations of power are woven into an overarching pattern of patriarchy which seeks not simply the domination of women, but domination of the market, of competitors, of human relationships, of the earth itself.

The Southern African Anglican Church is neither coy nor reserved about using insights from liberation theology. The reasons could hardly be more obvious since that Church has known, through its martyrs and victims, the structural sin of racism along with accompanying gender and class inequalities. Love, warns the Southern African Anglican Theological Commission,

> involves an attitude towards the other partner in which the happiness and welfare of the other is of prime importance, and which is expressed in appropriate acts. In view of the frequent distortion of sexuality by abusive power both within and outside marriage, a Christian sexual **ethic** is committed to the liberation of sexual

expression as mutual enrichment rather than as dominance and submission.[24]

The teaching of that church, its authors continue,

> must refer especially to ways of sexual intimacy as expressions of love and of self-discovery in discovering the other. Above all else, it must stress the mutual commitment of both partners to each other and the need to avoid any sense of domination of one partner by the other. Ethical judgments about sexual behaviour must be consistent with those about racism, sexism and other sins.[25]

The emphasis on mutuality in these extracts assumes both equality between women and men, and a relational view of the person such that only in relation with an 'other' can self-discovery and sexual growth be achieved. Domination in sexual relations is deemed sinful, and given the telling context which Southern African Christians know only too well — the domination of racism — this judgement about domination in sexual relations is all the more powerful. The linking of racism, sexism and oppressive 'power-over' provides the overall view within which the redemption of the world brought about by Christ is able to be understood.

The report of the Presbyterian Church of the USA explicitly confronts a 'gender **dualism**' (see **4.2** and Chapter 6) which it sees as an invention of patriarchy. 'The integrity of gender relations' has been distorted by 'elevating the male over the female' in a 'gender hierarchy', because 'in a culture of inequality, there has to be a group which rules and a group which is ruled over. In a patriarchal system, good order means that men must be in command.' A consequence of the gender hierarchy is that

> In our society men are typically socialized to be masterful, seek control, and assert power over others. Many men feel uncomfortable when such control is not theirs. Women, too, are socialized around power — not to exercise power, but to welcome dependency and subordination for their own good. In a patriarchal society and family system, women organize their lives exclusively around men and find their worth in fulfilling their duty to take care of male needs. Trained for dependency and service to others, women are encouraged literally to be self-less, that is, without their own sense of self-worth, and to locate their identity only through others.[26]

The language of the social sciences is seen as a theological resource in this work. The notion of **socialization** becomes fundamental in coming to an understanding of the whole context including, for church members, the churches themselves, within which sexual experience is understood and acquired. The assumption that 'dominant–subordinate relations' are 'normative' is understood as an ideology whereby unjust assumptions pass themselves off as natural and unchallenged.[27] These assumptions belong to an oppressive system and Christians are called instead to help to dismantle them, trusting in the power and justice of God.

5.4 THE ISSUE OF CONSENT

Consent to sexual activity with another person is clearly fundamental to the morality of what takes place. The giving or withholding of consent is central to the determination of whether or not a crime of harassment or rape has taken place. What is often overlooked, however, is the wider social expectation that when sexual activity is initiated, consent be given, and given on demand. This expectation is a manifestation of 'power-over' (see above, **5.2**) and an example of structural sin. It results in consent being given because of a false consciousness with regard to the socially mediated prompts which, in the case of **heterosexual** practice, favour male pleasure. This is a claim which will be substantiated by querying the role of the individual in decision-making, the impact of social pressure, and the possibility of the positive mediation of the churches in influencing sexual practice.

According to one of the deepest assumptions to permeate Western societies, societies are comprised of individuals who make choices. Passionate ethics begins with relationships, not simply with individuals (see **2.12**). There is a predisposition towards individualism, assumed alike by armies of psychotherapists, legal systems and Christian evangelists. The value of this view is that everyone supposedly counts for something and is not reduced to invisibility among the collective mass of people. What this view at times wilfully ignores is that no choices can ever be made in a purely mental or private space. Choices are massively influenced. It is not necessary to embrace the philosophical theory of **determinism** to see that the influences affecting our choices may predominate over any personal preferences, or moral intuitions, or calls of conscience. It is not simply that we end up doing what we perceive everyone else to be doing. Rather, we end up believing we are still choosing for ourselves when only the rhetoric of choice remains. This too is false consciousness. Christian power-in-community offers a glimpse of a sharing in the non-coercive life of Christ where genuine freedom is restored. Such communities should provide role models for men and women which challenge submission with mutuality and which honour vulnerability. This is the love which is provided by God and made known in Christ. This is God's love set forth in the community of Christians of which St John spoke:

> My dear friends, let us love one another, because the source of love is God. Everyone who loves is a child of God and knows God, but the unloving know nothing of God, for God is love. This is how he showed his love among us: he sent his only Son into the world that we might have life through him. This is what love really is: not that we have loved God, but that he loved us and sent his Son ... (1 John 4.7–10)

Anyone who thinks the Church normally provides such love has got to be kidding. But that would not invalidate the icon (see **2.6**) which remains a Christian vision and hope. The power and love in the Christian community should always be a safe place for the exercise of consent, for membership consists of those committed to the mutual love of each other 'in Christ'. Sadly we know the churches are rarely safe places, for power as power-over is still widely exercised within them.

5.5 HARASSMENT

Violence against women is 'the annihilation of connectivity, the dulling and erasure of human relationality through **objectification**'.[28] It is described in chilling detail in *The Cry of Tamar*. The descriptions of force (see above, **5.1**) and 'power-over' (see above, **5.2**) set out in this chapter now enable us to focus more clearly on the pervasive evil of violence against women and children. What is sexual harassment? At work, it includes 'unwelcome sexual advances, requests for sexual favors, and other verbal or physical conduct of a sexual nature'.[29] It 'occurs on the streets, in the subways, and every place where women dare to move freely in society'.[30] Just as the issue of consent cannot be reduced to a matter of individual choice in particular situations, so harassment cannot be reduced to a matter of individuals being subjected to particular instances of threatening male behaviour. It creates fear. The widespread tolerance of such fear is itself unacceptable. Harassment and the threat of it keeps women in their place. It creates an environment of stress, insecurity, and fear that reduces all a woman's identity, role, and worth to her sexuality alone. It erodes her confidence, her initiative, and even her health, with direct consequences for her ability to work competitively and well. As such, sexual harassment becomes an effective tool of social control and economic oppression. There is no other form of violence against women, except perhaps domestic violence, which functions so immediately and directly to constrain women's economic independence and social freedom.[31]

Harassment is a serious problem in the churches.[32] The Church-wide Assembly of the Evangelical **Lutheran** Church in America approved a policy statement committing that church to working towards a harassment-free atmosphere among its congregations. Believing that Christian baptism 'into the family of God calls us to stand firmly and pastorally against all forms of abuse and to respect and empower our brothers and sisters in Christ', the Lutherans recognized that 'sexual harassment and sexual abuse betray God's creation, inflict grievous suffering on the victims and rend the fabric of the whole community of the people of God'. It resolved to undertake a programme of action against harassment, and required that

> each congregation commit itself to become a safe place by working to:
>
> a) provide an atmosphere where sexual abuse can be discussed with the freedom and compassion of the gospel, and where specific acts of ministry can be encouraged;
> b) engage in education and prevention of all forms of sexual abuse and harassment;
> c) provide pastoral care for survivors and referrals for treatment of offenders;
> d) create policies and procedures that assist and support the members of the congregation and its leadership to cope in healing and redemptive ways with these abuses ... [33]

Harassment offends against the most simple and basic beliefs of Christian faith. The Golden Rule of Jesus rules it out completely. It is simply not possible to 'always treat others as you would like them to treat you' (Matthew 7.12) if one is exercising 'power-over' of a sexual nature. The love of neighbour as oneself cannot be reconciled with harassment, nor can countless other Christian teachings.

5.6 RAPE

Rape is the most obvious example of the use of force, of 'power-over' a victim. In the United States it is claimed that one in three women and one out of fifteen to twenty men have been raped. Fifty to ninety per cent of rapes are unreported. Major reasons for this include the fear of reprisal, the ordeal of giving evidence, and the belief that justice is unlikely to be obtained. In less than 50 per cent of reported rapes is a suspect ever apprehended. Of these less than 50 per cent go to trial and of these only 10 per cent are convicted.[34] When rape is regarded as an individual act, albeit a culpable one, the wider problem of unequal power relations of men over women is bracketed out. What is required is greater understanding of these relations, which locates acts of rape in the distorted personal, social and political relationships which, on a Christian understanding of the reign of God, belong to a disordered and gravely sinful world that is passing away.

The fear of rape 'is simply a part of the fabric of everyday life for women'.[35] Rapes are more likely to occur in the home than in a public place and are much more likely to be carried out by acquaintances than by strangers. The impact of rape on the lives of victims is incalculable. Victims of rape are thirteen times more likely to have made a suicide attempt. Rape has long been associated with military violence, political domination and racist oppression. Rape is more likely than not to be premeditated, especially if more than one assailant is involved. The assumption therefore that men are the real victims (i.e., of the passions women culpably arouse in them) is absurd. Women of all ages are raped and the so-called 'sex-appeal' of victims is irrelevant. 'A man assaults someone who is accessible and vulnerable',[36] irrespective of stereotypes of attractiveness. It is widely thought that rape is a sex crime. Even this assumption is less than wholly accurate. Rape is 'an act of aggression and intimidation accomplished by sexual means'.[37] What is and is not sexual is a matter of debate. Nicholas Groth's work on rapists led him to conclude that sexual gratification was 'secondary or absent'. Rather, 'we look at rape as the sexual expression of aggression, rather than as the aggressive expression of sexuality'.[38]

Rape is a spiritual, as well as a physical crime. Wherever the body is not regarded as sacred, a climate which favours rape is encouraged. A view of the person as an inseparable unity of body and spirit cannot but see violence against the person as violence against the spirit as well as the body. The negation of the person in the effort to dominate and subdue it is sometimes as difficult to recover from as the assault itself. With rape,

> the violation . . . of the most private parts of the body — the parts connected with procreation, birth, and sexual pleasure — constitutes a violation of nothing less than one's spiritual core of being. It is the sexual nature of the violation that makes it so profoundly a crime against the spirit.

There is a disturbing connection between religious and sexual submission which in the context of the threat of rape becomes complex and acute. Doubtless there is a difference between human submission to divine power and female submission to male power, but through centuries of Christianity the two have become intertwined and must now and forever be separated. The two best known examples of religious submission in Christian faith are the prayer of Christ in Gethsemane and the reply of his mother on learning she would be pregnant by the Holy Spirit. Jesus prayed, 'Yet not my will but yours' (Mark 14.36) and Mary, informed that 'The Holy Spirit will come upon you, and the power of the Most High will overshadow you; for that reason the holy child to be born will be called Son of God' (Luke 1.35), responded 'I am the Lord's servant . . . may it be as you have said' (Luke 1.38).

Attitudes of unquestioning obedience and submission are frankly dangerous, and are advantageous to any user of force. Among Christian mystics, the language of submission is graphically used, and sometimes drenched with sexual metaphors. We will not engage in debate about whether these outpourings represent frustrated human sexual desires, or whether they provide evidence that the mystics were making good religious sense of their sexuality.[39] There is a simpler point — being overwhelmed by God and being overwhelmed by anyone else must be absolutely separated.[40]

5.7 THE PLIGHT OF SUSANNA

The story of the rape of Tamar by David's son Amnon (2 Samuel 13.1–22), together with its patriarchal assumptions, its psychological and social realism, and its personal consequences for perpetrator and victim, is the founding narrative of *The Cry of Tamar*.[41] The anguish of Tamar calls us back from theoretical considerations to consider the traumas of real victims of rape, past and present. That is why a similar narrative, the attempted rape of Susanna, will be examined here instead. In particular we will be looking at how power is distributed among the participants and misused by men before and after the act of rape is attempted.

In the book of Daniel and Susanna[42] two judges who had just been appointed from among the elders of the Israelite community regularly frequented the home of an aristocrat Joakim in connection with their legal practice. At siesta time 'when the people went away', Joakim's wife Susanna used to walk in her husband's garden. Both the judges were besotted with Susanna and were determined to fuck[43] her. Each discovers the other ogling Susanna, so they decide they will fuck her together. Opportunity knocks when, one very hot day, Susanna decides to have a bath in the garden pool and sends her servants away. The concealed judges pounce on Susanna and tell her if she does not consent to having sex with them they will ensure her death by giving evidence that they have seen her having sex with a young man in the garden. Susanna refuses to yield to them and cries out 'at the top of her voice', knowing that an audible cry is the only defence against the assumption of consent. But the judges also cry out so her voice is not heard. The judges bring false accusations against her and at the trial their word is believed. Susanna is given no opportunity even to plead. She is condemned to death. Raising her voice to God she cries out in a last despairing cry for justice. The young Daniel persuades the people to re-open the trial while he interrogates the judges. He establishes Susanna's innocence by eliciting from each of the judges irreconcilable statements about where in the garden Susanna and her supposed lover had been seen. The judges are killed and Susanna is 'found innocent of a shameful deed' (v. 63).

The 'dulling and erasure of human relationality through objectification' (see above, **5.4**) is well exemplified in this neglected story. The insistent power of male desire converts Susanna, like millions of women before and after her, into an object to be possessed. She is no longer a person to be honoured, and her assailants make no attempt to converse with her. Their obsession with Susanna led them to ignore the trust the community had placed in them to be dispensers of justice, not the perverters of the course of it. Guardians of the law themselves, they were aware their actions would break both the seventh commandment forbidding adultery and the ninth commandment forbidding the giving of false evidence against one's neighbour (Exodus 20.14,16). Not even baser reasons for leaving her alone, like fear of detection, deterred them. They were 'inflamed with **lust**. Their minds were perverted; their thoughts went astray and were no longer turned to God, and they did not keep in mind the demands of justice' (vv. 9–10). We may speculate that their inability to share their feelings about Susanna (v. 10), or to own up to them, intensified them. They became voyeurs. 'Day after day they watched eagerly for a sight of her' (v. 12).

The story illustrates how male power and social power may collude to the detriment of women. The judges occupied important positions in the Israelite state and religion. They were like senior bishops, or Vatican officials, or High Court Judges today. They were able to use their office in order to gain access to Susanna. They were guests in her husband's house. They could rely on their false evidence being unchallenged (although they reckoned without the upstart young hero Daniel). They were prepared to misuse a position of trust in order to bring about either the rape or the certain death of an innocent woman. 'Because they were elders of the people and judges, the assembly believed them and condemned her to death' (v. 41).

Susanna, we are told, was 'a very beautiful and devout woman' (v. 1), but it is Susanna's body, not Susanna which occupies the attention of the rapists (and the narrator) in the story. The bathing scene (vv. 15–18) with its sensuous oils and ointments is not prurient, yet neither is it entirely innocent since it invites the aroused male reader into the scene even before the elders can get there. Is the alleged sex-appeal of the victim to be the excuse for the incident? There is a tension in the narrative between Susanna the devout woman who comes to the trial 'with her parents and children and all her relatives' (v. 30) and Susanna the object of sexual gratification whose relations and relationships count for nothing. Although 'a woman of great beauty and delicate feeling', at the trial it is her body which is of interest to the court — 'those scoundrels ordered her to be unveiled so that they might feast their eyes on her beauty. Her family and all who saw her were in tears' (vv. 32–33). The court is no place of justice. There is an obvious continuity here between the treatment Susanna receives and the treatment given to women who, when they bring charges of rape, have been cast as culpable arousers of men's desires. Susanna is even presented with this mythic explanation of her ordeal before it starts. 'We are overcome with desire for you; consent, and yield to us' (v. 20). The possibility of consent is offered to her. We have already noted the fragility of the meaning of the term 'consent' (see above, **5.4**). In her own words, she is in 'a desperate plight' (v. 22). Her predicament is very like that of all women who come face to face with sexual attackers. They do not know whether they are going to be killed. The only difference in Susanna's case is that if she resists and survives, her death will be brought about by judicial means.

Susanna was yet another woman unsafe even in her own home. This is where the rape of Tamar (2 Samuel 13) and one-third of all rapes occur. The privacy of the garden, its locked gates, even the presence nearby of maidservants, provide no defence against the assailants' determination. She is depicted as making a swift and pious decision. Faced with death or being placed at the mercy of her assailants (v. 22), she exclaims 'My choice is made: I will not do it! Better to be at your mercy than to sin against the Lord!' (v. 23). She then 'called out at the top of her voice'. Whatever the religious motivation may have been, Susanna's action was the right one, since resistance to attempted rape increases the likelihood of avoidance, while surrender in the hope of avoiding further injury is likely to be counter-productive.[44] Women's socialization into passivity and silence aids rapists. But Susanna's judgement that she should not 'sin against the Lord' is, for modern readers, contentious. Does the writer attribute to Susanna the thought that she would bear the guilt of being raped? Is she held, at this point of extreme danger to her body and to her life, to put questions of theological **purity** above her own safety? Not necessarily. If the crime of rape is seen as a spiritual crime, the violation of the soul through the violation of the body, there is good theological justification for seeing her violation as a sin against the Lord. The demand of piety is that of resistance, not submission to male demands.

Susanna's deliverance was brought about by her quick-thinking refusal to submit. She realized her 'power-within' (see above, 5.2). The deliverance brought about by the precocious young prophet was from the false evidence of the frustrated rapists, who now conspire with each other to pervert the course of justice. Such is their power that Susanna is given no opportunity to refute the false evidence against her. We have had reason to advocate a sexual ethic based on the virtue of justice (see 2.12) and something like a justice-ethic now emerges in Daniel's accusations which God inspires him to bring (v. 45). One of the elders is accused of what in narrative ethics (see 2.5) would be called 'a failure of character'. He is told that he has become 'hardened', and that 'the sins of your past have now come home to you'. He has already given previous 'unjust decisions'. Both of them are accused of using their power to prey on women, 'terrifying them into yielding to you' (v. 57).

It would be a mistake to regard Susanna's story as one which is wholly free from patriarchy. The narrator is as anxious to establish the esteem of the young prophet as he is to vindicate Susanna. Even when Daniel uses all his forensic skills to find out the truth, Susanna's own story remains unheard. Nonetheless there are highly illuminating parallels between Susanna's 'desperate plight' and that of women who are harassed, abused and raped today. While the details of the exercise of 'power-over' will vary, the fact of the exercise of 'power-over' remains.

5.8 BATTERING

Battering is 'abusive behavior that *intimidates and controls the battered partner, for the purpose of establishing and maintaining authority*'.[45] Once again the heritage of previous generations of Christians is an ambiguous one. Wife-beating was long allowed in English law as a means of correction and control, while the beating of children is not merely authorized in the Bible — failure to carry it out is regarded as neglect of parental duty (see below, **5.10**). While the beating of children in the schools of Europe is now a criminal offence, the beating of children and wives and/or partners in the home is so widespread it has been called an 'epidemic'. In common with the analysis in this chapter, battering, like other forms of violence against women and children, 'is a matter of power, and its aim is not primarily to discharge anger or stress, but to assert ownership and enforce control'[46] (see **1.7**). Thus it is one more expression of domination, and historically the ideology of male headship and the duty of submission has been used in support of it.

Battering is probably better understood now than it has ever been. This is a fortunate consequence of the lifting of the veil of secrecy off violent patriarchal behaviour. There is now a widely agreed 'cycle of violence'[47] which is likely to include tension-building, an acute incident, a respite phase involving possible admission of guilt and apparent remorse, leading only to repetition of the cycle. The cycle imposes intolerable strains on victims, and counsellors and clergy are often unaware that the assailant's confession of violence, together with sincere repentance and the promise of reform, may be no more than a further strategy of control, especially if the battered partner has threatened to leave or has actually left. In fact the respite phase of the cycle of violence is actually the best time to leave a violent relationship, as well as the time when it is least likely to happen.[48]

5.9 CLERGY ABUSE

More grim statistics greet the reader on numbers of clergy engaging in sexual relationships with parish staff or parishioners. It seems that between one in eight and one in three clergy have 'crossed sexual boundaries' with their parishioners.[49] This behaviour is called 'abuse' because of the obvious power dynamics which are an inescapable element of such relationships.[50] The growing awareness of the abuse by clergy of parishioners and children has become one of the most notorious scandals of the 1990s. If anything positive can be said about the constant stream of tabloid stories about clergy abuse, it is that the mystique of ordained male priesthood no longer has any credibility in the world even if deference towards it continues inside the churches. Greater awareness that clergy are as prone to err as the rest of us (and with more opportunity and sometimes a cocktail of religious prejudices which condone it) has also led to a greater awareness that traditional sexual morality cannot, and does not, deal with it. And that is because, once again, the issue is one of power.

Cooper-White has herself been involved in over 100 cases of clergy abuse and she confirms that power rather than sex lies at the root of them all. She writes:

> As with rape, a pastor's sexual or romantic involvement with a parishioner is not primarily a matter of sex or sexuality but of power and control. For this reason, I have called it clergy sexual abuse rather than a private matter of sexual activity between consenting adults. Even when adultery is involved, unfaithfulness is not the primary issue. I have found that a majority of ministers who enter into romantic or sexual relationships with parishioners do so primarily because there is an imbalance of power between them at the onset, and because they need to reinforce and heighten the intensity of that power dynamic. This need is driven by internal forces and is reinforced by societally conditioned expectations that women will function as a nurturing, sexual servant class to support men's external achievement.[51]

5.10 CHILD ABUSE

A recent analysis by Hilary Cashman of the extent of child sexual abuse inside the British churches shows the practice to be as widespread and as horrific as it is in the United States.[52] A child is sexually abused 'when another person, who is sexually mature, involves the child in any activity which the other person expects to lead to their sexual arousal'.[53] At least one child in ten is thought to be a victim of sexual abuse. Ninety per cent of abusers are male and they abuse both male and female children. 'It is likely that the rate of child sexual abuse within Christian communities is similar to the rate in the non-Christian population.'[54]

The Judaeo-Christian tradition has sanctioned abusive power over children. 'A father who spares the rod hates his son, but one who loves his son brings him up strictly' (Proverbs 13.24). 'Folly is deep-rooted in the hearts of children; a good beating will drive it out of them' (Proverbs 22.15). The distinction made between authority and force (see above, **5.1**) helps with the interpretation of these texts. Even so, the texts do not merely license the corporal punishment of children, they have provided direct encouragement of physical abuse in the name of paternal authority. And physical and sexual abuse blur into each other. The further connection between the uses of patriarchal power in the home and in the churches gets striking confirmation from the young victims of abuse studied by Margaret Kennedy.[55] The churches operate an hierarchical male power-structure. 'Such a patriarchal structure has a particular resonance for the abused child or abuse survivor, especially where the abuser was her father.'

Just as there is a cycle of violence in the battering of women which can lead to the erroneous expectation that reform may be on the way, there is a similar cycle of abuse of children. Unfortunately,

> abusers rarely give up abusing. This is one of the truths so grim that we do not want to hear it. It is more hopeful to believe that a few months of therapy will do the trick and the happy family can be safely reunited. It is children who pay the price of this belief.[56]

Over 40 per cent of homeless girls in a survey by the Campaign for Homeless People were found to be fleeing from sexual abuse.[57]

5.11 PORNOGRAPHY

Pornography takes its place in this chapter because it is another expression of 'power-over', a vast, even ubiquitous phenomenon of male domination which presents women as sexual objects available to men. Pornography has been variously defined. Once again we are pleased to use a report of the Presbyterian Church of the USA to speak for Christians generally, both in defining and analysing pornography from a detailed theological perspective. According to the authors of the report *Pornography: Far from the Song of Songs* (adopted by that church at its 200th General Assembly in 1988), pornography

> includes any sexually explicit material (books, magazines, movies, videos, TV shows, telephone services, live sex acts) produced for the purpose of sexual arousal by eroticizing violence, power, humiliation, abuse, dominance, degradation, or mistreatment of any person, male or female, and usually produced for monetary profit. Any sexually explicit material that depicts children is pornography.[58]

Pornography is described and understood as an issue about male power over women. Thus defined it is recognized, among other features, by 'graphic displays of sexual behavior ("graphic" meaning vivid, exaggerated, or excessively descriptive) that eroticize (make sexually arousing) self-pleasure through the exploitation of power over another person', and by 'the sexual subordination or mistreatment of women or men'.[59] It is significant that 'power over' is used here before it came to have a semi-technical meaning (see above, **5.2**).

For the Roman Catholic Church, pornography is an offence against **chastity**. The Catechism says it consists 'in removing real or simulated sexual acts from the intimacy of the partners, in order to display them deliberately to third parties'.[60] One must not expect too much detail in the solitary paragraph devoted to pornography in the Catechism, but there must surely be doubt about the adequacy of this short definition. The definition signals unintended approval of 'simulated sexual acts' since it is the removal of these from the context of intimacy and not their pretended and deceitful character which, at least according to the text, make simulated sex wrong. Second, pornography need not display 'acts'. The third and most important reason for querying the definition is its assumption that what makes pornography morally objectionable is its voyeuristic character, the display to third parties, which makes it wrong, and not the objectification or subjugation involved in the display.

The definition in the Catechism does not focus on the elements of the misuse of power found in the Presbyterian approach. Pornography is wrong for other reasons. It offends against chastity, because it perverts the conjugal act, the intimate giving of spouses to each other. It does grave injury to the dignity of its participants (actors, vendors, the public), since each one become an object of base pleasure and illicit profit for others. It immerses all who are involved in the illusion of a fantasy world. It is a grave offence. Civil authorities should prevent the production and distribution of pornographic materials.[61]

Chastity is 'the successful integration of sexuality within the person',[62] so the offence against chastity which the user of pornography commits is a failure to control desire. It may be helpful to speak here of 'eruption' and 'disruption'. The eruption of desire, whether or not produced by the use of pornography, is thought to bring about the disruption of the unity of the person (his or her will, intellect and emotions). This failure is inconsistent with and therefore (we might add) against the interests of the user. A further reason for the wrongness of pornography in the Catechism is that it divorces sex from love and so devalues the latter. The 'grave injury' which pornography inflicts on 'the dignity of its participants' is the nearest the document comes to condemning the violence against women which is almost inevitable in pornography. There is no equality of injury inflicted (among 'actors, vendors, the public'), yet the document seems to imply this. That is because there is no comprehension of the role of pornography in enforcing the subjugation or exploitation of women. For these reasons the treatment of pornography in the Catechism, while illuminating, is clearly inadequate.

One of the most difficult tasks facing Christian theologians is to come to the point of admitting that patriarchal theology and pornography are actual 'bedfellows' in dominating women. Mary Hunt, reflecting on the publication of the infamous 'Letter to the Bishops of the Catholic Church on the Pastoral Care of Homosexual Persons' in 1986, calls this publication 'theological pornography'. Claiming that pornography 'objectifies persons', 'trivializes sexuality' and 'leads to violence', she finds that the Letter, and to different degrees, the patriarchal and heterosexist tradition of Catholic moral theology, qualifies as pornography on the basis of her three criteria.[63] It can hardly be denied that much theology *is* pornography in this sense. That is why Rosemary Radford Ruether, having drawn attention in the theological past to men's depiction of women speaks of 'this theological "gangbanging" of women' in the tradition.[64] Women have been blamed for bringing sin into the world (1 Timothy 2.14), believed to be born from defective male seed, deprived of legal status, excluded from professions, burned and drowned as witches, legally beaten as wives (clergy could do it harder since correction of clergy-wives was deemed more necessary), and so on.[65] This legacy, she says,

> justified almost limitless violence against them whenever they crossed the male will at home or in society. Woman as victim is the underside of patriarchal history, seldom given respect or concern from agents of morality or law enforcement. Women particularly have been subjected to the double bind of blaming the victim in innumerable and convoluted ways that women even today have a difficult time refuting.[66]

The parallels between theology and pornography are disquieting and disturbing, certain to elicit angry denials. Fortunately there is a non-patriarchal theology, just as there is a non-patriarchal construction of sexuality. Once the distorting power bias against women is removed, the possibility remains that explicit, sexually arousing material might be produced and enjoyed without worry that men or women are being objectified or humiliated. This is confirmed by work done in Canada and the United States which utilizes *three categories* of pornography, viz., (i) sexually explicit and violent; (ii) sexually explicit and non-violent, but subordinating and dehumanizing; and (iii) sexually explicit, non-violent and non-subordinating, based on mutuality and equality.[67] The third is able to be seen as erotic, and not strictly pornographic, since (at least at the level of categorization) no exploitative elements exist in this category. One suspects that the classification of potential or actual pornography into these categories will be a perplexing task, but the classification has been recognized in Canadian courts when plaintiffs have argued they have been harmed by material in categories (i) and (ii), and research into the consequences of the use could find no evidence of negative behaviour resulting from the use of category (iii).

We are now in a position to begin to specify what is and what is not wrong with pornography. Some criticisms of pornography are non-starters. The condemnation of pornography sometimes proceeds from a disowning of the sexual desires that are deliberately aroused by the use of it. Since sexual desire is good (see Chapter 6) there is no mileage in disowning our desires or projecting our disgust at them on to the objects (generally women's bodies) that excite them. Again a particular psychological view of the person deploys the dualisms of reason and passion, will and desire, and fears pornography because it weakens the resolve of reason and the will to control passion and desire. There is no denying that the possible use of pornography will arise in the lives of most men and some women as *temptation*, and thus as conflict, but when the conflict is expressed as the conflict between reason, or the will, or the mind, with passion, desire and the flesh, the problem is presented once more as a problem of control. There are good reasons for rejecting this view as well. It is one more version of the patriarchal problem of controlling wife, children, household and property: this time the control problem is lodged in the master's own body. Some condemnation of pornography is based on hatred of the body, especially those of women. This attitude expresses a particular patriarchal mind-set which is already violent towards women. One type of criticism of pornography shares with pornography the fear and hatred of women.

Another failed condemnation of pornography lies in straight bourgeois prudery. Some enlightened models of the human person so de-emphasize the power and disruption of bodily desires that they are given no official existence. The disembodied mind is then in poor shape to deal with any erotic imagery because it is not supposed to be part of the official world at all. The religious equivalent of this view draws a veil over the erotic potential of all human bodies because the disruption to spiritual tranquillity which they cause is explained as sin. The evil of pornography lies in the power relations it normalizes, the objectification of persons which it validates, the hates and fears which it aggravates, and the lack of connectivity which it exploits. These are evils enough without being further compounded by theological mistakes which make the body, and desire, and erotic arousal, sins as well.

Pornography as depicted in *Far from the Song of Songs* is

> a powerful symptom of injustice and alienation in human society. Through words and images, pornography debases God's intended gifts of love and dignity in human sexuality. Although humankind was created male and female, equally and fully in the image of God, the history of humanity reveals a fundamental pattern of dominance and subjugation.[68]

Pornography 'represents human discord, far from the mutual sexual delight depicted biblically in the Song of Songs'. It is 'a striking sign of human brokenness and alienation from God and from one another', and the central issue 'is not so much the disturbance of traditional norms of sexual morality as it is the gross distortion of power revealed in its graphic sexual images'.[69]

Lodged against the destructiveness of pornography is the Song of Songs in which 'highly sensuous love poetry ... where man and woman take pleasure and celebrate one another's bodies, has been seen through the centuries as symbolic of the relationship of God and the people of Israel, of Christ and the church'.[70] The 'people of the covenant' (both Jews and Christians)

> expect human beings to live in such a way that they express toward each other the compassion that God has extended to them. The term for this life is *shalom*, which means health, wholeness, unity, peace. In living as covenant people in *shalom*, there can be no separation of body and spirit. And there can be no easy separation of **eros** and agape or connecting sexuality only to eros, surrounding it with taboos, or expressing it through patriarchal oppression or pornographic exploitation.[71]

5.12 THEOLOGICAL REFLECTION: THE DOORMAT OR THE DOOR?

The theology which exercises domination, often by claiming divine authority, has now been exposed. Hand in hand with patriarchal power is a type of explanation of suffering which falsifies its real cause. The experience of being abused, or battered, or raped is sometimes explained as divine punishment, or a means to a greater good, or God's will, or an opportunity to develop the virtue of patience, or endurance, or to suffer with Christ, etc. Marie Fortune has called this 'doormat theology'.[72]

It is necessary to state how widespread doormat theology is. We have already had occasion to be wary of rape and submission **metaphors** in mystical theology. But doormat theology tramples over several of the central doctrines of the faith. Not only is unjust suffering glorifed in patriarchal theology, forgiveness and repentance are corrupted by it. The need to forgive one another as Christ forgave us can become an oppressive expectation which adds to the burden of the victim[73] and postpones the real work of repentance. 'Facile' forgiveness[74] ignores the horror of sin. 'Reluctance or slowness to forgive, therefore, is not a falling short of a Christian ideal; it is rooted in the reality of sin and the meaning of forgiveness.'[75] The 'rush to resurrection' is another example of facile and corrupting treatment of Christian belief. 'Because we believe in the healing power of Christ's resurrection, we may expect Christianity to heal all grief speedily.' Yet this very emphasis on supernatural power easily 'denies the depth of the damage done'.[76]

Counterposed to doormat theology is a place of safety, a sheepfold whose door is Christ himself. In this realm where there is ultimate protection from predatory violence Jesus is both the door and the shepherd of the sheepfold. He said:

> 'In very truth I tell you, I am the door of the sheepfold. The sheep paid no heed to any who came before me, for they were all thieves and robbers. I am the door; anyone who comes into the fold through me will be safe. He will go in and out and find pasture. A thief comes only to steal, kill, and destroy; I have come that they may have life, and may have it in all its fullness. I am the good shepherd; the good shepherd lays down his life for the sheep.' (John 10.7–11)

Short of eternity no such place of safety exists. But the gospel depicts Jesus Christ as the entrance to a realm where violence is left outside along with wolves and hired shepherds who are uncommitted to their sheep (vv. 12–13). The followers of Jesus belong to such a realm even though it is not confined to them and violence among them is only partially renounced. They 'appear as people threatened, but Jesus is their protector'.[77] The text enables us to glimpse what the reign of God might mean when it is finally inaugurated. Here is a place of safety where fullness of life is celebrated and predation of all kinds is barred. There is no suggestion that fullness of life should accommodate pointless suffering.

What is to be made of the shepherd laying down his life for the sheep? Is this doormat theology, or the door to an enclosure where divine love surrounds and transforms human love? That depends on how it is interpreted. If the laying down of one's life is the model of Christian service, that too is susceptible to misuse. But Christ's sacrificial death need not and should not be understood as a summons to put up with suffering. Rather, as Marie Fortune has said,

> Sometimes Jesus' crucifixion is misinterpreted as being the model for suffering: since Jesus went to the cross, persons should bear their own crosses of irrational violence (for example, rape) without complaint. But Jesus' crucifixion does not sanctify suffering. It remains a witness to the horror of violence done to another and an identification with the suffering that people experience. It is not a

model of how suffering should be borne but a witness to God's desire that no one should have to suffer such violence again.[78]

In the sheepfold, the bearers of violence and the abusers of power are banished. 'Power-in-community' is restored. 'Power-over' belongs only to the good shepherd who exercises it.

5.13 SUMMARY

This chapter began with two contrasts, between authority and force, and between 'power-over' and 'power-with'. These contrasts have helped to locate sexual morality in a wider social context which brings into view the pattern of destructive relationships which may infect, and at times engulf, personal relationships between men and women. The contrast between Jesus' refusal of patriarchal power and the Church's use of it has been noted. Some churches were slow to acknowledge the connection between sexual sin and the misuse of power. The term 'structural sin' has been used to speak theologically of the wider social situation which awaits redemption. It has been noted that consent to sexual relationships, while vital in personal and legal terms, may take place in contexts where alternatives are obliterated, and social expectations of compliance are strong.

The fearful catalogue of violence, generally violence by men against women, is understood as the exercise of patriarchal power, and uncomfortable parallels between the misuse of this power within the churches and outside them has been noted. The record of the churches as places of safety, as segments of the wider society which practise 'power in community', has been found wanting. The presence within them of attitudes of domination and control, which lead to violence against women, has been noted. Harassment and rape have been seen to be pervasive, and the plight of the biblical character, Susanna, has been taken as an illustration of the working of 'power-over' in a particular case. An analysis of pornography and the reasons for condemning it as evil has also arrived at the conclusion that it is a manifestation of male power over women, confirming them as objects, and expressing hatred and fear towards them. The chapter ends where it began, pointing to the figure of Jesus Christ. His summons to the reign of God draws his followers to a place of safety where fullness of life may be enjoyed, where violence is excluded, and relationships patterned and informed by the self-giving love of Christ himself.

Notes

1 See the section 'From "sex" and "gender" to "power" and "difference" ', in Elaine Graham, *Making the Difference: Gender, Personhood and Theology* (London: Mowbray, 1995), pp. 22–4.

2 James P. Mackey, *Power and Christian Ethics* (Cambridge: Cambridge University Press, 1994), p. 7.

3 *Ibid.*, p. 4.

4 *Ibid.*, p. 24.

5 *Ibid.*, p. 36.

6 *Ibid.*, p. 37.

7 *Ibid.*, p. 54.

8 *Ibid.*, p. 59.

9 *Ibid.*, p. 160.

10 *Ibid.*, p. 169.

11 *Ibid.*, p. 202.

12 *Ibid.*, p. 95.

13 Pamela Cooper-White, *The Cry of Tamar: Violence against Women and the Church's Response* (Minneapolis: Fortress Press, 1995), p. 31. The terms are drawn from the writings of Starhawk, but considerably developed by Cooper-White. The analyses of violence against women in this chapter are partly dependent on the detailed and chillingly convincing treatment of the topic in this book.

14 *Ibid.*, p. 32.

15 *Ibid.*, p. 33. The quotation is from Matthew Fox's *Original Blessing*.

16 *Ibid.*

17 *Ibid.*, p. 31.

18 *Ibid.*, p. 38.

19 *Ibid.*, p. 41.

20 John Milbank, *Theology and Social Theory: Beyond Secular Reason* (Oxford: Black-well, 1990), p. 6.

21 Church of Scotland Panel on Doctrine, *Report on the Theology of Marriage* (1994), para. 7.7, p. 273.

22 *Ibid.*, para. 8.4, p. 275.

23 Adrian Thatcher, *Liberating Sex: A Christian Theology* (London: SPCK, 1993), pp. 70–5.

24 The Southern African Anglican Theological Commission, *The Church and Human Sexuality* (Marshalltown, South Africa, 1995), para. B4.3, p. 12.

25 *Ibid.*, para. E10, p. 17.

26 General Assembly Special Committee on Human Sexuality, *Keeping Body and Soul Together: Sexuality, Spirituality, and Social Justice* (1991), p. 29.

27 *Ibid.*

28 Cooper-White, *The Cry of Tamar*, p. 18.

29 *Ibid.*, p. 67. This is part of a longer definition, found in the 1964 American Civil Rights Act.

30 *Ibid.*, p. 68.

31 *Ibid.*

32 *Ibid.*, ch. 6.

33 The words are taken from a handout, 'Sexual Harassment and Abuse', of the Commission for Women of the Evangelical Lutheran Church of America. See Cooper-White, *The Cry of Tamar*, p. 289, note 42.

34 Cooper-White, *The Cry of Tamar*, p. 80.

35 *Ibid.*

36 *Ibid.*, p. 84.

37 *Ibid.*

38 In Cooper-White, *The Cry of Tamar*.

39 D. Z. Phillips, *Religion without Explanation* (Oxford: Blackwell, 1976), p. 53.

40 See Cooper-White, *The Cry of Tamar*, pp. 89–95.

41 *Ibid.*, pp. xiii–xiv, 1–14, *et passim.* See also Thatcher, *Liberating Sex*, p. 69, and Tracy Hansen, 'My name is Tamar', *Theology* 45, no. 767 (Sept./Oct. 1992). Hansen compares Tamar's experience with her own as an abused child. She is able to see the suffering of God in the story and the ministry of Jesus to her through all those who helped her through the long trauma that followed (p. 376).

42 Protestant Christians include the work in the Apocrypha, because it was written in Greek. The Roman Catholic and some Orthodox churches regard the work as canonical. Article 6 of the Church of England lists The Story of Susanna among the books which 'the Church doth read for example of life and instruction of manners'. That is precisely how the book is being used here.

43 The violence of their intentions is best conveyed by this violent word. It is preferable to 'seduce' (v. 11), for the latter term implies possible consent, i.e., seduction is an act of *inducement* to engage in sex. The judges were rapists, not romantic Don Juan figures.

44 For the evidence, various sources are cited in Cooper-White, *The Cry of Tamar*, pp. 86–7.

45 *Ibid.*, p. 102 (author's emphasis).

46 *Ibid.*

47 First described by Lenore Walker, *The Battered Woman* (New York: Harper Colophon, 1979); see Cooper-White, *The Cry of Tamar*, p. 106.

48 *Ibid.*, pp. 107–8.

49 *Ibid.*, p.128, and the sources noted on p. 290.

50 On the abuse of power in such relationships, see Marie Fortune, *Is Nothing Sacred? When Sex Invades the Pastoral Relationship* (San Francisco: Harper & Row, 1989), and Peter Rutter, *Sex in the Forbidden Zone: When Men in Power — Therapists, Doctors, Clergy, Teachers, and Others — Betray Women's Trust* (Los Angeles: Jeremy Tarcher, 1989).

51 Cooper-White, *The Cry of Tamar*, p. 129.

52 Hilary Cashman, *Christianity and Child Sexual Abuse* (London; SPCK, 1993); and see Cooper- White, *The Cry of Tamar*, ch. 7.

53 A. Baker and S. Duncan, 'Child sexual abuse: a study of prevalence in Great Britain', *Child Abuse and Neglect*, 9 (1985), p. 458: see Cashman, *Christianity and Child Sexual Abuse*, pp. 29–30.

54 Cashman, *Christianity and Child Sexual Abuse*, p. 48.

55 Margaret Kennedy, 'Christianity — help or hindrance for the abused child or adult?', *Child Abuse Review*, 5.3 (Winter 1991–92), pp. 3–6; cited by Cashman, *Christianity and Child Sexual Abuse*, p. 15.

56 Cashman, *Christianity and Child Sexual Abuse*, p. 42.

57 M. Hendessi, *4 in 10: Report on Young Women Made Homeless as a Result of Child Sexual Abuse* (London: CHAR, 1992), in Cashman, *Christianity and Child Sexual Abuse*, p. 47.

58 The Office of the General Assembly, The Presbyterian Church (USA), *Pornography: Far from the Song of Songs* (Louisville, Kentucky, 1988), p. 11.

59 *Ibid.*, p. 16.

60 *Catechism of the Catholic Church* (London: Geoffrey Chapman, 1994), para. 2354, p. 504.

61 *Ibid.*

62 *Ibid.*, para. 2337, p. 500. This is the meaning of chastity in the Catechism.

63 Mary Hunt, 'Theological pornography: from corporate to communal ethics', in Joanne Carlson Brown and Carole R. Bohn (eds), *Christianity, Patriarchy, and Abuse* (Cleveland, Ohio: The Pilgrim Press, 1989), p. 91.

64 Rosemary Radford Ruether, 'The Western tradition and violence against women', in Brown and Bohn, *Christianity, Patriarchy, and Abuse*, p. 33.

65 *Ibid.*

66 *Ibid.*, p. 37.

67 See Catherine Itzin, 'Should we legislate against pornography?', *The Times Higher Education Supplement* (10 December 1993), p. 18. The arguments are developed further in Catherine Itzin (ed.), *Pornography: Women, Violence and Civil Liberties* (Oxford: Oxford University Press, 1993).

68 Itzin, *Pornography*, p. 6.

69 *Ibid.*

70 *Ibid.*, p. 7.

71 *Ibid.*

72 Marie F. Fortune, 'The transformation of suffering: a biblical and theological perspective', in Brown and Bohn, *Christianity, Patriarchy, and Abuse*, p. 144.

73 Cooper-White, *The Cry of Tamar*, pp. 114, 253.

74 Cashman, *Christianity and Child Sexual Abuse*, p. 80.

75 *Ibid.*, p. 81.

76 *Ibid.*, p. 74.

77 D. Moody Smith, *The Theology of the Gospel of John* (Cambridge: Cambridge University Press, 1995), p. 33.

78 Fortune, in Brown and Bohn, *Christianity, Patriarchy, and Abuse*, p. 145. John has in any case removed 'the cultic language of the sacrificial altar'. He 'has chosen to present the old message in a new and different mode'. See Smith, *Gospel of John*, p. 119.

Suggestions for further reading

Joanne Carlson Brown and Carole R. Bohn (eds), *Christianity, Patriarchy, and Abuse* (Cleveland, OH: Pilgrim Press, 1989).
Hilary Cashman, *Christianity and Child Sexual Abuse* (London: SPCK, 1993).
Pamela Cooper-White, *The Cry of Tamar: Violence Against Women and the Church's Response* (Minneapolis: Fortress Press, 1995).
James P. Mackey, *Power and Christian Ethics* (Cambridge: Cambridge University Press, 1994).
The Office of the General Assembly, The Presbyterian Church (USA), *Pornography: Far from the Song of Songs* (Louisville, KY, 1988).

6

GENDER

6.1 GENDER AND PRE-MODERN CHRISTIANITY

Despite the fact that almost every Christian denomination in the West has been preoccupied with issues of **gender** for the past thirty years, in the debates over the ordination of women, **homosexuality** or contraception and abortion, the concept of gender has rarely been examined in those debates except at a remarkably superficial level. This failure to engage with the nature of gender contrasts with the development of a vast body of critical theory around the issue in the human and social sciences.

In the West understandings of gender have been influenced by Greek philosophy's tendency to categorize the world in **dualistic** terms (see **4.1**). Male and female were perceived to be binary opposites who created life and culture, which must also be constructed in such a way: mind–body, culture–nature, reason–emotion, production–reproduction and so on. The first in each pair was associated with the world of men and transcendent spiritual reality, the second with women — the first was superior to the second. Recent scholarship has questioned whether all ancient Greek philosophy was as radically dualistic as this, but certainly the theories of gender offered by Plato and Aristotle were, and it was these which were taken into the heart of early Christian theology.[1] However, there it encountered another more radical tradition which rejected the notion of male and female binary opposition and hierarchy (Galatians 3.28) and the family unit in which those divisions were lived out and upheld (Matthew 10.37–39). It was this politically and religiously subversive theology that made Christianity particularly attractive to women and it was through women that Christianity first infiltrated the upper classes of Roman civilization.[2] Tension between these two notions of gender are evident in the writings of Paul and in the Gospels and polarized the early Christian community.

Rosemary Radford Ruether notes a tendency among the early Christian apologists, who were concerned to reconcile Christianity and the existing social order, to 'privatize and spiritualize the radical character of the Christian vision'[3] by endeavouring to persuade women to endure the restrictions and oppressions that came with being wife and slave because inwardly and spiritually she was free and equal. Eventually the polarization became institutionalized, the radical vision of gender being preserved in the **ascetic** life which was of course open only to a small minority. However, as Gillian Cloke has noted, not even female ascetics were immune from the theology that developed which held women responsible, through Eve, for the destruction of God's image (man) and saw them as slaves to their bodies and sexual temptation.[4]

But the indisputable holiness and heroism of some women in the early Church had to be accounted for by the male theologians who articulated a negative view of femaleness. The solution to this conundrum was twofold: active and creative women had obviously managed to transcend their nature and become masculine. Palladius described Melania the Elder, a prominent church mother, as 'the female man of God'.[5] This perception of active, intellectually formidable women as 'manly' enabled some church fathers to relate to these women as equals and sometimes accept guidance from them. Certainly the ascetic tradition continued to provide a place, often the only place, for women to exercise independence, leadership and authority in the Church. Later, medieval women ascetics like Hildegard of Bingen and Catherine of Siena might in their writings reflect traditional views of the weakness and inferiority of women, but these strong, independent, innovative and subversive theologians did not apply these restrictions to themselves! Women who did not have the freedom to be as active or independent as Melania but still demonstrated holiness by repenting of their bodiliness and **sexuality** with abnormal self-abasement were also admired for they seemed to many church fathers to represent the ideal soul, completely submissive to God. All souls were feminine (i.e., submissive and supplicatory) before God and therefore it was possible for male ascetics to learn something from these embodiments of femininity.[6]

Medieval scholastic theology continued to be dependent upon classical Greek philosophy. Thomas Aquinas, whose theology was built upon the foundation of the philosophy of Aristotle, reasserted Aristotle's conviction that women were failed or defective males,

> The particular nature of the active male seed intends to produce a perfect likeness of itself, and when females are conceived this is due to weak seed or unsuitable material, or external influences like the dampness of the south wind.[7]

Men alone represented true humanity. This led theologians to assert that, contrary to what appears to be stated in Genesis 1.27, women did not bear the image of God and could only be incorporated into true humanity through men.

6.2 MODERN DISTINCTIONS BETWEEN SEX AND GENDER

Modernity brought both the consolidation of **patriarchal** concepts of gender and the philosophical ideas which would eventually lead to the birth of **feminism**:

> Many of the traditional spheres of comparative independence for women — such as the domestic economy, the wisdom of women healers and midwives, and the centres of learning founded on religious communities — were either placed under male-dominated authority or marginalised as civil society and factory industry effected a split between the public and private realms. The subsequent association of women with nature, matter, sexuality and domesticity further condemned women to a subordinate and marginal role, although the portrayal of women also deliberately evoked their **purity** and innocence, especially in the discourse of Romanticism.[8]

As religion was privatized and pushed into the domestic sphere women, who had previously been identified with anti-spirituality, came to represent the spiritual. The emerging scientific mind identified itself as male and its subject, nature, as female (most explicitly in the work of Francis Bacon) and set about to dissect and subdue it. Yet the philosophy of the **Enlightenment**, with its emphasis upon democracy, equality, individualism, human rights and reason, also provided some with the concepts and language to question the subordination of women. Detailed and in-depth study of gender began in the nineteenth century and reached its zenith in the second half of the twentieth century with what is often labelled the second wave of feminism (the first wave having taken place in the nineteenth and early twentieth centuries). Interest focused on the nature–nurture debate: are men and women biologically determined to be different or are differences between men and women **socially constructed** — are we taught or forced to behave differently? During the 1960s and 1970s it became social scientific and feminist orthodoxy to distinguish between '**sex**' and 'gender', a distinction which demonstrates who was winning the nature–nurture debate.

> 'Sex' has to do with basic biological differences, such as that men ejaculate, women ovulate, gestate and lactate ... 'Gender' refers to what a particular society makes of the relationships between males and females ... [It] can be argued that the dominant gender construction of Christian culture for men has been that they are active, independent, intelligent, brave, strong, good and, needless to say, godlike. God in turn is male-like ... [women's] religiously sanctioned gender construction has been that they are passive, dependent, bodily, emotional, weak, peculiarly responsible for evil and sin (though not for pride, the sin of the intellect!) and childlike.[9]

6.3 ANDROGYNY

The severing of the link between sex and gender led some to advocate **androgyny** as an ideal. Recognizing that so-called male and female character traits are not grounded in biology, the androgynous vision is one in which both sexes display the most admirable character traits of both genders and thus become integrated and whole human beings. Genders must be bended and notions of masculinity and femininity subverted. Celebrities such as Boy George, David Bowie, Annie Lennox and k. d. lang incarnated in their own appearance the androgynous vision. People would be free to be 'themselves', unshackled from sexual stereotypes and patterns of behaviour. However, there are serious flaws in the androgynous vision. Ultimately it appears to be another form of dualism (see **4.1**) for it suggests that wholeness and integration come through transcending the prison of the sexed body. By locating the place for transformation in the individual psyche it seemed to ignore the existence of political and legal oppression of women. It ignores the fact that 'masculine' and 'feminine' are not regarded as equally desirable characteristics in patriarchal society and are therefore not easily interchanged.

Alison Webster believes that often the aim of those who advocate androgyny is to 'blur gender stereotypes just enough to benefit men a bit more (e.g. by allowing them to have a more fulfilling emotional life), but not enough to actually change anything'.[10] She believes that most women are content with being 'only' women: what they want is social, political and theological justice. As Roland Martinson points out in his theological reflections upon the concept of androgyny, men's and women's realities are different, diversity is not something to be afraid of but to be celebrated as enriching. The point is to create justice, equality and **mutuality** in communities which respect the different experiences of men and women, whilst giving each individual the freedom to work out their 'uniqueness in relationship'.[11] We have incorporated this kind of justice into our proposals for passionate ethics (see **2.4**, **2.12**). Martinson believes that the Old Testament view of reality as **covenantal** provides the best basis for establishing right relationships between the sexes:

> The entire created order is organically and volitionally connected to its source who has promised never to leave nor destroy it. Life within the existing creation is organic and volitional. It is based on interdependent patterns and promises. Both the patterns and promises are malleable and interconnected. The cultural and historical, which are the arenas of social construction, are to be based on covenants; that is, they are to be grounded in vows mutually agreed upon, respectful of all parties, open to renegotiation, inclusive of the full range of life and death issues and subject to internal and external sanctions. In this view of reality females and males are unique, of equal value and mutually interdependent one of another, biologically and culturally ... Existence is essentially connected and interdependent.[12]

6.4 MEN AND MASCULINITY

One of the most interesting consequences of the second wave of feminism is that it has prompted men to reflect upon masculinity. One response to the undoubted distress and confusion caused to some men by the feminist movement has been exemplified by Robert Bly and his conviction that men must rediscover an essential masculinity represented by the mythical figure of Iron John, a wild man.[13] Bly has been criticized for reinforcing an **essentialist** notion of masculinity and for offering a purely individualistic and therapeutic solution to the problem of gender. However, most sociological and theological studies of masculinity adopt a social constructionist view of masculinity. Michael Hester in a theological reflection examines the repercussions of the construction of masculinity under patriarchy (see **1.5**). He argues that men are conditioned to stand like Joseph at the nativity play, 'strong and still and say nothing'.[14] What Hester calls the 'Myth of Manhood' can be represented by ten commandments:

1. Thou shalt not be weak, nor have weak gods before thee.
2. Thou shalt not fail thyself, nor 'fail' as thy father before thee.
3. Thou shalt not keep holy any day that denies thy work.
4. Thou shalt not love in ways that are intimate and sharing.
5. Thou shalt not cry, complain or feel lonely.
6. Thou shalt not commit public anger.
7. Thou shalt not be uncertain or ambivalent.
8. Thou shalt not be dependent.
9. Thou shalt not acknowledge thy death or thy limitation.
10. Thou *shalt* do unto other men before they do unto you.[15]

Of course not all men fit all of these descriptions. Men's identities are also influenced by class, **sexual orientation**, economic status and race, and therefore there are considerable differences among men, but this is how Western society constructs maleness. The repercussions of this myth of maleness are considerable. Men often find it difficult to be intimate with each other and with women because vulnerability is considered to be a weakness in a man. Relationships tend to be built around tasks to be performed, rather than mutual encounter. C. S. Lewis, who sought to draw hard and fast distinctions between different types of love, wrote that, 'Lovers are normally face to face, absorbed in each other; Friends, side by side, absorbed in some common interest.'[16] That description of friendship would be quite alien to most women.

> As sexual beings, men tend to focus on sexual activity and the 'genitalization' of sexuality. Since our genitals are external we are more controlled by visible, physical, and active sexuality. We separate sex from intimacy. Sexual pleasure is limited because we experience sex as an act, not as being part of being close.[17]

James Nelson has made the male body the centre of some reflections upon the social and theological construction of masculinity. He notes that the erect phallus, 'big, hard and up', has been the dominant symbol of masculinity and God. But in reality men are not big, hard and up for most of the time, their penises are soft, small and down. He suggests that this other side of male experience has the potential to put men in touch with what he calls the *via negativa* spiritual tradition (see **9.9**). This emphasizes that the way to God is through emptying, darkness, absence and vulnerability: 'One might add that those genital emblems of manly courage, the testicles ("he's got balls"), are the most vulnerable part of a man's body. Indeed, we need more testicular masculinity — a vulnerable, generative, quiet and faithful "hanging in there".'[18]

Fear of being feminine, of being labelled homosexual, plays its part in preventing intimacy between men and in prompting men to behave in ways that are 'big, hard and up'. It leads to egocentricity, i.e., being concerned only with oneself and the fulfilment of one's own ambitions. Hester points out that trying to live up to the myth of masculinity has direct consequences on men's health.

> As infants our death rate is significantly higher, perhaps because we receive less nurture and touch. In childhood boys have a more difficult time establishing a secure gender identity under the pressure of avoiding 'effeminacy'. In adolescence our search for identity is often more dangerous and violent. The vast majority of murders are committed by men 18–24 years old. On average men die seven years sooner than women. Our incidences of suicide, chemical dependency, incarceration, and violent death are vastly higher. We postpone getting help for physical and emotional illnesses and are then hospitalised 15 percent longer. Our difficulty in expressing emotions is directly linked with higher incidence of major diseases. Nine of the ten leading causes of death in America are dominated by men.[19]

Men are to some extent the victims of patriarchy too. Hester looks for models of 'redeemed masculinity' in the scriptures. In the story of Jonathan and David (1 and 2 Samuel) there is a model for male friendship based upon intimacy, passion and face-to-face encounter which Jonathan and David formalized in a covenant. Both Hester and Nelson find in Jesus 'a compelling picture of male sexual wholeness, of creative masculinity, and of the redemption of manhood from both oppressiveness and superficiality'.[20] Jesus, they maintain, built his life around intimate relations with men and women and this enabled him to balance power and vulnerability, creativity and productivity, dominance and submission. Mutuality was at the heart of his model of relating. Nelson argues that the manner in which Jesus embodies masculinity raises questions over the 'big, hard and up' construction of **Christology** that developed around him. Jesus was portrayed as the barely human Superman in much Christology because he is proclaimed as the **incarnation** of a God who is 'big, hard and up'. If divinity is small, soft and down as he seems to indicate then what constitutes humanity as God intended it to be when he created it in his image needs to be re-examined.

6.5 GENDER AND THE CHURCHES

Jacqueline Field-Bibb offers a detailed analysis of the debates over the ordination of women in the Roman Catholic, Church of England and Methodist Churches. She argues that the opposition to the ordination of women arose as a necessary consequence of the institutional churches having adopted a solely **androcentric** set of symbols and metaphors for God and humanity[21] and having privileged male experience in the realm of theology.[22] Those who oppose the ordination of women often believe that gender difference is essential to our bodily and psychological make-up and not socially constructed, and that priesthood or ministry requires 'male' qualities such as initiative, creativity and innovation.[23] Those who argue along these lines are usually at pains to affirm the equality of men and women. The sexes are equal but different, with different roles to play. This is the position of Pope John Paul II in his *Letter to Women* (see **1.6**).

This letter, the most radical Vatican statement on women to date, demonstrates how much of an impact feminism has made on the churches. Even at the conservative heart of the ecclesiastical establishment it is considered necessary to acknowledge the equality of women and to condemn obstacles to full equality in the workplace and society as a whole, as well as violence against women. Yet we took this letter as a prime example of patriarchal theology (see **1.6**). The Pope is clear that men and women are not the same: they are different and **complementary**, 'not only from the physical and psychological points of view, but also from the ontological. It is only through the duality of the "masculine" and the "feminine" that the "human" finds full realisation.'[25] What the Pope calls the 'genius of women' reaches its highest expression in Mary, who is represented by him as exemplifying classic 'feminine' traits. She is obedient, receptive, passive and her life is characterized by service.[26]

Most advocates of the theory of 'complementarity' (see **7.2**) base their case on Genesis 1.27. Feminist theologians and others have questioned whether this verse can bear such an interpretation and suspect other influences upon the advocates of complementarity, particularly the psychological theory of C. G. Jung who believed that whole and healthy individuals balanced 'masculine' and 'feminine' principles within their psyche. This is made possible by confronting our unconscious masculine or feminine elements in a person of the opposite sex. Jungian psychology is obviously highly influential in the theology of sexuality articulated in a Church of Scotland report which states that 'in an ideal marriage, the unconscious male within the woman would be complementary to her partner's unconscious feminine element; in such a union, two would indeed become one'.[27] Feminist theologians have pointed out that advocates of complementarity, whilst paying lip-service to the notion of equality, actually present a construction of femininity which will always leave women socially, politically and theologically subordinate to men. Women are objectified as passive, receptive, nurturing and serving — it is men the actors and initiators who are in control. One of the very few church documents to subject the theory of complementarity to critical analysis is the Presbyterian (USA) report *Keeping Body and Soul Together*, which was not adopted by the General Assembly of the Church (see **2.2**). It notes:

> In this gender dualism, neither partner functions — sexually or socially — as a fully integrated person, but rather as a fragmented complementary half. By the logic of patriarchal sexual relations, the sex act has to do not only with sex, but more importantly with a total patterning of what it means to be male and female and properly ordered. As so-called complementary beings, each functions as a half-personality, bringing what the other lacks in social interaction. In sexual intercourse, two half-personalities supposedly become one whole, but male ascendancy is, nevertheless, secured.[28]

Feminist theologians also point out that biblical passages such as Galatians 3.28 might be thought to subvert all notions of complementarity.

The other popular argument against the ordination of women also endorsed by Pope John Paul II in his *Letter to Women* is that, as God chose to become incarnate in male form, women will never be able to act as an 'icon' (see **2.6**) of Jesus at the eucharist. This is further underlined by the fact that Jesus did not choose any women to be apostles, his representatives. Advocates of this view either explicitly or implicitly argue that Jesus' gender, as opposed to his ethnic origins, religion, appearance and so on, is a fundamental aspect of the incarnation. In other words, God revealed something about the essential nature of the divine in the gender of Jesus. Opponents of this view argue that it is Jesus' humanity and his message, not his gender, which are essential components of the incarnation. Feminist theologians would want to draw attention to the power given to all men by the argument that maleness somehow reflects the true nature of the divine in the way that femaleness does not.

The issue of ordination is connected to that of inclusive language. Some Christians argue that it is no accident that Jesus referred to God as 'father' and that the whole thrust of biblical language around God is male. God may be beyond gender but should never be identified with the female. Whereas 'feminine' elements such as compassion and mercy can be incorporated into the male God, to label God as feminine would be to associate God with nature, the sexual, the body, all of which are antithetical to the God of **theism**.

6.6 GENDER AND FEMINIST THEOLOGY

Christian feminist theology (see **2.8**) broadly speaking reflects upon the Christian faith from the standpoint of feminism. Feminists maintain that,

> our culture, and Christian theology as one manifestation of that culture, is in fact riddled with what Gerda Lerner calls 'a conceptual error of vast proportion'. For where the male has been thought to represent the *whole* of humanity, the half has been mistaken for the whole, so that what has been described has been distorted in such a way that we cannot see it correctly.[29]

6.6.1 The androcentric fallacy

Lerner calls this conceptual error the '**androcentric fallacy**' and argues that it is built into all the mental and physical constructs of Western culture. Merely adding women to these constructs simply serves to disguise their patriarchal nature and does nothing ultimately to liberate us from the conceptual error. What is needed is a complete restructuring of our thought, theology, political and social systems to reflect the fact that humanity consists of both male and female. This involves, at the present time, privileging women's experience as a source of knowledge to restore some of the balance. The work of the psychologist Carol Gilligan has been very influential upon feminist theology. Her studies have convinced her that men and women think of themselves and their relationships with the world around them very differently. She believes that men have problems with relationships. This is because they think of themselves as being isolated, independent, enclosed selves around which the world revolves. Since they tend to view life in terms of competition, what threatens them is other people. Women, in complete contrast, understand themselves in terms of being in relationship with others and are threatened by anything that seeks to rupture their sense of interdependence.[30]

Christian feminists are presented with a theological tradition riddled with the androcentric fallacy: 'Feminist theology shows that scripture, creeds and tradition are more correctly termed *male* scripture, creeds and tradition.'[31] The whole Christian tradition must be tested against women's experience which women must learn to trust and articulate. Feminist theologians have become very aware in recent years that there is no such thing as a universal women's experience and therefore for women there will never be one universal theology (it is part of the strategy of patriarchy to deny or minimize difference). **Womanist theology** has emerged to articulate the experience of Afro-American Christian women. **Mujerista theology** articulates the theological reflection of Hispanic American feminists. Asian feminists, African feminists, Latin American feminists, **lesbians**, disabled women, are all drawing attention to the differences among women (including power differences) and the theological insights that arise from reflections upon that difference.

6.6.2 Redemption from patriarchy?

Some Christian feminists have questioned whether, 'given the complexity of women's experience, is it still a reliable or usable category upon which to base an alternative theological perspective?'[32] Isherwood and McEwan answer that question by locating authority in feminist theology not in any theological or doctrinal prescriptions which have the agreement of all women but in liberating praxis, a concept taken from **liberation theology**. Truth can only be known or affirmed through action, and therefore the ability of feminist theology to inspire and reflect liberating action in specific contexts is the criterion for judging its truth. Relativism and rampant individualism is avoided by emphasizing that the task of doing theology is a communal exercise, and the interconnectedness which is an important aspect of women's experience demands that it is in this context that an individual seeks to interpret her experience. Some feminist theologians, such as Mary Daly and Daphne Hampson, having reviewed the Christian tradition from a feminist standpoint, have concluded that it is beyond redemption from patriarchy. Both, for example, have drawn attention to the way in which the Christian emphasis upon self-sacrifice and voluntary powerlessness has served to reinforce the subordination of women. Women are required to give up that which they do not usually have — a sense of self, and

> it is one thing for a person to choose a path which may lead to suffering 'for Christ's sake'. It is quite another to suggest to someone who is powerless that her powerlessness should be her identity ... Women need to actualise themselves.[33]

We were careful to sound a note of caution about self-sacrificial love in our account of feminist ethics (see **2.8**). More than one feminist theologian has suggested that for women the primary sin is not pride as it may be for men, but 'hiding', failing to speak their own truth, allowing themselves to be marginalized and subordinated. Empowerment, not self-sacrifice is what women need and the evidence suggests, Daly and Hampson maintain, that Christianity cannot supply it. Therefore women's energies are better spent developing alternative spiritualities. Others remain convinced that there is much within Christian tradition that acts as a critique of the dominant patriarchal ideology and that suggests other ways of being and other forms of theology which have existed in the Christian community. Elisabeth Schüssler Fiorenza argues that most biblical texts are rhetorical in nature, by which she means that they have emerged out of disputes in communities. By reading between the lines we can begin to trace the nature of the dispute and the position of those who have been written out of history.[34] So when the biblical writers become preoccupied with portraying women as subordinate to men or unauthorized to exercise ministry on a par with men, or when they rail against fertility cults and the women who flock to them, we can get some idea of the debates and practices to which they were contributing or denouncing. To give but one example, the four canonical Gospels describe Mary Magdalene as the first witness of Jesus' resurrection, but Paul in 1 Corinthians 15.5 names Peter as the first witness. The non-canonical *Gospel of Thomas* reports that there was a power struggle between Peter and Mary which Mary won. All this may suggest that there was a dispute within the early Church over whether women could exercise the power and authority of an apostle. Some believed that they could and looked to the figure of Mary as a symbol of this, while others did not. Thus Christian feminists adopt a **hermeneutic** of suspicion when reading the Bible (see **10.2**). They ask constantly 'who does this teaching or story benefit and what part might it play in a dispute?'

There are in the Christian tradition, from the Old Testament through the Gospels and their portrayal of Jesus and through church history, strands of opposition to patriarchy. Anonymous Hebrew women co-operate with an anonymous Pharaoh's daughter to defy the orders of the Egyptian ruler and thereby save the infant Moses from death (Exodus 1–2.10). Ruth and Naomi defy convention in order to remain together and secure their future (Ruth). The Syrophoenician woman refuses to be dismissed by Jesus and challenges his arguments for not helping her, changing his mind. It is traditions like these which women seek to rescue. Women seek to remember their lost history and thereby not only root themselves and their struggles in the Christian tradition but also wrest the Bible and tradition from the exclusive hands of those who use it to justify subjugation of women today. For example, womanist theologians have found in the story of Hagar (Genesis 16.1–16; 21.9–21) — the Egyptian slave of Abraham who struggles not only against the system that enslaves her but also against a woman, Abraham's wife, Sarah, who is ranked above her in the patriarchal pyramid, in order to ensure her survival and that of her son, and who in the process becomes the first person in scripture to have seen God — not only what Phyllis Trible calls a 'text of terror', which silences and marginalizes the slave, but also a model of resistance (see **10.2**).

6.6.3 Beginning with women's experience

Christian feminists are also engaged in a wholesale re-evaluation and recasting of Christian theology on the basis of women's experience. All agree on the power of language both to express and to shape our thought and indeed to affect our behaviour. Sallie McFague has explored the way in which traditional images of God as king, father, all-powerful, all-knowing, perfect, static and transcendent, not only reflect the power or experience of the male but also serve then to legitimate the **hierarchical**, patriarchal structures in Church and society which have led not only to the marginalization of women but also to a complete disregard for the earth except as a resource to be dominated and exploited.[35] She is convinced that only by adopting new models for God which undermine the 'big, hard and up' (see **6.4**) images of God will human beings be given the spiritual resources to prevent nuclear and ecological disaster. She offers three alternative models for God: Mother, Lover and Friend. These models emphasize a co-operative rather than hierarchical relationship between God and humanity. They also transcend the dualism (see **4.1**) which separates God from the world. These models convey that God loves bodies and is concerned about them. Indeed, McFague uses the **metaphor** of the world as God's body (see **3.4**) to undermine the traditional notion of God being 'above' matter and concerned with the spiritual rather than the physical. Feminists in Latin America have found in the image of God as mother a model of liberation which does not simply dissolve into violence:

> God's female maternal womb, fertile, in labour and compassionate, enables this liberation to come about with force and firmness, but also with creativity and gentleness, without violence ... struggle is tempered with festivity. Permanent and gentle firmness ensures the ability to be strong without losing tenderness. An uncompromising resistance can be carried on without excessive tension and sterile strain — even with joy.[36]

Chung Hyun Kyung shows that Asian women are reclaiming the imagery of the doctrine of the Trinity — God as a community rather than an individual. This too is an image which is conducive to peace. It empowers them

> to get out of their individualism. It also encourages them to honour their responsibility and rights as a part of the community ... Monopolised power destroys community by destroying mutuality. Therefore, in this image of God as the community in relationship, there is no place for only one, solitary, all-powerful God who sits on top of the hierarchical power pyramid and dominates all other living beings.[37]

In the wisdom tradition of the Hebrew scriptures, where wisdom personifies an attribute of God as female — Hochma (in Hebrew) or Sophia (in Greek) — other feminists have found a female model of God which emphasizes immanence, as opposed to transcendence, co-operation rather than hierarchy and embodiment rather than dualism.[38] Mary Grey has utilized the Sophia myth in developing a model of **revelation** alternative to that which has dominated Christianity — the 'Logos' model which emphasizes that revelation is sent into the world from outside of it by God and passed down a hierarchical chain which has tended to be dominated by men. In the Sophia model, revelation occurs in connectedness, in listening to each other and our ancestors in faith speaking through the tradition. Grey believes this model of revelation reflects women's experience of the ways in which knowledge comes about and in which God works much more than does the Logos model. For some feminists the ultimate stumbling block in the Christian tradition is Jesus. How can a religion which makes a woman's salvation ultimately dependent upon a man be liberating for women? Feminist Christians maintain it is possible to deconstruct the patriarchal construction of Christianity and refashion it from a feminist viewpoint to produce a Christology which does not do violence to women. Many Asian, Latin American, African and Womanist women view Jesus as a brother or friend who stands in solidarity with their struggle and suffering. Others regard Jesus as a prophet, perhaps a prophet of Sophia, who undermined the foundations of patriarchy in the way he worked and spoke about God. This prophet founded a new community based upon friendship rather than kinship and treated women accordingly. Rita Nakashima Brock argues that the traditional Christology which emphasizes the uniqueness of Jesus reflects patriarchy's need for heroes. She believes that the Gospels themselves testify to the fact that Jesus did not act alone nor did he simply descend from heaven.

> If Jesus is reported to have been capable of profound love and concern for others, he was first loved and respected by the concrete persons of his life. If he was liberated, he was involved in a community of mutual liberation.[39]

In separating Jesus out from the community that nurtured and sustained him, the Church has also lost his vision of the kingdom which he came to proclaim — a radical form of community based upon mutuality and friendship. Brock's contention is that it is the community, rather than Jesus alone, who incarnates God's power.

Grace Jantzen has begun work on a new feminist theology of salvation. She has noted that in the Hebrew scriptures God's will for humanity is often talked about in terms of flourishing (see, for example, Proverbs 11.28, 14.11, and Psalms 37.36, 92.12 and 103.17), a specific image which is virtually absent from the New Testament, although analogous language of fullness and abundance is used. As a metaphor it has received hardly any attention from theologians ancient or modern, although theologians of liberation are now reclaiming it. Jantzen believes 'that the contrast between salvation and flourishing is a gendered contrast'.[40] Whereas the metaphor of flourishing suggests abundance, energy, and movement from strength to strength that is self-sufficient, salvation (which is also of course a metaphor, even though it is rarely recognized as such) suggests the need for rescue by someone, for outside intervention. One takes an optimistic view of the human state, the other a pessimistic. One assumes interconnectedness ('flourishing is impossible by oneself alone'[41]) and is aware of the dynamics of flourishing ('who suffers that I may flourish?'), the other is individualistic and depoliticized. One is concerned with this world and the embodied beings within it, the other is concerned with the next world and the souls that may get into it. 'The interconnections between the construction of masculinity and the socio-economic system of competitive individualism have received much attention. What has been less frequently noted is how neatly it coheres with a theology built on the model of personal salvation.'[42] Jantzen draws upon Luce Irigaray's observation that patriarchy has always been fixated on other worlds, thus distracting itself from this world and our responsibilities in it and to it. Women are identified with despised and distrusted matter and men with the 'pure' realm of spirit. The metaphor of flourishing is therefore part of the subjugated knowledge of women's spirituality, resurrecting and insurrecting itself against male-constructed notions of 'salvation'.

And so the feminist reconstruction of Christian doctrine goes on. Mariology, understandings of atonement, sacraments, sainthood — feminist theologians are engaging in a comprehensive reworking of the Christian tradition. Notice how feminist theology is based upon the concept of difference. It assumes that women's experience is different to men's but most feminist theologians would maintain that that difference is based upon experience rather than on 'nature'. Men and women under patriarchy have different experiences of life and therefore different psychologies. The male experience has normative weight in theology as elsewhere, so now it is time to do theology on the basis of female experience.

6.7 RECENT THEORIES OF GENDER AND THEIR CHALLENGE TO THEOLOGY

Feminist theologians (Western ones at least) may have taken on board a social-constructionist view of gender, but recently the social sciences have been questioning this position. Janet Sayers has argued that the problem with a social-constructionist view of gender is that it fails to deal adequately with the effect that embodiment has upon women. Some women find their period menstruation extremely difficult: they may suffer a great deal of pain, find themselves to be extremely tired and clumsy or impatient and restless. She suggests that this affects their normal life and that there must be a way of responding to this, for example in the workplace, without thereby penalizing women for being different. Elaine Graham comments: 'This suggests that what is required is not an abandonment of the connection between bodily experience and personal identity — even gender identity — but a severing of bodiliness from an association with **ontological** inferiority and gender polarity.'[43] The issue is not difference but justice.

Emily Martin and others have suggested that we need to develop a much more complex understanding of gender which does justice to the feminist assertion that embodiment cannot or should not be transcended.[44] A 'dialectical' account of gender, such as Martin proposes, argues that there is a complex interaction between biology, society and individual in the creation of gender. It recognizes that biology is no more static and fixed than society or an individual's consciousness. Gender is therefore a process and gender identity may be affected by body changes. Ruth Hubbard has drawn attention to the way in which biology and society interact in the way we have traditionally brought up boys and girls. Girls have generally been made to wear skirts that prevent them running around and have been told to restrict their movement to avoid being unladylike. (They may then be told to watch what they eat to avoid getting fat and encouraged to don more and more restrictive clothing.) Boys, however, have been encouraged from an early age to engage in vigorous outdoor pursuits. They have been given clothes that enable them to do it, and if they are then encouraged to eat heartily, boys and girls are going to develop different muscles and their body posture, reflexes, etc. are going to be different.[45] Lacqueur (following Foucault) argues that, although we in the modern West may regard our bodily identity as fixed and culture as something changeable which is imposed upon us with a particular interpretation of our body, past ages took a diametrically opposed view. Bodies could change, gender or sex could not and were not therefore regarded as being rooted in the body — this idea only took off with the Enlightenment.

Secular feminism has developed a strategy known as 'writing the body' which seeks to reclaim women's bodies as a source of knowledge. Luce Irigaray has used women's experience of bodily sensuality to develop a source of self-knowledge and speech for women outside the restricting boundaries of patriarchy. Drawing upon the philosophy of Lacan she argues that under patriarchy a person's sense of self is developed around what she calls 'phallogocentrism' which renders women invisible and void as subjects. Women are reduced to the 'Other' and have no opportunity to create for themselves a sense of self. They are created by and in the image of men. Irigaray believes that the symbol of patriarchy, the phallus, 'big, hard and up' (see above, **6.4**), represents monolithic structures and lack of imagination and diversity, whereas women's bodies are places in which pleasure is not confined to one area or organ but is diffuse. Unlike men, women have many sexual organs; the two lips of the vulva replace the phallus, symbolizing plurality, inclusiveness, diversity, difference. It is through their bodies that women discover *jouissance*, uninhibited, unconfined sensuality that prefigures 'the feminist Utopia in which the feminine is not repressed by the "symbolic" or cultural realm, but released like the unconscious under analysis'.[46] The body in Irigaray's thought is symbolic of an alternative female identity. Irigaray then seeks, in contrast to most feminists, to emphasize rather than downplay difference between the sexes. Only by doing this, she believes, can women create a female symbolic system to stand alongside and in contradistinction to that of the 'phallus'. The body is the site of the creation of identity. Feminists must therefore return the body to the centre of gender theory.

Another French feminist, Monica Wittig, focuses on the lesbian woman as a subverter of patriarchy. Under patriarchy women are defined by and exclusively in terms of men — as wives, daughters, sisters, etc., but the lesbian, in refusing to be defined in terms of men, exposes the extent to which heterosexual relationships are not grounded in 'nature' but socially constructed. The lesbian subverts what Wittig calls 'the Straight Mind' (see Chapter 7).

After surveying the many contemporary theories of gender Elaine Graham endeavours to work towards a theology of gender drawing upon these secular accounts. She warns that these accounts demon-

strate that 'gender is a complex, dynamic and self-reflexive phenomenon; and a "theology of gender" will not be a straightforward
application of selected categorical statements about empirical differences'.[47] In particular she highlights the challenge that theories such
as those mentioned above pose to the concept of an essential human
nature which exists outside culture. Is it possible, she asks, to accept
this and yet still maintain an ethical system that protects the dignity of
persons? Gender, for all that it may be constructed and complex, is
not an unimportant or marginal aspect of being human: 'The
decisive impact of gender as a form of social relations is suggestive of
a model of human nature as profoundly relational, requiring the
agency of culture to bring our personhood into being.'[48] Human
nature in being profoundly relational images the model of God as
Trinity. We might ask how may our experience of the complexity and
fluidity of gender and the self influence our understanding of God in
whose image we are made? Gender theory also challenges theology
to integrate the body into theories of knowledge and action whilst
recognizing that our bodies are historically and culturally conditioned subjects.

What is clear is that the 'equal but different' position beloved of
church documents and public statements is no longer satisfactory
because difference is expounded in such a way as to guarantee
inequality. We have seen that there is a strong and consistent tradition within Christianity which acknowledges that, from a 'God's eye
view', gender is a constructed, subvertable commodity. However,
Christians who have stood in that tradition have never been entirely
successful in holding an unstable view of gender with an appreciation
of the importance of the body (see **4.4**). Often they have envisioned
that the way to reach beyond gender is through denial of the body.
The situation is made more complex by the fact that individual
women experience their bodies differently: some find menstruation
a pain, others enjoy the experience, and the same goes for childbirth
and motherhood. There are differences among women and differences among men. The future for a theology of gender lies in
recognizing that, and prioritizing the achievement of justice for all
whilst developing an ethical system not based upon theories of
nature or other 'gendered' systems — passionate ethics as we have
called them (see **2.12**). Justice is an ingredient of this ethic (see **2.4**,
2.12). Yet at the same time we need to hold on to the importance of
the sexed body as a source of knowledge and theology. Theology
itself will have to change its method for this to happen. Gradually we

shall weave together a patchwork quilt of theologies out of our different experiences, from which patterns may eventually emerge. Perhaps the churches are so reluctant to think seriously and deeply about gender because in the process everything else — Christian doctrine, ethics and practice — becomes destabilized. Women promise/threaten to change Christianity completely and for ever.

6.8 SUMMARY

This chapter has explored the extraordinarily complex topic of gender. We have noted how little attention is given in church documents to the issues of the nature and construction of gender. We have pointed out how theology's future challenge is to combine a recognition of the social construction of gender with a full appreciation of bodiliness. The diversity and richness of feminist theology has been introduced. The 'equal but different' approach to gender in most church documents has been exposed to be totally inadequate.

Notes

1 P. Allen, *The Concept of Woman: The Aristotelian Revolution 750 BC–AD 1250* (Montreal: Eden, 1985), p. 19.

2 Rosemary Radford Ruether, 'An unrealized revolution: searching scripture for a model of the family', in A. Thatcher and E. Stuart, *Christian Perspectives on Sexuality and Gender* (Leominster: Gracewing/Fowler Wright, 1996), pp. 442–50.

3 Ruether, 'An unrealized revolution', p. 448

4 Gillian Cloke, *This Female Man of God: Women and Spiritual Power in the Patristic Age AD 350–450* (London: Routledge, 1995).

5 *Ibid.*, p. 214.

6 *Ibid.*, pp. 216–17.

7 Thomas Aquinas, *Summa Theologiae*, I. 92.1.

8 Elaine Graham, *Making the Difference: Gender, Personhood and Theology* (London: Mowbray, 1995), p. 15.

9 Ann Loades, *Feminist Theology: A Reader* (London and Louisville: SPCK and Westminster/John Knox Press, 1990), pp. 5–6.

10 Alison Webster, *Found Wanting: Women, Christianity and Sexuality* (London: Cassell, 1995), p. 18.

11 Roland Martinson, 'Androgyny and beyond', in Thatcher and Stuart, *Christian Perspectives*, p. 118.

12 Martinson, 'Androgony and beyond', p. 119.

13 Robert Bly, *Iron John* (Longmead: Element, 1991).

14 J. Michael Hester, 'Men in relationships: redeeming masculinity', in Thatcher and Stuart, *Christian Perspectives*, p. 87.

15 Dick Vittitow, quoted in 'Men in relationships', p. 88.

16 C. S. Lewis, *The Four Loves* (London: Collins, 1960), p. 58.

17 Hester, 'Men in relationships', p. 89.

18 James B. Nelson, 'On doing body theology', *Theology and Sexuality*, no. 2 (March 1995), p. 54. See also *The Intimate Connection: Male Sexuality, Masculine Spirituality* (London: SPCK, 1992), pp. 85–112.

19 Hester, 'Men in relationships', p. 87.

20 Nelson, *The Intimate Connection*, p. 108, and Hester, 'Men in relationships', pp. 95–6.

21 One of the contentions of feminist theology is that the Church has forgotten that all talk about God is metaphorical. This has led to the belief that God is 'really' male. See Sallie McFague, *Models of God: Theology for an Ecological, Nuclear Age* (London: SCM, 1987), pp. 29–58.

22 Jacqueline Field-Bibb, *Women Towards Priesthood: Ministerial Politics and Feminist Praxis* (Cambridge: Cambridge University Press, 1991).

23 Graham Leonard, Ian MacKenzie and Peter Toon, *Let God Be God* (London: Darton, Longman and Todd, 1989).

24 *Letter of Pope John Paul II to Women* (London: Catholic Truth Society, 1995).

25 *Ibid.*, p. 12.

26 *Ibid.*, p. 15.

27 The Board of Social Responsibility of the Church of Scotland, *Report on Human Sexuality* (Edinburgh: Church of Scotland, 1994), para. 3. 1.8.

28 The General Assembly Special Committee on Human Sexuality of the Presbyterian Church (USA), *Keeping Body and Soul Together: Sexuality, Spirituality and Social Justice* (1991), p. 2.

29 Loades, *Feminist Theology*, p. 1.

30 Carol Gilligan, *In a Different Voice? Psychological Theory and Women's Development* (Cambridge, MA: Harvard University Press, 1982).

31 Lisa Isherwood and Dorothea McEwan, *Introducing Feminist Theology* (Sheffield: Sheffield Academic Press, 1993), p. 80.

32 Graham, *Making the Difference*, p. 54.

33 Daphne Hampson, 'On power and gender', in Thatcher and Stuart, *Christian Perspectives*, pp. 130–1. See also Mary Daly, *Gyn/Ecology* (London: The Women's Press, 1979).

34 Elisabeth Schüssler Fiorenza, *But She Said: Feminist Practices of Biblical Interpretation* (Boston: Beacon Press, 1992).

35 McFague, *Models of God*.

36 María Clara Bingemer, 'Women in the future of the theology of liberation', in Ursula King, *Feminist Theology from the Third World* (London and Maryknoll: SPCK and Orbis, 1995), p. 316.

37 Chung Hyun Kyung, 'To be human is to be created in God's image', in King, *Feminist Theology*, p. 253.

38 Elizabeth A. Johnson, *She Who Is: The Mystery of God in Feminist Theological Discourse* (New York: Crossroad, 1993).

39 Rita Nakashima Brock, *Journeys by Heart: A Christology of Erotic Power* (New York: Crossroad, 1991), p. 66.

40 Grace M. Jantzen, 'Feminism and flourishing: gender and metaphor in feminist theology', *Feminist Theology*, 10 (September 1995), p. 83.

41 *Ibid.*, p. 2.

42 *Ibid.*, p. 94.

43 Graham, *Making the Difference*, p. 88.

44 Emily Martin, *The Woman in the Body* (Milton Keynes: Open University Press, 1989).

45 Ruth Hubbard, 'The political nature of "human nature"' in D. L. Rhode, *Theoretical Perspectives on Sexual Difference* (New Haven: Yale University Press, 1990), p. 69.

46 Graham, *Making the Difference*, p. 137.

47 *Ibid.*, p. 222.

48 *Ibid.*, p. 223.

Suggestions for further reading

Gillian Cloke, *This Female Man of God: Women and Spiritual Power in the Patristic Age AD 350–450* (London: Routledge, 1995).

Lisa Isherwood and Dorothea McEwan, *Introducing Feminist Theology* (Sheffield: Sheffield Academic Press, 1993).

Elaine Graham, *Making the Difference: Gender, Personhood and Theology* (London: Mowbray, 1995).

James Nelson, *The Intimate Connection: Male Sexuality, Masculine Spirituality* (London: SPCK, 1992).

Alison Webster, *Found Wanting: Women, Christianity and Sexuality* (London: Cassell, 1995).

7

HOMOSEXUALITY

7.1 DEADLOCK IN THE CHURCHES

Perhaps there is an issue in every generation and part of Christianity that forces its adherents to ask hard and divisive questions about the authority of scripture and tradition and the nature of **revelation**. For the first generation of Christians it was the 'Gentile question'; for Western Christians in the nineteenth century it was scientific discovery, particularly Darwinism; for the same group of Christians a century later it is **homosexuality**. Almost every mainstream Christian denomination in the West has had to reflect upon this issue. So complex are the questions it raises that it would be true to say that in most the debate is deadlocked. This is evident, for example, in the report produced by the commission on human **sexuality** set up by the UK Methodist Church, published in 1990, which after rehearsing all the arguments around the subject of homosexuality concluded that the division of opinion among members of the commission prevented it from offering a recommendation. Three years later, faced with polarized motions at its conference, one of which suggested that **lesbian** and **gay** people be excluded from church membership, the Methodist delegates passed two different motions which are open to be interpreted as completely contradictory:

1. This conference reaffirms the traditional teaching of the Church on human sexuality; namely **chastity** for all outside marriage and **fidelity** within it. The conference directs that this affirmation is made clear to all candidates for ministry, office and membership ...
2. Conference recognises, affirms and celebrates the participation and ministry of lesbians and gay men in the Church. Conference calls on the Methodist people to begin a pilgrimage of faith to combat repression and discrimination, to work for justice and

human rights and to give dignity and worth to people whatever
their sexuality.

This stance was reaffirmed at its 1994 conference, which refused to
endorse a proposal to carry out a study into discrimination against
lesbian and gay people within the denomination. A similar impasse
has been reached in the Episcopal Church of the USA which has
followed the pattern of many church ruling bodies in recent years
(such as the UK Methodist Church and as was recommended to the
Church of Scotland by the authors of the 1994 report on the theology
of marriage) in passing the decision-making (e.g. over whether
lesbian and gay people should be ordained) to the local churches.
The Evangelical Lutheran Church in America in a social statement
on human sexuality follows the Methodist report in rehearsing the
various arguments and offering no recommendations, only a prayer
that the Holy Spirit will guide the Church on this issue.[1]

In many Protestant denominations the focus has shifted off the
acceptability of the homosexual laity and on to the clergy, not as
some have argued because the issue of homosexuality among the
laity has been resolved, but because church authorities implicitly
recognize that their control over the laity is limited, whereas they
have much more power over the lives of ordained ministers. So
hostile and divisive has been the debate that some Christians have
sought to make attitudes to homosexuality a test of orthodoxy. In
1996 unsuccessful attempts were made to try the retired American
Episcopalian bishop Walter Righter for heresy for ordaining an
openly gay and partnered man. To commit heresy is to commit an
offence against Christian doctrine. For many people a negative
attitude to homosexuality is as essential to the Church as belief in the
Trinity or the divinity of Christ. In the Roman Catholic Church
theologians who have questioned the Vatican's line on homosexuality have been disciplined or silenced.

The classification of people according to their sexual preferences
is a modern phenomenon and is a consequence of the belief of
modern psychology, represented most clearly by Freud, that sexuality (see **9.3**) is a — perhaps *the* — central dimension of a person's
character and the force behind most of their behaviour. Previous to
this there had certainly been men who had **sex** with men and women
with women but their actions were interpreted in terms of social or
moral nonconformity, not as the consequence of an innate drive.
Ancient Greece and Rome interpreted sexual activity according to a

far more sophisticated set of criteria than modern Western culture. Gender was certainly a part of it but so was age, preference for active or passive positions, nationality and a person's social and economic status. Michel Foucault argued that the homosexual as a personality type was invented in the late eighteenth and nineteenth centuries by the medical community who were then taking over from the Church the role of classifying and controlling society.[2] The homosexual was **socially constructed** as suffering from some sort of pathological condition which led to a displaced 'normal', i.e., **heterosexual** desire. A number of theories have developed in the last one hundred years to explain the 'causes' of homosexuality, from the psychological to the biological and genetic. Ironically, the classification of 'homosexual' gave individuals who were described in this way a context in which to develop a personal and political sense of self, from which they were then able to argue for toleration. In the late 1940s and 1950s the famous Kinsey Report revealed that homosexual activity was far more common and widespread than had previously been thought,[3] and subsequent studies suggested that homosexual people were in fact no less psychologically or physically healthy than heterosexual people, leading both the American Psychiatric and Psychological Associations and the World Health Organization to remove homosexuality from their list of mental disorders. In the 1950s and 1960s homosexual people themselves began to challenge explicitly the pathological construction of their **sexual orientation**, and to present themselves as a social and cultural minority to whom equal civil and social rights should not be denied. The term 'homosexual' was rejected as pathological and people referred to themselves as lesbian and gay. The churches have had to come to terms with the emergence of a distinct and increasingly self-confident and articulate group of people. This chapter is going to analyse critically three different Christian responses to the 'problem' of homosexuality.

7.2 THREE APPROACHES TO HOMOSEXUALITY: (I) 'INTRINSIC MORAL EVIL ... OBJECTIVE DISORDER'

This view is best represented by the Vatican's stance on homosexuality, as summarized in the Catechism:

> Basing itself on Sacred Scripture, which presents homosexual acts as acts of grave depravity, Tradition has always declared that 'homosexual acts are intrinsically disordered'. They are contrary to the **natural law**. They close the sexual act to the gift of life. They do not

proceed from a genuine affective and sexual **complementarity** [see below, **7.5.1**]. Under no circumstances can they be approved.[4]

Such a view was developed more fully in the *Letter to the Bishops of the Catholic Church on the Pastoral Care of Homosexual Persons* issued in 1986 by the Congregation for the Doctrine of the Faith. In many respects this letter was a rebuke to Catholic bishops in England, Wales and the United States of America who, struggling to come to terms with the emergence of a gay and lesbian identity, had sought, following the example of a 1975 Vatican declaration on sexual **ethics** to draw a distinction between the homosexual condition, which was morally neutral, and homosexual 'acts', i.e., homosexual genital acts, which were not. They also condemned **homophobia** — the fear of homosexuality that leads to discrimination and violence — and argued that the Church had a particular duty to a group which had been oppressed and an obligation to help a homosexual person 'come out', i.e., live openly and honestly as a gay man or lesbian woman and integrate their sexuality in their whole personhood.[5] The Vatican letter described those bishops' approach to homosexuality as 'overly benign' and declared that 'Although the particular inclination of the homosexual person is not a sin, it is a more or less strong tendency ordered toward an intrinsic moral evil; and thus the inclination itself must be seen as an objective disorder'.[6]

The Vatican grounds its judgement on homosexuality in the story of creation in Genesis, in particular the statement in 1.27: 'In the image of God he created him; male and female he created them.' It says

> Human beings, therefore, are nothing less than the work of God himself; and in the complementarity of the sexes, they are called to reflect the inner unity of the Creator. They do this in a striking way in their co-operation with him in the transmission of life by a mutual donation of the self to the other ... To choose someone of the same sex for one's sexual activity is to annul the rich symbolism and meaning, not to mention the goals, of the Creator's sexual design. Homosexual activity is not a complementary union, able to transmit life; and so it thwarts the call to a life of self-giving which the Gospel says is the essence of Christian living.[7]

Therefore, the letter goes on rule out church support for civil legislation which would give homosexual people and their relationships legal equality with heterosexual people, on the grounds that such legislation puts the 'nature and rights' of the family in 'jeopardy'. Although condemning violence towards homosexual people the Vatican suggests that such violence is often a natural reaction to homosexual people demanding civil rights.[8] Homosexual people are called to live 'a chaste life', by which the letter means **celibate**. The letter instructs bishops to refuse support or physical space to lesbian and gay groups which dissent from the Church's teaching. In 1992 the same congregation issued a document to bishops in the USA alone (*Some Considerations Concerning the Catholic Response to Legislative Proposals on the Non-Discrimination of Homosexual Persons*), which instructed bishops actively to oppose all civil legislation designed to give lesbian and gay people equality under the law. Lesbian and gay people, it stated, have no absolute human or civil rights because they are objectively disordered and a danger to society, like the mentally ill or people suffering from contagious diseases. In any case it is only those lesbian and gay people who 'come out' who attract discrimination.

The great Protestant theologian Karl Barth also addressed the issue of homosexuality in the context of a theology of male–female complementarity (see below, **7.5.1**) which he developed in reflection upon the story of creation. However, Barth's theology is even more radical in its application than that of the Vatican. Barth was convinced that the partnership between men and women established at creation is not only expressed in marriage but in family relationships, working relationships and friendships. Therefore every form of relationship which separates women from men is disobedient to the divine command — including religious communities and single-sex clubs. When this happens men become 'philistinish' and women 'precious'.

> These first steps may well be the symptoms of the malady called homosexuality. This is the physical, psychological and social sickness, the phenomenon of perversion, decadence and decay, which can emerge when man refuses to admit the validity of the divine command in the sense in which we are now considering it.[9]

For Barth then, as for Paul, homosexuality is the by-product of minds turned away and against God. In the face of the reality of the homosexual condition pastors, legislators and judges must first of all do all they can to protect the young, but also call upon God's forgiving and transforming grace with regard to the person who has entered upon this 'whole way of life'. He seems to suggest, therefore, that homosexuality can be 'healed': the proper response of the Church is to call people away from the idolatry of which homosexuality is a part, into relationship with the true God who commands that men can only be truly human in relationship with women, and vice versa.

Those Christians who take this stance on homosexuality argue that biblical law is completely clear and consistent in condemning homosexuality. Leviticus 18.22 and 20.13 describe male homosexual acts as an 'abomination' to be punished by death. The story of Sodom (Genesis 19) indicates that homosexuality was regarded as a worse sin than heterosexual rape. The Judaeo-Christian stance against homosexuality was one of its most distinguishing marks. Ancient Judaism and early Christianity were surrounded by pagan cultures which tolerated and even idealized the practice. Growing toleration of homosexuality in Western cultures is attributed to the decline of traditional religion. Homosexuality is attributed either to deliberate perversion or to psychological or biological abnormality which must be 'treated' and 'healed'. Some may recognize a distinction between crime and sin, and whilst proclaiming the unacceptability of homosexuality from a Christian point of view, believe that the state has no right to penalize homosexual people.

A very interesting alternative methodological approach which came to the same conclusion was adopted by John Giles Milhaven in 1970. In the 1960s and 1970s advocates of new morality, like Joseph Fletcher, recognized no a priori laws except the divine command to love (see **2.7**). John Giles Milhaven takes this principle and applies it to the question of homosexuality. Since **situation ethics** (see **2.7**) must be grounded upon experience and his own experience of homosexuality is limited, he goes to 'experts' in order to ascertain the information necessary to make a judgement on what the most loving reaction to homosexuality is. However, the experts Milhaven chooses to take most seriously are those who believe that homosexuals are suffering from a severe emotional disorder. He acknowledges that there are challenges to this view but 'one who loves does not demand certainty before deciding how to help the one he loves. He uses the best evidence at hand.'[10] And since the best evidence at hand in Milhaven's view is that homosexual feelings reflect immaturity and disorder, and since a person with genuine love for him- or herself and for others would not wish to encourage such a state, a Christian has no option but to condemn homosexuality as wrong. It is wrong not because it frustrates nature but because it frustrates the person concerned. It prevents that person reaching the full emotional and sexual maturity which God wishes for his creation. There is nothing sinful about homosexual impulses, as we all have sinful impulses, but it is sinful to choose to act upon them.

7.3 RESPONSES TO THE FIRST APPROACH

Leaving aside the issue of complementarity (see below, **7.5.3**), there are several critical responses which can be made to the Vatican's argument. Five of them are dealt with in this section.

7.3.1 *Sex and pleasure*

As the Roman Catholic theologian Gareth Moore has noted, the assumption that sexual activity's primary purpose is procreation (see **1.10**) begs the question of why it is a pleasurable activity at all.[11] It cannot be, as some have argued, that God made sexual activity pleasurable in order that we would be enticed to engage in it, because the same does not apply to other measures essential to ensure the survival of the human race, such as work. Furthermore,

> if God has made the act of procreation pleasurable so as to induce us to do it, that means the inducement to perform this activity must, in God's design, be pleasure. There cannot be anything wrong with doing it in just the way that God intends. And the pleasure that we do it for must be that of the sexual activity itself, not the pleasure of procreating, of begetting or conceiving.[12]

Procreation is itself not an activity but the result of an activity. We may rejoice in having conceived but this is not the same pleasure as enjoying the sexual activity that led to the conception. Sex is in the right circumstances a pleasurable activity, whether or not it leads to procreation; this is the way God has arranged it, therefore it must be fully in conformity with God's purposes to enjoy sexual activity as a good in its own right.

We have already noted that Aquinas was unable to accord any value to the personal dimension of sexual **desire** and pleasure (see **2.4**). Yet throughout the Bible the pleasurable image of a feast serves as a powerful **metaphor** of God's coming reign. Feasting is not eating for survival — on the contrary, the pleasure of a feast lies in enjoying food (and other things) purely for its own sake. Indeed, delighting in things for their own sake is what enables human beings to flourish. When we cannot enjoy things for their own sake and have to do them simply to survive we are diminished as human beings, for they become burdens around our necks. This is not to deny that there are important ethical issues around doing things for their own sake (does my ability to enjoy food, clothes, country walks, etc., have negative consequences for others? If so then I need to alter my habits) but it is simply to point out that doing things for their own sake is a natural human good. Moore points out that God's words in Genesis 1.28, 'Be fruitful and multiply', are not in fact an instruction, as many Christians have argued, but a blessing along with dominion and food: 'The divine purpose is not that people should have children, be powerful and eat cereals and vegetables whether they want to or not, but to bring about human well-being by satisfying human wants.'[13]

7.3.2 The 'purpose' of sex

We have already had reason to criticize extensively the natural law tradition of Christian ethics (see **2.3**), together with its application to **masturbation**, abortion and contraception (see **2.9–2.11**). We now criticize the ability of natural law to arrive at an adequate account of the purposes of sexual activity. Following Moore, we note that for Aquinas natural law means in fact two things: acting rationally and following laws which are evident in the behaviour of animals. Human beings share with the animals inclinations to do certain things, including having sex. God has established a natural law amongst animals regulating their behaviour. They therefore become a guide to sinful human beings on how to regulate their own behaviour. The idea that we can read off from the natural world laws of behaviour which God has established in his creation is a highly dubious one. It ignores the fact that concepts of what is or is not 'natural' are in fact socially constructed. Human beings observe the world, classify it and then invest those classifications with meaning. We have taken small biological differences between men and women and invested them with enormous meaning. The fact that these notions are social constructions can be proved by observing cultures where men engage in activities which people in Britain and the USA might label as women's activities, or by observing that most of us in Britain and the USA no longer consider the medical profession unsuitable for women or the nursing profession unsuitable for men, and yet three or four generations ago it would have been considered unnatural for women to want to be doctors or men to want to be nurses.

There are also hermaphrodites — people who do not fit into the biological categories of male or female. They are part of the 'natural order' yet we refuse to recognize them as such. We regard them as sick or an unfortunate anomaly,

but that only means that the classification that *we* make and that *we*

insist on allows for only two possibilities, male and female. We do
not make room for a third possibility, even though nature does . . .
We insist on binary opposition . . . because it is fundamental to our
social organisation.[14]

And it is not just gender differences (see Chapter 6) that we have
invested with meaning. Skin colour and ethnicity have also been
subject to binary division on the basis of 'natural law'. Most of us
would now shudder at the idea that nature teaches us that black is
inferior to white or Aryan superior to Jew, but again within living
memory these were accepted by large numbers of people (including
the Church) as natural facts.

The investing of nature with meaning which is then claimed to be
'obvious' is clearly evident in Aquinas' use of natural law. He uses
natural law to argue that there is only one kind of sexual intercourse
permitted by nature: between men and women for the purpose of
procreation. Yet he is very clear that it is totally improper for human
beings to adopt the sexual positions of animals. This is because there
is certain behaviour that is proper only to one species and it is
improper for one species to imitate the behaviour of another. But
how is one to judge whether a certain form of behaviour is naturally
common and therefore obligatory for all animals and when it should
be reserved to one particular species? Animals may or may not
engage in 'homosexual' behaviour (and in fact there is plenty of
evidence that they do), but if they do not the fact that some humans
do could be used to argue that it is one of those forms of activity
which is reserved for humans alone and is therefore quite proper.

Augustine contended that animals have sex only for procreation.
He thought that the 'procreative purpose' of sexual activity was
uniform throughout creation. Moore also questions these contentions. It is assumed that animals have a concept of purpose which
they set out to achieve, but there is no evidence for this. Aquinas'
assertion that everything has its natural end, and that the end of
sexual organs and semen is procreation, is similarly questionable.
Sexual activity appears to have been ordered towards a number of
ends: pleasure, expressing love or affection, relaxation, etc. Aquinas'
argument on semen falls on the fact that not all semen is needed for
procreation — most of it is indeed what he denies it is, superfluous to
requirements. To waste something of which there is an abundance
can therefore not be seen as sinful, otherwise bathing and watering
ornamental plants (in non-drought conditions) would be sinful.
Similarly the often-rehearsed argument that sexual organs have

specific purposes (e.g. the penis to ejaculate into the vagina and cause conception) is also hard to sustain. The penis has at least two functions: sexual, and the expulsion of waste. Why should parts of the body only have one divinely ordained function? Do human beings not have control over their bodies as they do over creation? If not, if we are forbidden to use our bodies creatively, then we have no business in trying to alter the shape and appearance of our bodies at all. Moore contends that it is impossible to speak of voluntary sexual activity having a divine purpose. In voluntary human activity the purpose is the purpose of the persons performing it. God may have a purpose in laying down laws to guide our sexual activity, and his purpose is revealed in the laying down of laws but not in the sexual activity of voluntary agents — their purpose is their purpose.[15]

Sexuality is a gift from God. There is a proper and improper way of using a gift which demonstrates gratitude or ingratitude. A year ago a group of people presented one of us with a splendid red hat. Instead of being worn regularly, it was hung above a desk. So the hat which could be worn on the head has become an ornament, a piece of art. The givers of this gift would not, we think, be offended that the hat is rarely worn — we think they would be amused and delighted with the use of their gift. If, however, the hat had been cut up and used as a dish rag or if the cat had been allowed to use the hat as a litter tray they would have justifiably been offended and hurt. Contempt would have been demonstrated for their gift and lack of gratitude. When we apply this insight to the realm of sexual activity it is easy to see that rape and abuse of any sort is a gross and debasing misuse of the gifts God has given us, including the gift of people. We are given people to love, so to fail to love them or to treat them in ways incompatible with love is a clear misuse of a gift. But what about homosexual activity? This activity need not be any more inherently offensive to the giver than the hanging of the hat on the wall, provided it is done in love and leads to gratitude to God.

Assuming that human beings have a nature, it also seems to be part of their nature to act unnaturally, to intervene in and mould nature to their own purposes. Indeed, as Michael Vasey has pointed out, the creation accounts in Genesis suggest that humanity is created both as part of nature but also as 'a little "god" within it. It is part of our nature to order, to understand and to create. Nature (creation) waits for humanity's creativity to bring it to perfection ... '.[16] Human culture and nature is not then a **dualism**. Culture, although prone to sin, is part of the creation and therefore of the nature that God has made. Does the concept of the natural have no place in theological discourse about sexuality? Moore thinks that it must because it is part of self-understanding. He suggests that human beings do share a nature, in that we know that certain things are bad for us (e.g. breathing in water) and certain things good for us (e.g. exercise).[17] Living according to our nature enables us to survive but also to flourish. We are social animals and in order to flourish we need to live together as friends. Of course for various reasons which Christians would want to label sin we also sometimes want to do what is bad for us to obtain short-term pleasure, e.g., to take drugs. We know that taking certain drugs can lead to diminishment and death. This enables us to say that such behaviour is unnatural and people engaging in it should be encouraged out of it for their own good and for that of others who are diminished by their actions. The same will be true of sexual behaviour if it can be established that a particular form is bad for people. We will only learn whether this is so through observation. Contrary to what Victorians were led to believe by scientists, masturbation does not actually lead to madness.

7.3.3 The homosexual 'condition'

The Vatican adopts a pathological model of homosexuality. Homosexuals suffer from a 'condition'. They cannot help being homosexual and therefore cannot be blamed for it and even if they engage in homosexual acts they must be treated with care and compassion because they are suffering from an illness which propels them to do such things. There are several problems with this approach. It uncritically assumes heterosexuality as natural and normative. To say or imply that homosexuals are sick is to imply that healthy people will not be homosexual. A homosexual person on this model is one whose 'natural' heterosexual desires have 'gone wrong' and been transmuted into sexual desire for the same sex. This in turn assumes that heterosexual and homosexual desire are mutually incompatible, or binary opposites. Kinsey, however, has shown this assumption to be without foundation. Hence homosexuality cannot be conceived as being perverted heterosexual desire, for it is possible to be predominantly homosexual and still experience heterosexual desire, and vice versa. To label something as sickness also implies that it is distressing to the person suffering from it.[18] But this is not the case with homosexuality. It is possible to be gay or lesbian and be perfectly happy. Any unhappiness or suffering that a homosexual person experiences is not likely to be the consequence of homosexuality itself but of reactions to it, which may of course be internalized.

The other problem with the sickness approach to homosexuality is that it denies lesbian and gay people the moral agency (as does the view that homosexual desire is the result of demon possession) which the Christian tradition has always considered to be an essential part of being human, to be lesbian or gay is therefore to be less fully human than heterosexual people. The construction of homosexuality as a condition also opens the door to the possibility of 'healing' (even though many would argue that it is no more healable than a physical condition, such as the loss of a leg, there is within Christian tradition a strong and often unconscious belief that healing of even the most severe physical injuries and conditions is possible). A number of organizations have grown up in recent years claiming to be able to 'cure' people of homosexuality. The psychologist Elizabeth Moberly[19] has been very influential in evangelical circles for suggesting that homosexuality is a psychological disorder, the result of an early inability to realize a proper relationship with the parent of the same sex. The solution to this is to form strong but non-erotic relationships with members of the same sex which, along with prayer and counselling, will result in the proper development of the arrested heterosexual desire. However, there is no consensus of opinion among psychologists and others about what causes homosexuality, or indeed that it is in any way a psychological condition. Gerd Brantenberg wittily parodies the numerous different psychological approaches to lesbianism:

> If one grows up alone with one's mother, the male will become a distant and peculiar figure, whom one will later have inhibitions approaching ... Several lesbians have had no father. If one grows up in a family with only sisters, the intimacy with them will easily lead to joint masturbation in the shared bedrooms ... It turns out that a lot of lesbians have only sisters. If one only has brothers, close contact with the male sex in the tender years will easily lead to the development of a nervous fear of all males, and one becomes a lesbian. A considerable number of lesbians have had only brothers ... [20]

And so on. Moberly and others do not approach the issue of homosexuality objectively. They come to it with pre-existing ideas about its moral status. It must be healable because it is against God's will: therefore the nature of the illness has to be uncovered. This still begs the question: is it against God's will? Moore directly attacks Milhaven's uncritical reliance on certain psychological theories which claim that homosexuality is a condition of stunted emotional growth which manifests itself in a flight from love (of women, that is, because Milhaven seems to focus on gay men). Milhaven chooses to reply to these psychological theories whilst dismissing others. The ability to love can only be judged from the basis of action, not from a supposed hidden state of mind. Many gay men have extremely good relations with women, and most gay and lesbian people are extremely loving and self-giving people.

> If Milhaven's test is love, it cannot be said that homosexuals, as such, are any less likely to pass it than heterosexuals as such; still less is it true that, as Milhaven wants to show, they are bound to fail it because of the very nature of homosexual desire and activity as purportedly shown by a disputable psychological theory.[21]

7.3.4 *Orientation and practice*

The Vatican's attempt to distinguish between a homosexual orientation and homosexual practice is echoed in many Christian circles. The distinction is often adopted for compassionate motives, enabling Christians to accept homosexual persons whilst still maintaining a negative view of homosexual activity. The fact that the orientation–practice approach immediately creates another dualism should arouse our suspicions. Alison Webster draws a parallel between sexuality and the Christian faith, pointing out that most Christians would reject the view that you can be a Christian without demonstrating any practical outworking of your belief: 'Just as Christians would say that religious beliefs without practical application are worthless, so lesbians and gay men are justified in arguing that the term "sexual orientation" has no meaning outside of a relational context.'[22] So the implicit message from the churches is that, despite assurances to the contrary, to be homosexual is to be as worthless as a Christian faith which results in no recognizably Christian behaviour.

This brings us to another point. Most church documents on the subject of sexuality tend to reflect the patriarchal habit of reducing sexual intimacy to genital acts. When Christians talk of 'homosexual acts' they are usually thinking about anal or oral intercourse or mutual masturbation. Yet one of the most important insights that has come out of the feminist and gay movements is that sexuality is about much more than that — it is the seat, the root, of all our relationality, as active in our absorption in a work of art, piece of music, prayer or chat over a tea and cake as in making love (see **9.3**). To label

homosexual 'acts' as evil or even 'just' inferior to heterosexual ones
is to label all homosexual acts and relationships defective and therefore to classify gay and lesbian people as less human than heterosexuals and less able to reach out of their relationality to God.

Moore argues that the only grounds upon which a Christian could
condemn homosexual sexual activity would be proof that it was
vicious. Many do claim that it is exactly that. There is an association in
the British mind at least between homosexuality and child abuse,
even though it has been shown over and over again that heterosexuals
are statistically more likely to abuse children. The 1992 Vatican letter
endorses and perpetuates this slur by instructing the USA bishops
that it is legitimate to take sexual orientation into account when
appointing teachers or sports coaches, or recruiting people for the
military or in the fostering and adoption of children.

Another commonly believed fallacy is that lesbians and gay men
are incapable of forming long-term relationships. It has been suggested that the perpetuation of such untruths contravenes the ninth
commandment, 'Do not give false evidence against your neighbour'
(Exodus 20.16)[23] There is no evidence that gay or lesbian people are
any more vicious or virtuous than heterosexual people and therefore
it is extremely difficult, if not impossible, to justify condemnation
from a Christian perspective.

7.3.5 Homosexuality and the Bible

But what about the scripture? Seven proof texts are usually cited by
those, like the Vatican and Barth, who wish to argue that homosexuality is clearly and unambiguously condemned in the Bible: Genesis
18.26–29.29 (Sodom and Gomorrah); Leviticus 18.22 and 20.13;
Deuteronomy 23.17–18; Romans 1.18–32; 1 Corinthians 6.9, 10;
1 Timothy 1.8–11; Jude 7. However, before turning our attention to
these passages it is important to draw out at least two questionable
assumptions that lie behind the statement that scripture condemns
homosexuality (see **10.1**). The first is that these are the only passages
in scripture that *deal* with homosexuality. People who come to the
scriptures assuming that they condemn homosexuality will see only
those passages which appear to do so. Others, particularly lesbian
and gay scholars, have found other texts which may be just
as relevant. The story of David and Jonathan (1 Samuel 18.1–5;
2 Samuel 1.17–27) idealizes a passionate covenanted love between
two men, which disturbed and scandalized King Saul. The story of

the healing of the centurion's servant in Matthew 8.5–13 and Luke 7.1–10 may well have a homosexual subtext. The person being healed is referred to in Greek as *paîs*. This word can mean 'child' of either sex but it was also the word used in Hellenistic culture to refer to a man's slave lover. John's gospel portrays a close emotional relationship between Jesus and the beloved disciple. Some have seen within the Hebrew scriptures a constant theme of sexual subversion whereby the history of salvation only proceeds because people break the laws around sexual behaviour.[24]

What are the implications of this? Possibly that within the biblical text we may detect an ongoing debate about sexual morality which foreshadows what is going on in the churches today. Law codes are a notoriously misleading guide to a society's views, for they are often politically and/or personally motivated. The same is also true of the Christian tradition when it is claimed that it has always condemned homosexual behaviour. John Boswell has done much to show that the waters of Christian history are not that clear on the issue. In particular he has uncovered the existence of liturgies for 'same-sex unions', in manuscripts dating from the eighth to the seventeenth centuries, a fact which raises enormous questions about the Church's attitude to same-sex passion in previous eras.[25]

The second assumption to challenge is that the passages condemning homosexuality have more authority than other commandments which Christians have happily jettisoned. Passages around the condemnation of male homosexual behaviour in Leviticus condemn the trimming of beards and the mixing of fibres in clothes. Yet these are happily ignored by Christians along with the food laws. ('As someone memorably put it, the next time you see a clean-shaven fundamentalist in a poly-cotton shirt eating a prawn cocktail, be sure to shout, "Abomination".'[26]) Direct obedience to all biblical laws has never been a Christian principle: the need to discern the authority of scripture has always been recognized (see **2.2**).

But the matter is even more complex, as an analysis of the seven texts will make clear. The use of the story of Sodom and Gomorrah in the debate about homosexuality is interesting because when it is referred to in other biblical books it is not once linked with homosexuality. The sin of Sodom is inhospitality, which appears to be expressed first in the desire of the men of Sodom to rape the (male) messengers from God and then in the rape of Lot's daughters. The story condemns rape, not homosexuality. In order to understand fully the Sodom story it is necessary to understand the thought that lies behind the Levitical texts. Sexual acts are never simply a private matter. Even in our own day, though we like to pretend that they are private, they have social meaning and in that context can take on a symbolic significance. The authors of the book of Leviticus, members of the priestly school writing after the Babylonian exile, construct a social and symbolic meaning for certain sexual acts as part of their concerted attempt to enable Israel to survive as a distinct nation. This they do by building a theology around the notion of Israel's separateness from other peoples. Israel is a separated, holy and *pure* people. This involves avoiding all that is impure. The understanding of **purity** (see **1.8**) is built around concepts of normality and kinds. Deviations from the norm such as disability, women bleeding, and fish without scales and fins (such as prawns) are therefore impure. The mixing of kinds such as cross-dressing or sex between humans and beasts is also impure. The 'spilling' of semen is also perceived to be abnormal and therefore impure. What Leviticus condemns is not sex between men but lying with a man as with a woman. This alerts us to the symbolic meaning given to **gender** distinctions (see **6.2**) in Leviticus. Men and women stand in binary opposition to one another, the male superior to the female. Indeed, male power is maintained by defining itself positively against the negativity of being a woman. Ancient Israelite society was built around this fundamental distinction. Sex was part of the symbolic enactment of these social relations: men on top, women underneath. Homosexual sex disrupted and threatened the social system. Nothing could be more demeaning to men than to 'play the part of a woman' in sex (which is why male rape was often used upon prisoners of war in the ancient world). Moore notes 'we cannot have an attitude to this law and others like it without having an attitude to the social organization it presupposes'.[27] And Christians have very clear and distinct attitudes to purity and social organization particularly as it relates to men and women.

We have already noted (see **1.8**) that the New Testament abolishes the whole symbolic system of purity (Mark 7.18; Acts 11.15). Nothing is unclean in and of itself.[28] Similarly the teaching of Paul (Galatians 3.28) echoes the implicit teaching of the Gospels that divisions between male and female are abolished. No one group should dominate over the other. Thus the rationale upon which the condemnation of homosexual acts in Leviticus is based is rejected. Deuteronomy 23.17–18 condemns male prostitutes in the service of the cult of the goddess Astarte. What is being condemned is not homosexuality but a particular cult and its practices.

Many Christian people have little difficulty accepting that the authority of the Old Testament law is not binding on Christians, but they would point out that homosexuality is also condemned in the New Testament, most unambiguously in Romans 1.18–32. Here Paul condemns those Gentiles, male and female, who have rejected the real God in favour of idols, the result of which is that 'God gave them up to dishonourable passions', including homosexuality. Paul's argument is based on cause and effect. The Gentiles have exchanged true worship for false worship and therefore they have exchanged natural sexual relations for unnatural ones. Homosexuality, though, is singled out as being a symbol of a more general godlessness and it is surely significant that when homosexuality is condemned in the New Testament it is never condemned alone but is included in lists of vices (1 Corinthians 6.9–10 and 1 Timothy 1.8–11). In these passages Paul is condemning a whole way of life which includes and is symbolized by homosexuality. What we find in Romans 1 is in fact a conventional polemic against Gentile culture, very similar, for example, to Wisdom 14.12–27. For Paul homosexuality takes on its repugnant meaning in the context of Gentile rejection of God and godless behaviour. Paul draws upon the notion of natural law. He assumes that Jew and Gentile will be aware that there is a 'natural' use for sexual organs. Male and female homosexual behaviour is a culpable rejection of this natural law. In the twentieth century we experience homosexuality in a different context. We will see (if we bother to look) men and women who have not rejected God, who are not thieves, murderers or deceivers but kind, generous and devoted to God. Therefore we cannot simply lift Paul's condemnation of homosexuality and apply it to twentieth-century lesbian and gay people.

The difficulty in interpreting 1 Corinthians 6.9–10 lies in the translation of the terms *malakoi* and *arsenokoitai*, which are rendered as 'sexual perverts' or 'homosexuals' or 'effeminate and abusers of themselves' in different translations of the Bible. The meaning of these words is obscure and certainly there is no justification for the modern trend to interpret the words as meaning active and passive homosexual. *Malakoi* is probably better translated 'loose living' and has no direct associations with homosexual behaviour. The meaning of *arsenokoitai* is much more difficult to establish. Some believe it refers to male prostitutes, others that it is a general term for homosexuality. However, what we have said about the use of Romans must also apply to this passage and 1 Timothy 1 (which uses only the word *arsenokoitai*). Jude v. 7's mention of Sodom and Gomorrah has been interpreted by some as referring to homosexual sex. In fact in context the reference is obviously to sex with angels.

There is no single 'mind' of scripture[29] on sexuality and it is dishonest simply to read off apparent references to homosexuality within the scriptures without paying attention to their (often **patriarchal**) context and asking whether it is compatible with the Christian vision. A **hermeneutical** framework is needed in order to deal with the scriptures with integrity (see Chapter 10). It has been suggested that, as Christians affirm that God's revelation has most clearly and fully been revealed in Christ, all the texts of scripture must be tested against the teaching and behaviour of Christ.[30] Jesus abolished both the purity codes and undermined the patriarchal basis of his religion. He welcomed those whom society rejected, judging them only on their loving acts. Jesus, the argument goes, would not have rejected gay and lesbian people.

Gareth Moore believes that all Christian ethics must be built around the central command of Jesus to love your neighbour as yourself. Love becomes the criterion by which to judge sexual relationships. The report prepared by the South African Anglican Theological Commission and endorsed for study by the Synod of Bishops, after reviewing the biblical teaching on many different aspects of sexuality, argues that

> in view of the vast difference between the situation of the first century and that of today, care must be taken to interpret scripture in accordance with its main themes and principles rather than by a literal acceptance of specific texts.[31]

If we are to reinterpret scripture it must be because we can show that our reinterpretation reflects a deeper love for God and other people. This reflects two central biblical principles: love and righteousness (which includes holiness *and* justice), which must be kept in balance. Just as the Church has interpreted scripture to address racism, apartheid, sexism and economic injustice, so it must now address human sexuality. Regarding homosexuality, which is one of the topics considered by the Commission, it acknowledges the dispute between **essentialists** and social constructionists (it is one of the few church reports to show any awareness of this debate — see below, **7.6**), but notes that 'neither of these two lines of scientific research is condemnatory of homosexuality'.

> Good theology begins with real people in relationship with God, so that the church needs to listen to the experiences of homosexuals

... The witness of the Bible and the Christian tradition needs to be explored afresh in the light of new understandings of homosexuality. The key to a fresh approach will be found in the themes of God's love and compassion (*hesed*), and righteousness. The starting-point should be the loving and caring practice of Jesus himself with his concern to build community by reconciling to God and each other those whom the world has condemned.[32]

7.4 THREE APPROACHES TO HOMOSEXUALITY: (II) 'FALLING SHORT'

The second approach taken by Christian theologians in the second half of the twentieth century towards homosexuality has been that homosexual relationships, whilst not necessarily being sinful, are imperfect when compared to heterosexual relationships. This position is taken by those who recognize the difficulty of applying scriptural texts which themselves are ambiguous to relationships and categories of personhood unknown in the ancient world. They also believe that neither scripture nor theology have the competence to interpret the world on their own. The social and medical sciences must be looked to for the data about the world in which we live, upon which Christian theology then reflects. Scientific evidence suggests that homosexuality is not a pathological or psychological disorder but a consistent sexual condition of a minority, and theologians have to take this fact on board when assessing the morality of homosexuality. However, this fact does not overturn the general gist of scripture or the theory of natural law. Charles Curran, the Catholic theologian, in developing a 'theory of compromise', argues that taking on board scientific evidence means recognizing that, although homosexuality is an objective moral disorder and that ideally homosexuals should refrain from 'practising' homosexuality, in fact because of the presence of sin in the world and because of the fact that 'homosexuality exists as a result of sin' (i.e., poor relationships in a person's background, etc.) homosexuals cannot be held culpable for engaging in homosexual acts and should be encouraged into stable unions.[33] Heterosexuality remains the ideal rooted in creation but homosexual people are allowed some freedom to seek loving sexual relationships, a freedom granted because of the sinful context in which they exist.

Still within the broad category of 'falling short', the Protestant theologian Helmut Thielicke takes a different approach. Beginning with scripture he notes the problems associated with the passages normally applied to homosexuality. However, like Curran he believes that 'the fundamental order of creation and the created determination of the two sexes make it appear justifiable to speak of homosexuality as a perversion',[34] and it therefore belongs to the disorder of creation which follows the fall, along with disease and suffering. But Christians cannot denounce the homosexual condition because we all share in the disorder of a fallen creation. The homosexual must not idealize or accept 'his' condition as normal but must be willing to be treated or healed. However, since healing does not appear to work, Christians must simply accept the condition as incurable and as 'a divine dispensation and see it as a task to be wrestled with, indeed — paradoxical as it may sound — to think of it as a talent that is to be invested (Luke 19.13f)'.[35] Thielicke acknowledges that the New Testament gives us no guidance as to how to approach the issue of whether homosexuals should be permitted to engage in sexual acts because the notion of homosexuality as a condition is an extremely modern one. He does however use the analogy of the covenant between God and Noah (Genesis 9.1ff). Sin has entered the world disordering it and yet God does not abandon creation but relates to it in and through its disorder. Homosexuals too must behave as ethically as possible within their disordered but irreversible condition. (He recognizes that celibacy cannot be enforced because it is based upon a special calling.) This involves adopting the same norms as heterosexual couples, i.e., monogamous partnerships. But it would be better for the homosexual to sublimate his desires and channel them into caring professions.

As far as church reports are concerned, the 'falling short' argument is central to the statement by the House of Bishops of the General Synod of the Church of England, *Issues in Human Sexuality*. Once again their stance is rooted in a theory of complementarity based upon Genesis 1 – 3.[36] Like Thielicke the bishops acknowledge the ambiguity of many scriptural texts traditionally used to condemn homosexuality and the problem of applying judgements based upon cultural assumptions so different from ours to the present day, and yet conclude from an overview of scriptural teaching on sexuality that

> there is, therefore, in Scripture an evolving convergence on the ideal of lifelong, monogamous, heterosexual union intended by God for the proper development of men and women as sexual beings ... it is quite clearly the foundation on which the Church's traditional teaching is built.[37]

Sexual desire and activity are considered by the bishops to be 'obviously' for the purposes of procreation and created so by God. Biology and theology therefore collude in a similar view that 'heterosexual physical union is divinely intended to be the norm'.[38] This is not the only purpose of sexual desire. It creates a bond between the couple and a pattern of self-giving which can become sacramental. However the bishops are clear that 'scripture, tradition and reasoned reflection upon experience' reveal that it is impossible to regard the 'homophile' (the word the bishops use to describe lesbian and gay people and experience) orientation or relationship as on a par with the heterosexual. The bishops respect the right of conscientious gay and lesbian people to conclude that 'they have more hope of growing in love for God and neighbour with the help of a loving and faithful homophile partnership'[39] as long as those relationships are **monogamous** and the intention is for them to be permanent. However, this right of conscience is not extended to gay or lesbian clergy. Clergy are obliged to live a way of life in conformity with what the Church commends. Clergy should also be accessible to everyone and at present a 'homophile' orientation would, they claim, alienate a substantial number of people.

7.5 RESPONSES TO THE SECOND APPROACH

A range of responses is prompted by the characterization of homosexuality as a 'falling short'. We start first with the weight placed on the notion of complementarity. We have already touched on some of the difficulties associated with this notion (see **6.5**). It is now time to address the issue in more depth.

7.5.1 *Complementarity*

All church documents which use it base their theory of complementarity on Genesis 1. To read and use this passage with integrity we must endeavour to read it in its context. It is another piece of writing by the priestly school of authors and the theme of separation runs throughout this account of creation. Light is separated from dark, the day is separated into distinct parts, species are created as distinct kinds and the crown of creation is the formation of male and female. We have already seen (see above, **7.3.4**) that the division between male and female was crucial for the social ordering of ancient Israel and so the priestly writer wishes to ground this distinction in the ordering of creation (like the Jewish Sabbath which is the clearest sign of Jewish identity). As Moore points out he does not root other biological differences, like left- and right-handedness and fair and dark hair, in creation because these do not bear heavy social symbolic significance.[40] This is true even today where so-called complementary characteristics of men and women (usually based on Jungian psychology) have been shown to be largely socially constructed and constructed by men: 'Hence men and women turn out to be complementary; they fit each other socially because the women occupy the space defined and left for them by the men.'[41]

These definitions therefore reflect a social situation of dominance and submission which Christianity is committed to abolishing (see Chapter 5). It is also to bear false witness (Exodus 20.16) to say that women exhibit so-called 'feminine' qualities and men 'masculine' ones (see **6.5**). The notion that 'true' self-giving love demands that we reach out to someone 'other' than us, different in key respects, also lies at the heart of the theory of complementarity. In everyday life complementarity is often grounded in sameness. For example, we generally like items in our dinner service to have the same pattern. According to Genesis 2, it is the similarity between Adam and Woman, not their sameness, that makes them complementary. Whether complementarity is grounded in sameness or in similarity, it remains a Christian principle that people are valuable and lovable in themselves, irrespective of whether they are the same or different from us. As Moore notes,

> true complementarity in a relationship is a matter of will, the willingness to give and take, to take each other's character, likes, dislikes and interests into account ... It is something that can be worked at [rather than God-given and grounded in gender differences], and its end is that the partners go well together, in that they find their relationship a pleasure.[42]

Barth (see above, **7.3.1**) is more consistent in his approach towards complementarity than others for he argues that all relations must be complementary rather than just sexual ones. For the Vatican and the Church of England have yet to explain why complementarity is only applicable to sexual relations. Barth's approach founders on the example of Jesus and his close male friendships and also reinforces the patriarchal foundations of Christianity, suggesting that women should not be allowed to exist outside of relations with men. The idea that our ability to image God through male–female complementarity is a very recent interpretation of Genesis. Both Aquinas and Augustine located that ability in our power to be rational. The modern interpretation seems to suggest that single people, celibate, homosexual persons and children do not bear the image of God and the logical extension of that is the ridiculous idea that Jesus did not.

Michael Vasey has pointed out the difficulties of asserting that Genesis 1 and 2 provide a biblical mandate for monogamous marriage as an ideal, since the rest of the Bible does not echo it. The ideal of the modern marriage based upon companionship is absent.

> Jesus's mission is not about the establishing of stable marriages or secure and happy homes. He himself did not marry. It is precisely the passage in which Jesus quotes Genesis 2.24 that commends the renunciation of marriage. His primary thrust is the creation of an affectionate community within which marriage is almost an irrelevance.[43]

It is certainly not an ideal. This leads to a further difficulty with the 'falling short' approach: the use of scripture seems to be inconsistent. Neale Secor has noted: 'To equate functional sex differences with essential being is to resort to a literalist biblical anthropology which not only is inappropriate and perhaps completely meaningless in modern discussion, but is also embarrassingly inapposite to [the] otherwise nonliteralistic ethical methodology.'[44] Alison Webster has described complementarity as 'the foundation, the *theological structure* by which Christianity justifies its suppression of all expressions of same-sex love'[45] and asserts heterosexual normativity. The structure is built on sand and becomes decidedly shaky when analysed.

7.5.2 Homosexuality and culture

Perhaps the chief problem with both of the approaches we have examined so far is their failure to recognize the cultural dimension of homosexuality. There is a long-standing debate among lesbian and gay scholars over whether homosexuality has always existed in all times and cultures (essentialism) or whether homosexuality is the creation of society which chooses to interpret certain behaviour as characteristic of a distinct personality type (social constructionism). The first theory leaves open the possibility that homosexuality may be a matter of genetics and the possibility for gay Christians to claim that 'God made me this way'. However, it also involves a surrendering of moral agency, and ignores the vast differences among cultures in the way homosexual behaviour has been understood and expressed. In

Britain and the United States we would regard two men engaging in mutual masturbation to be engaging in homosexual activity. In Turkey such behaviour would not be interpreted in these terms. In Turkey for an act to be homosexual it would have to involve penetration of man by another — one would have to be 'playing the role of a woman'.[46] So even today the same act has different meanings in different cultures. Similarly in some parts of Africa certain forms of activity which in Western culture would be perceived to be lesbian would be regarded as simply friendly contact. The contemporary churches seem to speak as if it were as clear as crystal that the world is divided into homosexual and heterosexual people, and that what constitutes a sexual act is universally agreed, but this is far from the case.

7.5.3 The fear of bisexuality

Alison Webster has pointed out the Church has nothing positive to say to people like her who are quite capable of forging satisfactory relations with members of the opposite sex but choose to enter into relations with people of the same sex because they find them 'superior to heterosexual ones in terms of mutuality, equality, intimacy, communication and sexual pleasure'.[47] This seems to be a phenomenon more common among women than men and the Church's inarticulateness about it reflects its usual disregarding of the experiences of lesbians and indeed of women generally. Such people would not necessarily label themselves **bisexual** for that would be to hide the fact that they have made a deliberate relational choice.

Tom Driver wrote that 'bisexuality ... is the church's deepest sexual fear',[48] for bisexuals undermine the whole sexual system, the neat classification of people into homosexual and heterosexual, the pathologizing of homosexuality as a heterosexual disorder and so on. Bisexuality represents desire unfettered, and perhaps that is why those who experience it are so studiously unacknowledged in church documents, and on the odd occasion where they are acknowledged they are pathetically misrepresented as sexually indiscriminate and promiscuous.[49] Freud suggested that we are all born bisexual but socialized into heterosexuality and the Kinsey report certainly seemed to suggest that the majority of us cannot be neatly categorized into the polarities of homosexuality and heterosexuality. Michael Vasey has argued that the concept of the 'homosexual' only emerged as part of the change in understanding of masculinity which took place in the modern era. Previous to this, he points out, most homosexual activity — male and female — took place alongside marriage. Same-sex friendship or passion was regarded as essential: it was idealized and prioritized as the basis of society.

Changing understandings of masculinity, sex and public life have left some men who cannot identify with masculinity as constructed by modern capitalist society. Equally, there are women unable to identify with the passive femininity which was constructed to complement it. They are now classified as separate personality types.[50] Vasey suggests that the Church might be better employed critically examining the construction of heterosexuality into which most of us are socialized and asking whether it is compatible with the gospel, rather than circling endlessly around the issue of homosexuality. If sexual orientation is a social construction then the churches need to construct a sexual ethic which can be applied to all persons no matter with whom they are in relationship. Such an enterprise would be wholly consistent with what was called 'passionate ethics' (see Chapter 2), and some of its components have already been described (see **2.12**).

7.5.4 *Homophobia*

Finally a word needs to be said about the denunciation of homophobia that occurs in all church documents these days. We have to ask how convincing it is to deplore violence against homosexuals and yet, as the 1992 Vatican document does, bear the kind of false witness against gay and lesbian people that others use to justify 'queer bashing'. The churches' denunciation of homophobia will never ring true whilst they persist in condemning homosexual relations as morally evil or inferior. It is a bit like saying: the Church believes black people to be inferior to white people and their relations to be disordered and morally evil; we therefore think they should not be teachers or coaches and we will not be employing any ourselves; they are not to be given the same civil rights as white people and if they show any pride in their cultural heritage they are only asking for trouble — but of course we denounce racism! The fact that the churches have shown a remarkable reluctance to support any anti-discrimination legislation makes it difficult for lesbian and gay people to believe that their denunciations of homophobia are sincere.

7.6 THREE APPROACHES TO HOMOSEXUALITY: (III) NEUTRALITY

The third position taken by Christians on homosexuality in recent years has been that homosexual acts are neutral and can only be evaluated in terms of their relational significance. This position has been taken by those who have bothered to listen to the experiences of lesbian and gay Christians and come to the conclusion that statements such as that made by H. Kimball Jones that 'two homosexuals can never complement one another in the same sense that male and female can'[51] are simply false. As the ground-breaking British Quaker report on sexuality of 1963 stated, 'Homosexual affection can be as selfless as heterosexual affection, and therefore we cannot see that it is in some way morally worse.'[52] The Quakers came to the conclusion that the physical nature of a sexual act could not be the criterion upon which it was judged. Rather the quality of the relationship should be the criterion. Homosexual and heterosexual relations which involve force, coercion, or abuse of power are sinful. Homosexual and heterosexual relations in which the intention of both parties is mutuality and commitment cannot be designated as sinful.

The Presbyterian (USA) report *Keeping Body and Soul Together* starts its reflections upon gay and lesbian people in the Church by arguing that it is time for the Presbyterian Church to move out of the stalemate that other churches have found themselves in over this issue. Paying particular attention to the biblical objections to homosexuality, the report argues that the common proof texts need to be placed within a broader biblical perspective. Jesus broke through the religious and social stratifications of Jewish law, and Christians, according to Paul, are freed from slavery to the law.

> The freedom of the gospel makes possible a higher morality, not legislated by a code, but guided by the witness of love and justice exemplified in Jesus Christ. This gospel frames a theology of sexuality that affirms sexual expression which genuinely deepens human love and promotes justice. This theology of sexuality does not accord morality on the basis of sexual orientation, but rather on the moral quality of each and every relationship.[53]

Homosexuality should therefore be approached as a justice issue. Just as the Church has had to deal with racism and sexism, so now it must direct its attention to recognizing and ridding itself of **hetero-**

sexism. Heterosexuals and gay and lesbian people are called to the same standards of morality. All human beings, the report maintains, are created with a yearning to experience love with God and others. To deprive gay and lesbian people of the context in which to live out their God-given sexuality is an affront to justice and to the God who created them.

The homosexual–heterosexual distinction is another dualism which has allowed one group to claim superiority over the other and is therefore a bar to **mutuality**; it is also a distinction shown to be false by research which reveals that few of us are either exclusively gay or straight. The bodily integrity of gay and lesbian people must be protected as it must be for all women. This means refraining from forcing gay and lesbian people into celibacy or heterosexuality. The report suggests that if Christians take the line that no sexual intimacy is permitted between members of the same sex they deprive those people of responsible moral choice and yet, as the **Reformed tradition** has always acknowledged,

> Only when each assumes responsibility for our own choices can we genuinely offer or withhold our consent . . . God's call to gays and lesbians is to live responsibly in sexual, as well as nonsexual, relationships. We believe that God's justice requires respect for their right to do so.[54]

Moral responsibility cannot be determined on the basis of sexual orientation. Therefore, the report concludes, it cannot condemn all homosexual behaviour, nor can it approve all heterosexual activity. The Church is called to support lesbians and gay men in their desire to enter and sustain bonds of faithful relationships and to acknowledge the part it has played in creating an environment in which homosexual people are the victims of injustice. The report was not accepted by the Presbyterian Church's governing body.

A report from a working party of the central committee of the Church and Society Department of the United Reformed Church (UK) in the early 1990s, which has no official status, acknowledged that to a large extent the debate about homosexuality in the Church was built upon and symptomatic of a debate on the nature of biblical authority. However, the working party was 'not prepared to describe homosexual activity as intrinsically sinful in principle',[55] recognizing that homosexual relationships were capable of manifesting the same qualities as the best marriages. 'Our instinct is to affirm grace against law as a general rule, to take the risks of acceptance rather than those of rejection, to seek for humility rather than a righteousness tending towards self-righteousness.'[56]

This third approach has yet to be officially accepted by any but a handful of churches. One of these is the Universal Fellowship of Metropolitan Community Churches which was founded in 1968 by a gay Pentecostal minister, Troy Perry, in Los Angeles as a church for lesbians and gay men. One of the fastest growing churches in the world, its stance on homosexuality coupled with its willingness to re-examine Christianity from a non-homophobic, non-patriarchal point of view has made it increasingly attractive to a large numbers of heterosexuals as well.

7.7 LESBIAN AND GAY THEOLOGY

One of the most interesting developments around the issue of homosexuality and Christianity has been the emergence (beginning in the early 1980s) of **lesbian and gay theology**. Lesbian and gay people, tired of waiting for the churches to make up their minds on the moral status of their lives and inspired by the insights and methodologies of **liberation** and **feminist theologies**, have begun to break free of their dependence upon the churches. Recognizing that much of Christian theology has been built upon **heteropatriarchy**, they have sought to do theology instead on the basis of their own experience. Lesbian theologians have built up a sexual ethic around the concept of friendship (see **3.8**), arguing that this not only reflects the way in which lesbians understand their relationships but also stands in complete conformity to the gospel where friendship and not marriage is held up as the primary relationship.[57]

Robert Goss has argued that it was not Jesus' maleness that made him the Christ but his practice of solidarity with the oppressed. In the resurrection God affirms the validity of Jesus' life and message. At Easter Jesus becomes the 'Queer Christ', for if Christ does stand in solidarity with the oppressed then he must stand in solidarity with lesbian and gay people. At Easter Jesus comes out of the closet and becomes queer by virtue of being in solidarity with 'queers'. Note that this is not to say that Jesus of Nazareth was gay, although the gospel stories indicate that it is impossible to fit him into the modern construction of heterosexuality. To say that Christ is queer is to say that God identifies with lesbian and gay people and their experiences of injustice.

If Jesus the Christ is not queer, then his *basileia*[58] message of solidarity is irrelevant. If the Christ is not queer, the gospel is no longer good news but oppressive news for queers. If the Christ is not queer, then the **incarnation** has no meaning for our sexuality.[59]

Other lesbian and gay scholars have questioned the Church's knee-jerk idealization of monogamy (see **3.9**), noting that, for many, so-called 'casual sex' can be grace-filled and community-building.[60] So far the church governing bodies have studiously avoided interacting with the growing body of lesbian and gay theology and **spirituality** but it is clear that if the debate is to move out of stalemate they are going to have to.

7.8 TRANSVESTISM AND TRANSSEXUALITY

In truth these two topics do not belong in this chapter because, although they are associated in the popular mind with homosexuality, they are to be found among people of all sexual orientations. However since in recent years the concept of 'queer' has been developed to group together all those who challenge hetero-patriarchy, it is appropriate that these topics should be considered here. It should be noted that both these groups are often the victims of prejudice from within the lesbian and gay communities.

Transvestites are (usually) men (gay, straight and bisexual) who find sexual and emotional satisfaction in dressing in the clothes of the opposite sex. They never figure in church documents. Nothing perhaps reveals better how similar our culture is to the ancient Israelite culture of the priestly writers' vision. We continue to invest with tremendous meaning not only biological sexual differences, but also clothes. We still have notions of 'women's clothes' and 'men's clothes'. When a man wears 'women's clothes' we think there is something wrong, something dirty and unclean about him. He is likely to be the object of ridicule, marginalization and violence, and seen as a traitor to his sex. He cannot be a 'true' man. Yet if we are right that Christianity is essentially subversive of gender divisions and notions of purity the experience of transvestites should not be a problem to Christians. In any case there is a long and venerable tradition of saintly transvestism including St Joan, and a host of other female saints who assumed the dress of men in order to enter monasteries. Many outside the Church regard clerical dress as 'feminine' and therefore funny. In many cultures transvestites who enter homosexual relationships are accepted and regarded as having particular spiritual gifts, for example the berdache in Native American cultures.

Transsexuals are men and women, of all sexual orientations, who believe that they are trapped in the body of the wrong sex. Their bodies do not match the gender they feel themselves to be. Many now seek operations to transform their bodies into ones approximating to those of the opposite sex. Once again they are virtually ignored by the churches, dismissed as sick, unfortunate anomalies. We have to ask to what extent a transsexual's dilemma is caused by the rigid gender divisions that society (with the help of the Church) perpetuates. Yet whilst we do live in such a dualistic structure, people who do not conform to the role that their sex is supposed to play are always going to feel uncomfortable and often completely alienated from their sex, and the Church should support their right to alter their bodies in order that they might flourish. Some transsexuals find a family resemblance between themselves and eunuchs, who though reviled in ancient society are promised inclusion in the Kingdom of God (Matthew 19.10–12; Isaiah 56.3–5; Acts 8.26–40).

7.9 SUMMARY

In this chapter the complex and divisive issue of homosexuality has been examined from the perspective of the three most common church responses to it. The 'moral evil' and 'falling short' approaches have been shown to be extremely weak theologically and logically and to be highly dependent upon a view of reality which the gospel itself may challenge. In particular we have drawn attention to the patriarchal basis of the theory of complementarity upon which both responses are based. We have also drawn attention to the failure of both to acknowledge the cultural nature of homosexuality and the hermeneutical problems involved in 'reading off' a Christian attitude to homosexuality from a few scriptural texts. We have also drawn attention to a third approach to homosexuality which involves privileging the experience and theological reflection of those who live out the issue in their bodies and communities — lesbian and gay people themselves. Feminists are beginning to discern what a non-patriarchal Christianity will look like, lesbian and gay scholars are attempting to fashion a non-homophobic faith. Passionate ethics is both non-patriarchal and non-homophobic. Finally we have attempted to reflect theologically upon the situation of those whom most Churches choose studiously to ignore — bisexual, transvestite and **transgendered** persons. We have suggested that they may be so ignored because in their own persons they challenge so many of the 'foundations' and assumptions upon which the current debate around homosexuality is built. Passionate ethics will seek to privilege the insights and experiences of people so brutally marginalized.

Notes

1 Division for Church in Society, Department of Studies of the Evangelical Lutheran Church in America, *The Church and Human Sexuality: A Lutheran Perspective* (Minneapolis: ELCA Distribution Service, 1993), first draft.

2 Michel Foucault, *The History of Sexuality: Volume 1, An Introduction* (Harmondsworth: Penguin Books, 1981).

3 Alfred Kinsey *et al.*, *Sexual Behaviour in the Human Male* (Philadelphia: W. B. Saunders Co., 1948).

4 *Catechism of the Catholic Church* (London: Geoffrey Chapman, 1994), para. 2357, pp. 504–5.

5 See for example, Social Welfare Commission of the Catholic Bishops of England and Wales, *An Introduction to the Pastoral Care of Homosexual People* (London, 1979), and the National Conference of Catholic Bishops (USA), *To Live in Christ Jesus* (Washington, DC: United States Catholic Conference, 1976). Both sets of bishops have in the 1990s reaffirmed the stance they took in their documents of the 1970s, which has been interpreted by some as a veiled gesture of dissent from the Vatican's 1986 letter.

6 Congregation for the Doctrine of the Faith, *Letter to the Bishops of the Catholic Church on the Pastoral Care of Homosexual Persons* (London: Catholic Truth Society, 1986), para. 3.

7 *Ibid.*, paras 6–7.

8 *Ibid.*, para. 10.

9 Karl Barth, *Church Dogmatics* (Edinburgh: T. & T. Clark, 1961), Part 3, vol. 4, pp. 164–6.

10 John Giles Milhaven, 'Homosexuality and love' in Edward Batchelor, Jr, *Homosexuality and Ethics* (New York: Pilgrim Press, 1980), p. 67.

11 Gareth Moore, *The Body in Context: Sex and Catholicism* (London: SCM Press, 1992), p. 66.

12 *Ibid.*

13 *Ibid.*, p. 71.

14 *Ibid.*, p. 33.

15 *Ibid.*, pp. 85–6.

16 Michael Vasey, *Strangers and Friends: A New Exploration of Homosexuality and the Bible* (London: Hodder and Stoughton, 1995), p. 49.

17 Moore, *The Body in Context*, pp. 78–81.

18 *Ibid.*, p. 198.

19 Elizabeth Moberly, *Homosexuality: A New Christian Ethic* (Cambridge: James Clarke, 1983).

20 Gerd Bratenberg, *What Comes Naturally* (London: The Women's Press, 1987), pp. 31–3.

21 Moore, *The Body in Context*, p. 203.

22 Alison Webster, *Found Wanting: Women, Christianity and Sexuality* (London: Cassell, 1995), p. 20.

23 Thatcher, *Liberating Sex*, p. 132.

24 Stuart, *Just Good Friends*, pp. 126–37.

25 John Boswell, *The Marriage of Likeness* (London: HarperCollins, 1995), also published as *Same-Sex Unions in Premodern Europe* (New York: Villiard Books, 1994).

26 Margaret Bradman, 'The Bible and homosexuality' in Cristina Sumner, *Reconsider: A Response to 'Issues in Human Sexuality' and a Plea to the Church to Deal Boldly with Sexual Ethics* (London: Lesbian and Gay Christian Movement, 1995), p. 3.

27 Moore, *The Body in Context*, p. 40.

28 William Countryman, *Dirt, Greed and Sex: Sexual Ethics in the New Testament and Their Implications for Today* (London: SCM Press, 1989).

29 For the opposite assumption, see The Methodist Church, *Report of Commission on Human Sexuality* (Peterborough: Methodist Publishing House, 1990), paras 84, 88.

30 A. Thatcher, *Liberating Sex: A Christian Sexual Theology* (London: SPCK, 1993), pp. 22–7.

31 South African Anglican Theological Commission, *The Church and Human Sexuality* (Marshalltown, South Africa, 1995), p. 9.

32 *Ibid.*, p. 22.

33 Charles E. Curran, 'Homosexuality and moral theology: methodological and substantive considerations', in Batchelor, *Homosexuality and Ethics*, pp. 89–95.

34 Helmut Thielicke, 'The theologicoethical aspect of homosexuality', in Batchelor, *Homosexuality and Ethics*, p. 100.

35 *Ibid.*, p. 101.

36 House of Bishops of the General Synod of the Church of England, *Issues in Human Sexuality* (London: Church House Publishing, 1991), para. 2:5, p. 7.

37 *Ibid.*, para. 2:29, p. 18.

38 *Ibid.*, para. 4:14, p. 36.

39 *Ibid.*, para. 5:6, p. 41.

40 Moore, *The Body in Context*, p. 29.

41 *Ibid.*, p. 123.

42 *Ibid.*, pp. 128–9.

43 Vasey, *Strangers and Friends*, p. 117.

44 Neale Secor, 'A brief for a new homosexual ethic', in Batchelor, *Homosexuality and Ethics*, p. 157.

45 Webster, *Found Wanting*, p. 12.

46 Huseyin Tapnic, 'Masculinity, femininity, and Turkish male homosexuality', in Ken Plummer, *Modern Homosexualities: Fragments of Lesbian and Gay Experience* (London: Routledge, 1992), p. 40.

47 *Ibid.*, p. 27.

48 Tom Driver, 'The contemporary and Christian contexts', in Batchelor, *Homosexuality and Ethics*, p. 18.

49 *Issues in Human Sexuality*, para. 5:8, p. 42.

50 Vasey, *Strangers and Friends*, pp. 80–112.

51 H. Kimball Jones, 'Toward a Christian understanding of the homosexual', in Batchelor, *Homosexuality and Ethics*, p. 112.

52 Alastair Heron, 'Towards a Christian view of sex', in Batchelor, *Homosexuality and Ethics*, p. 137.

53 *Keeping Body and Soul Together*, p. 98.

54 *Ibid.*, p. 105.

55 Homosexuality Working Party, *Homosexuality: A Christian View* (London: United Reformed Church, n.d.), p. 5.

56 *Ibid.*, p. 6.

57 E. Stuart, *Just Good Friends: Towards a Lesbian and Gay Theology of Relationships* (London: Mowbray, 1995); Mary Hunt, *Fierce Tenderness: A Feminist Theology of Friendship* (New York: Crossroad, 1991); and Carter Heyward, *Touching Our Strength: The Erotic as Power and the Love of God* (San Francisco: Harper & Row, 1989).

58 *Basileia* is the Greek word usually translated as 'kingdom' or 'reign of God' in the Gospels.

59 Robert Goss, *Jesus Acted Up: A Gay and Lesbian Manifesto* (San Francisco: Harper-SanFrancisco, 1993), p. 85.

60 See for example, Sean Gill, 'Odd but not queer: English liberal Protestant theologies of human sexuality and the gay paradigm', *Theology and Sexuality*, no. 3 (September 1995), pp. 48–57, and Kathy Rudy, ' "Where two or more are gathered": using gay communities as a model for Christian sexual ethics', *Theology and Sexuality*, no. 4 (March 1996), pp. 81–99.

Suggestions for further reading

John Boswell, *The Marriage of Likeness* (London: HarperCollins, 1995), also published as *Same-Sex Unions in Premodern Europe* (New York: Villiard Books, 1994).

Robert Goss, *Jesus Acted Up: A Gay and Lesbian Manifesto* (San Francisco: HarperSan-Francisco, 1993).

Jeffrey S. Siker, *Homosexuality in the Church: Both Sides of the Debate* (Louisville, KY: Westminster/John Knox Press, 1994).

Elizabeth Stuart, *Just Good Friends: Towards a Lesbian and Gay Theology of Relationships* (London: Mowbray, 1995).

Michael Vasey, *Strangers and Friends: A New Exploration of Homosexuality and the Bible* (London: Hodder and Stoughton, 1995).

8

DESIRE

Contemporary Christians inherit a tradition which has at best been highly suspicious of **desire**, yet modern **feminist theology** has been engaged in the process of the redemption of desire. Can that which has been seen as the ultimate stumbling block to salvation become the royal road to God and the centre of theological discourse?

8.1 DESIRE AS PERVERSION

'Any account of desire, transgression, and deviation repeatedly encounters Augustine.'[1] We have already touched upon Augustine's understanding of desire (see above, **4.3**). For Augustine the tragedy of the **fall** was that disobedience resulted in more disobedience. Adam and Eve had disobeyed God and henceforth their children were ridden by the inability to obey. **Concupiscence** — 'the spontaneous desire for material or sensual satisfaction'[2] — is the cause and effect of original sin and infects us all by virtue of the fact that we came into existence through it. Christians have disagreed over whether the original sin was concupiscence or not. The Reformers argued that it was, the Catholic Church that it was lack of righteousness and holiness. It was important from the Catholic perspective to explain why concupiscence persists even amongst those who have been saved.

In any case, as a result of original sin, for Augustine and the Church which he influenced so remarkably, the human self is fractured by a disobedient will. Death is closely linked with desire in Augustine's thought, for it is the perversion of the will to desire to do wrong that brings death into the world. So depraved are our souls that we love to do evil for its own sake. Augustine's own teenage years taught him this. He felt himself 'driven' by 'impulses' which led him, among other things, to shake fruit off a pear tree at night with friends: 'My desire was to enjoy not what I sought by stealing but merely the excitement of thieving and doing what was wrong.'[3] Kenneth Burke has argued that in this incident Augustine detected a perfect parody or perversion of his conversion. It was a free or gracious act committed with no motive except the desire to do it. As such it is similar to and yet stands in stark contrast to God's creation and redemption which is motiveless. It was performed in company with a group of friends who were intent on wickedness, which is a parody of the fellowship of the Church.[4]

For Augustine the evil which comes into the world with desire is essentially the privation of good, but evil is certainly real and exercises force in the world. Privation involves the loss of what one ought to be and do. The concept of privation is closely related to that of **natural law** (see **2.3**). It is not therefore a privation that a cat cannot write or a word processor dance. It is a privation that rational human beings are incapable of acting rationally. Nothing is evil of itself (and this includes desire) but everything can be perverted. Perversion and privation are closely connected: 'Perversion becomes the negative agency within, at the heart of privation. Perversion thus mediates between evil as agency and evil as lack.'[5] Desire is perverted by selfishness and therefore becomes an experience of the absence of God, the ultimate good.

As Dollimore points out, Augustine's rejection of Manichaean **dualism** led him to locate evil within humanity itself and therefore the human self must be unceasingly policed.[6] The close proximity of evil or vice, to virtue, the former only being the perversion of the latter, makes them barely distinguishable in the fallen world. A realization of this close proximity will and should engender enormous fear of perversion. 'It is a perspective whose complex inheritance will help identify the sexual pervert as a modern incarnation of evil, the more dangerous for having been, before disclosure, indistinguishable from us.'[7]

The fate of humankind after the fall is to trudge back to the God from whom we have been diverted. Our wills must be realigned, refocused on what is higher rather than what is lower. This is why Augustine, and Aquinas who came after him, advocated the ideal of **celibacy** (see **3.10**). Sexual desire for both of them was the most obnoxious and least controllable form of concupiscence, for it assumes power not only over the whole body, and not only from outside, but also internally; and it disturbs the whole man, when the mental emotion combines and mingles with the physical craving, resulting in a pleasure surpassing all physical delights. So intense is the pleasure that when it reaches its climax there is almost total extinction of mental alertness; the intellectual sentries, as it were, are overwhelmed.

Notice here how the language of power (see Chapter 5) is used. **Lust** overpowers the human mind and drags the whole of ourselves down into the lower realm of the body, where focusing on higher things becomes impossible. This is what is so objectionable about sexual desire for Augustine. Augustine's discourse on desire is built upon a whole range of questionable dualistic assumptions: that God is absent in the experience of passion; that the mind and body are respectively higher and lower realms of being; that desire and will are mutually exclusive. As Gareth Moore has pointed out, desire is never beyond reason. If we do not think about God when having sex or listening to music or reading a book it is because we do not want to. We make a decision to give ourselves over to the intensity of the pleasure, to become absolutely absorbed in something because that increases the pleasure of doing it, but that does not mean that we are out of control, that we cannot think straight. Aquinas conceded this point when he stated that 'it is not contrary to reason if the act of thinking is sometimes interrupted by something which is done in accordance with reason'.[9] It is perfectly reasonable to be absorbed in another person if you love them, indeed, it is a condition of love that you are so. Love requires attention.

However, the influence of Augustine and Aquinas on subsequent Christian thought should not be underestimated. Thereafter desire was regarded as a subversive, destabilizing force. Male **sexuality** in particular became essentially an internal struggle between reason and desire, about an internal struggle rather than an external relationship. Desires needed to be suppressed, mastered and controlled and this internal struggle for control was acted out in male attempts to master others who represented the bodily and the sexual — women. Even though the idealization of celibacy was rejected by the Reformers, on the grounds that it was unbiblical and actually led to immorality, the legacy of Augustine and Aquinas lived on because the Reformers tended to promote marriage as the remedy for the sin of fornication and the means of producing holy seed. We have already noted (see **3.4**) that 'personal union' as a permissible meaning of marriage is recent, especially in the Roman Catholic Church.

8.2 DESIRE IN THE BIBLE

Augustine's construction of desire has no echoes in the Hebrew scriptures, where within the constraints of the two-pronged ethic of **purity** and **property** (see **1.7**, **1.8**) sexual desire is understood to be perfectly good and God-given. In the Hebrew scriptures, as in the writings of St Paul, there is no intimation of the later Christian view that sexual desire even within marriage was undesirable and sinful unless it led to reproduction and the containment of lust. But of course, like everything else in the Hebrew scriptures, desire is constructed in a **patriarchal** context. **Mutuality** is not part of the vision for desire except in one place — the Song of Songs (see **5.12**). This love poem, which is probably constructed out of a collection of various poems, dates in its final form to the post-exilic period. There are strong reasons for attributing female authorship to the poem, which may explain its radically different approach to the relationship between men and women.[10] The poem takes the form of a dialogue between a man and a 'black and beautiful' woman. Yet it was precisely because of its explicitly sexual nature that the poem nearly did not make it into the canon. That it did was due to the passionate pleading of Rabbi Akiva. He is said to have declared that 'All the ages are not worth the day on which the Song of Songs was given to Israel; for all the writings are holy, but the Song of Songs is the Holy of Holies.'[11] His argument was that the Song was in fact an allegory of the love between Israel and her God. First Judaism and then Christianity, as if they did not know how to handle a sacred book which revolved around humanity and not God (God is barely mentioned in the poem, a point we shall return to), and humanity in its bodily glory at that, allegorized it into a poetic description of Yahweh's relationship to Israel, Christ's to his Church, his consecrated virgin or to the Virgin Mary.

However, few scholars would now accept that the Song was written as an allegory. The woman is the main speaker, although it is difficult at times to tell who is speaking and, contrary to popular assumption, there is 'no indication that the male–female relationship described in the book is marital'.[12] Some scholars regard the Song as a deliberate subversion of the story of Eden. Phyllis Trible argues that 'The Song of Songs redeems a love story gone awry.'[13]

> We are presented with a garden that is not closed and barred, that
> is not a realm of delights from which we are expelled and over
> which for ever watches a cherubim with flaming sword to guard the
> way to the tree of life. Rather, this garden is open ... (4.16) ...
> There is no expulsion here; no constraint or curse in the Song; no
> taint or shame. The nakedness is not covered although neither is it
> unaware. In this garden of desire the fall is not our inevitable
> ancient memory. The garden is still that place of almost unutter-
> able beauty but we may walk within it.[14]

In Genesis the man seeks out the woman, leaving his home to do so,
far away from the sacred tree; in the Song the woman does the
seeking and takes her beloved back to the tree beneath which he was
born and to her own mother's house. Indeed, their relationship itself
is described in terms of a garden and fruit tree. Their embodied
passion is the tree and fruit of life. The fact that it is extremely
difficult to tell whether the man or woman is speaking in several
places demonstrates how little the constraints of patriarchy impose
themselves in this work. Fertility is not a concern of the Song; instead
it revolves around desire and the quest for its fulfilment. The woman
sets out actively to seek her beloved although she recognizes in a
dream sequence the dangers of her activity, for the sentinels who
find her in the streets beat and strip her (5.7), and her brothers,
angry with her subversive behaviour, make her keeper of the vine-
yards (1.6). The Song shudders with passionate imagery, glories in
the beauty of the body and the glory is mutual.

Heather Walton argues that the subversiveness of the Song even
undermines those who would hold it up as a legitimation of **heterosexual** relationships:

> The love is certainly heterosexual, there is no question of this, but
> not straight in a straightforward sort of way. The lovers are more
> than lovers, they are, or seek to be, brother and sister. They are, or
> seek to be, twins ... The paradigm in the Song is not a continued
> supposed **complementarity** of two binary opposite sexes but of an
> integration or even disintegration of gendered selves. The lovers
> frequently eat each other, pass into each other, echo each other
> and an illustration of this is the fact that scholars have disagreed
> over which lover is speaking when ... The binary opposite pre-
> suppositions of heterosexuality are not the rules of this game and
> when those binary opposites are so confounded heterosexuality
> becomes a redundant category.[15]

There may well be echoes of a desire to return to the pregendered

state of the first earth creature *hä'ädäm* (Genesis 2.7 and 5.1–2).[16]
But the Song recognizes the threatening nature of this gloriously free
female sexuality. The brothers and 'sentinels' cannot cope with it.
They either put her to work or humiliate her, they punish her and
even her beloved cannot always bear it: 'Turn away your eyes from
me, for they overwhelm me!' (6.5). As Walton notes, like the ancient
symbols of female power Kali and Isis, the woman in the Song is
beautiful, black, terrible, suffering and seductive. The Song of Songs
is the closest the Hebrew scriptures come to presenting us with a just,
equal and mutual passionate relationship between a man and a
woman but it is not naïve in its presentation of the subversive nature
of that desire.

One of the most interesting aspects of the Song of Songs is the
apparent absence of God. There may be one tiny explicit reference
to the deity which is easy to miss, particularly in English translation.
It comes in 8.6. The RSV renders this verse as follows:

> Set me as a seal upon your heart,
> as a seal upon your arm;
> for love is strong as death,
> passion fierce as the grave.
> Its flashes are flashes of fire,
> a raging flame.

In ancient Israel death and *sheol*, 'the grave', were often personified
as unrelenting, inescapable powers, so to compare love and passion
to these powers is to convey something about their depth and
intensity. In speaking of the fire-like qualities of love the Hebrew uses
the term *šalhebetyâ* which means 'a flame of *yah*' or 'Yahweh flame'. It
is unclear whether the term is comparing the love to the fire of the
deity or whether their love is regarded as being part of Yahweh's
burning love, but at least one scholar seems to prefer the latter
option.[17] If that is so, then God is everywhere in this poem, not as an
overpowering puppet-master presence, demanding central stage,
but as pulsating, longing, desperate and dangerous passion that is
summoned up between these people. This understanding of sexual
desire is the complete antithesis of Augustine's. Desire is not anti-
God but an experience of God. This is a common theme throughout
all the accounts of relationships within the Hebrew scriptures that
are not concerned with fertility.

The Song of Songs does not just celebrate desire, it celebrates what
within a patriarchal context would be labelled subversive desire. It is

impossible to read the history of the people of Israel as told in the Hebrew scriptures without noticing that sexual subversion is a consistent theme. Often, the breaking of laws and taboos is crucial in ensuring the survival and prosperity of the people of Israel. In the book of Ruth, for example, Ruth the Moabite, a member of a people which according to Genesis 19.30–38 was the product of an incestuous relationship between Lot and one of his daughters, and according to Deuteronomy 23.3–4 should not be allowed into the 'congregation of the Lord', manages to secure the birth of a baby who will be King David's grandfather by defying expected roles and customs; she transgresses the law by uncovering the 'feet' (a euphemism for genitals) of her father-in-law's relation Boaz, in conspiracy with her Israelite mother-in-law Naomi. Even the levirate law which Ruth was endeavouring to fulfil, the law which decreed that the brother of a man who dies childless should marry his widow in order to ensure the continuation of his brother's name, is a violation of the incest laws found in the book of Leviticus (18.16; 20.21).

A similar story is found in Genesis 38 in the story of Tamar who, when one of her deceased husband's brothers refuses to fulfil his obligation towards her and the other is not forced to do so by his father despite his promise to ensure this, disguises herself as a prostitute and sleeps with her father-in-law. When she reveals herself, her father-in-law declares that 'She is more right than I, since I did not give her to my son Shelah' (38.26). Tamar gives birth to twins, one of whom, Perez, becomes an ancestor of David. King Solomon is born out of the adulterous and murderous union between David and Bathsheba (2 Samuel 11 and 12). The Hebrew scriptures are littered with stories that demonstrate Yahweh's purposes being forwarded by deliberate floutings of sexual convention and law — law which it was believed had come from the deity. David Biale, commenting on the many stories which involve incest, notes,

> All of these stories no doubt preceded the Levitical incest laws by many centuries; what is therefore noteworthy is that they were included in the biblical text. The authors or editors who produced the text were surely aware of the flagrant contradictions between the laws and the narratives, but they must have seen those contradictions as serving an important cultural function. The creation of the Israelite nation was seen by these later authors as a result of the suspension of conventions, a sign, perhaps, of divine favour for a ragtag, ethically mixed people. Far from a disgrace to be hidden, sexual subversion, like the repeated preference for younger over

older sons, hints at the unexpected character of God's covenant with Israel.[18]

And in all of these stories God's presence is not explicit: 'It is as if God must step backstage in order to make space for human actors, and particularly women, to bend social custom and law ... God's absence implicitly sanctions these inversions and subversions.'[19] Once again the idea that God might be in the midst of or at least sanctioning subversive desire would have been anathema to Augustine.

'Yahweh is between you and me forever' Jonathan declares to David (1 Samuel 20.42). Whether the relationship between David and Jonathan was sexual or not is a matter of heated debate but their passion for one another which surpassed that for women (2 Samuel 1.25–26) was regarded as being dangerously subversive by Saul. They are portrayed as understanding God as existing in the midst of their passion for one another as did the lovers of the Song of Songs. Notice that this understanding of desire is only present in relationships which are subversive, it is not reflected in the accounts of marriage. Could it be that this is because in the lovers of the Song of Songs and David and Jonathan we have examples of love based upon mutuality? It is this understanding of desire that has been redeemed by feminist theologians seeking to untangle the dualistic net that has been woven by Christian theology around sexuality.

8.3 DESIRE AND THEOLOGY

María Clara Bingemer, a Brazilian feminist theologian, has argued that the redemption of the body and desire as a locus for revelation and theological reflection is perfectly consistent with the Christian assertion that 'God is love' (1 John 4.8). Indeed,

> If this is so, in the beginning God can only be the object of desire — not of necessity nor of rationality. Theology — which seeks to be reflection and talk about God and God's word — must therefore be moved and permeated in its entirety by the flame of desire ... Born of desire, theology exists as theology only if it is upheld and supported by desire.[20]

Rigorous rational analysis certainly has its vital place in theological discourse but its purpose is to reflect upon the desire, not to tame or suffocate it. For Freud, whose influence upon modern understandings of sexuality cannot be underestimated, our subjectivity (i.e., our sense of self) is born out of desire, the drive for life that propels our search for sex, for food, for everything. Christians would want to add that our desire for God is also, so to speak, 'inbuilt'. Our unconscious is the realm of desire and no attempts by our conscious reason, influenced by our parents, our society, our religion, etc. to suppress it, will succeed. It will speak to us in dreams or mental or physical disorders. Desire will out. Since the 1980s lesbian feminist theologians in particular have been developing a theology born of desire, or as they commonly term it, **eros**.

8.3.1 Bodily knowledge

The black lesbian feminist Audre Lorde was among the first to reclaim eros from the hands of men, where it has been made into 'the confused, the trivial, the psychotic, the plasticized sensation'. She re-membered and redefined it as deep knowledge of a capacity for joy, for satisfaction, a drive towards self-fulfilment. It is that which reveals what is possible, what ecstatic pleasure is available to us.[21] It is not a rational knowledge but a deep bodily knowledge.

> The considered phrase, 'It feels right to me', acknowledges the strength of the erotic into a true knowledge, for what that means and feels is the first and most powerful guiding light toward any understanding. And understanding is a handmaiden that can only wait upon, or clarify, that knowledge, deeply born. The erotic is the nurturer or nursemaid of all our deepest knowledge.[22]

Eros for Lorde includes sexual desire but cannot be limited to it. It is as evident in the writing of a book or the building of a bookcase as it is in making love.

8.3.2 Yearning for mutuality

The person who has done most theological reflection upon this understanding of desire is the lesbian theologian Carter Heyward. For Heyward eros is our desire for mutuality, for right relationship with one another, which is expressed perhaps most obviously in sexual attraction and intimacy but also in many other ways. Heyward identifies erotic power with the divine who urges towards right-relationship in a context riddled with **structural sin**.[23] Heyward thereby avoids one of the problems with Lorde's description of the erotic, which is the assumption that this power, this knowledge, is inherent in every woman, waiting to be uncovered like a long-forgotten treasure. This ignores the fact that we are interdependent. We have the terrifying power to create one another. We love because we are first loved. For most of us this does not come 'naturally', because we are brought up in the context of broken relationships — not only in our immediate family environment but also in the outside world. Rita Nakashima Brock uses the **metaphor** of the heart for the human self and describes most of us as 'broken-hearted', our hearts broken by our earliest relationships, by patriarchy, by racism or classism, by rejection and abuse in our later relationships. Erotic love bursts into the midst of this wrong-relation and calls forth in us a sense of connection, a yearning for mutuality and justice in *all* of our relationships.

8.3.3 Anger

Having been touched by the erotic we will then also become angry. Anger or rage is a deep physical reaction to the disconnection, injustice, violence and wrong relationship in our world. It is the pain of disconnection when we have known connection. Anger is

> a feeling-signal that all is not well in our relation to other persons or groups or to the world around us. Anger is a mode of connectedness to others and it is always a vivid form of caring. To put the point another way: anger is — and it always is — a sign of some resistance in ourselves to the moral quality of the social relations in which we are immersed. Extreme or intense anger signals a deep reaction to the action upon us or toward others to whom we are related ... Where anger rises, there the energy to act is present.[24]

Anger is an expression of love, hatred is an expression of absence of love. Hatred is the pain of disconnection when we have not known connection. Where there is only disconnection, connection is to be feared, the 'other' becomes a threat, one's own self becomes a threat, one fears being engulfed, being out of control, being taken over. Hatred is something to be overcome through the binding up of the broken-hearted. Anger is something to welcome and own, for it is our motivation to change the world. Mary Daly has put it well: 'Rage is not a stage. It is not something to be gotten over. It is a transformative, focusing force.'[25]

8.3.4 Embodiment

Eros reminds us of our own embodiment and the importance of embodying love. Studies have shown that infants deprived of touch are much more prone to death than those who are held, cuddled and generally warmly touched.[26] Generations of children in the United States and Europe were brought up with child manuals which discouraged parents from touching children. Morton and Barbara Kelsey believed that 'One of the reasons that sexual problems are so prevalent in much of Western society is the lack of warmth, affection and touch that we have received and that our parents and grandparents have received before us.'[27] The welcome exposure of the extent of child sexual abuse (see above, **5.10**) has, however, escalated into a panic to the point that we are in danger of making adults so frightened of touching children for fear of being accused of assault that the only touch some children will experience is the touch of pain and violation. Jesus is portrayed in the Gospels as one who touches, who heals through touch, who brings salvation to people through touch. His touch was healing because it was a just touch, a touch that reaches out of a yearning for mutuality. And those whom he touches, particularly women, respond by touching him back — anointing him with oil (Mark 14.3–4), responding to his needs. Eros is a feeling which reminds us of our physicality because it is experienced physically. In the Gospels a word often translated as 'moved with pity' or 'moved with compassion', or sometimes 'moved with anger', when referring to Jesus, literally refers to a person's bowels or entrails turning over. This is what we experience with eros — a connection deep within our bodies. It propels us out towards other bodies.

8.3.5 Play

Another element of eros is play. Western culture does not value play for adults. The capitalist work ethic teaches us that everything we do must produce some kind of good or it is suspect, indulgent, 'wicked'. Play, if it is for anything, is for children, they are allowed to do things just for the fun of it, to experiment, fantasize, pretend, imagine. Most of us were never as creative as when we were children, never as curious, never as open to different possibilities, never as connected with the rest of creation. Suddenly we are expected to grow out of all this. The power of the erotic is the power of play, of taking delight in doing and enjoying things in their own right, of

letting the imagination roam, of enjoying the being of another
which is essential if we are to flourish as human beings (see **7.2**).

A serious criticism of erotic theology has come from **Asian feminist
theologians**. Kwok Pui-Lan points out that the language of the erotic
may be a safe and exciting language for white North American and
European women but it is not necesarily so for Asian women:

> Asian women find it embarrassing to talk about **sex** and the erotic
> not only because decent women are not supposed to raise those
> issues in public, but also because many of our sisters are working as
> prostitutes in the hotels, nightclubs, bars, disco joints and cocktail
> lounges in the big cities like Manila, Bangkok, Taipei, Hong Kong,
> and Seoul.[28]

In view of this some feminist theologians have substituted the language of 'passion' for the language of the erotic. Their use of
'passion' accords with our own reasons for calling this book *People of
Passion* (see **1.5**) and advocating 'passionate ethics' (see Chapter 2).
The language of passion serves both to avoid a simplistic identification between the desire being described and sex, and to convey
something of the tragic dimension that is always involved in attempts
to love in a situation of structural sin. For we love in a context of
structured alienation — economic, sexual, racial, religious alienation. We have been formed in that context and we learn to relate in
a context in which sex, love and the erotic are constructed in terms of
domination and submission, of 'power-over' instead of 'power-with'
(see **5.2**). We are not taught to find equality or mutuality erotic. All
this and more conspires to prevent us relating justly with one another.
Our minds are so colonized by patriarchy that we are inevitably going
to stumble and fail in our struggle towards mutuality in our own
relationships. The 'passion of Christ', a phrase which includes both
his suffering and his love (see **1.5**) also reminds us that failure and
tragedy is part of the project of love, but it is not the last word.

8.4 DESIRE AND SIN

8.4.1 The social construction of desire

Part of the tragedy and joy of being human is that we are fundamentally relational. We are formed by our relationships, and not only our
immediate relationships (see above, **2.1**). We are influenced by the
society in which we live and the values it projects. To a large extent
desire is socially constructed, we are taught what and whom to desire.

Foucault famously revealed how much desires are created, classified and then policed by powerful social institutions. Men and women are taught what to desire and how to make themselves desirable through a mass of different media. In a capitalist society desire becomes part of the economic machine — we are persuaded to buy literally into a whole package of goods that will in some way consummate a desire that has been created for us and imposed upon us. Desire has then become a package of created artefacts which pass for true identity.

Capitalism depends upon our desire for goods which in turn create a new set of desires which we are led to believe will bestow happiness upon us. Herbert Marcuse, whilst drawing attention to the way in which capitalism restricts desire, pointed out that the liberalization of sex did not lead to the freedom of desire, on the contrary it simply became commodified and used to maintain capitalism. It is interesting that in the **gay** and **lesbian** communities liberation has come to a large extent to be measured by the number of bars, shops, restaurants, even gay villages that exist. At the moment there is a lot of talk in the USA and Northern Europe about the power of the 'pink pound' as a means of buying liberation. Is this liberation or simply a limited amount of freedom within an ultimately oppressive system?

Rosemary Radford Ruether has noted that the social construction of desire is manifest in many different ways. We are programmed to desire people of the 'right' **gender**, class, race and culture.[29] When we find ourselves desiring the 'wrong' type of people we may be filled with disgust and we will certainly be regarded as socially deviant and treated accordingly. Sue George has drawn attention to the way in which the 'naturalizing' of heterosexual desire serves patriarchy and capitalism:

> Far from having arisen 'naturally' the widespread desire for one's 'own' supposedly freely-chosen spouse, own children, own home, has been relentlessly orchestrated and marketed for the benefit of capitalist society: families bond together and consume. The pressure to live in a traditional family unit is also enforced at a practical level: the organisation of housing and economics makes it much easier in our society to live as part of a nuclear family.[30]

Recognition of the social construction of desire and the use of desire to bolster systems which may be ultimately oppressive should make Christians extremely suspicious of claims that certain forms of desire are 'unnatural' or 'natural'. Passionate ethics focuses not on such issues but the justice, mutuality and equality that is expressed in a relationship (see **2.12**). Desire is judged by its fruits. However, to judge those fruits justly requires enormous honesty and self-knowledge. It requires self-awareness and scrutiny which the Christian community has a duty to teach. Jonathan Dollimore demonstrates the close link that can exist between subversive sexual desire and deconstruction of other boundaries. T. E. Lawrence in his identification with Arabs and his desire for them rejected colonialism and the racist stereotyping of non-whites as alien, other and therefore dangerous. Yet, as Dollimore acknowledges, that is not just a noble tale of solidarity between black people and gay men. Attraction to the 'other' may just be a sweeter form of racism based upon **objectification** and stereotyping. White, rich European men may find sexual freedom and the consequent release of enormous creative energy by embracing their desire for young Moroccan men (as Gide famously did in 1895 under Wilde's watchful eye), but there is a strong element of colonial exploitation in the process. People's desire is always expressed within the context of a material world. In this world, political and social dynamics are at work. These dynamics cannot be ignored but are often very difficult to see because they are part of the structures under which we live.

8.4.2 Lust

In Matthew's version of the **Sermon on the Mount** Jesus addresses the issue of desire: 'You have heard that it was said, "You shall not commit adultery." But I say to you that everyone who looks at a woman with lust has already committed adultery with her in his heart' (5.27 NRSV). There is a strong tradition within modern Christianity of interpreting these words as condemnation of what in Catholic circles used to be known as 'impure thoughts'. Gareth Moore has challenged this popular reading. He notes first that Jesus is not talking about inward thoughts. He is talking about outward behaviour — looking is a physical act. Most women have to become very used to being looked at lustfully by men, from the schoolgirl who has to pass a group of male contemporaries in the playground to the woman passing the building site, to the woman in the office. Women are scrutinized by men, objectified and assessed from a distance. Such behaviour is obvious, intimidatory and humiliating. Moore also points out that the word translated 'woman' in most versions can also mean 'wife', and indeed in this context it is the most obvious translation since the passage is about adultery. So Jesus' focus may be the desiring of another person's wife. Moore's third point is crucial: it is wrong to impose upon this passage our dualistic distinctions between external action and inward thoughts. He points out that the Greek word *epithumeo* means 'seriously wanting something, setting desire on something, and acting accordingly'.[31] The heart in Hebrew thought was the organ of action. What is in the heart proceeds from it. Jesus is therefore talking about action not imagination, specifically seeking to possess another man's wife. This is not to say that our thoughts are not important. They are important precisely because they are intimately related to how we behave, but this was not what Jesus was concerned with here. He was concerned with lust. Lust is the sin of possessiveness, of treating another person as an object to be used for your own personal gratification (see **5.7**). Lust is the antithesis to mutuality, if mutuality is

> the experience of being in right relation. Mutuality is the sharing of power in such a way that each participant in the relationship is called forth more fully into becoming who she is — a whole person with integrity. Experientially, mutuality is a process, a relational movement. It is not a static place to be, because it grows with/in the relationship. As we are formed by mutuality, so too does the shape of our mutuality change as our lives-in-relation grow.[32]

Lust is desire perverted and thus there is a perilously close relationship between them. Both lust and desire are based on a sense of lack, an acknowledgement of incompleteness. Lust fixes itself on a person and schemes to attain him or her at all costs. The relational web in which both parties exist is ignored or dismissed. Individual satisfaction is made the ultimate concern. The Hebrew scriptures contain many stories of lust in which men use their disproportionate power to possess women. David murders Uriah in order to 'have' Bathsheba (2 Samuel 11). Tamar becomes the violent victim of Amnon's lust (2 Samuel 13.1–22). Two elders try to force themselves upon Susanna (see **5.7**). This is true even when two people lust after each other. Desire also longs for another but within a context of mutuality and the web of relationships in which both exist. Desire does not seek to 'have' another but to let a person 'be' and this may ultimately mean avoiding physical intimacy and letting them go.

8.4.3 Fantasy

What about fantasy/imagination? What is its proper place in our sexual lives? Imagination is the space where we play with ideas and assess whether we should orientate our heart towards them — in other words whether we should do something. We can use our imagination to play around with the possible and impossible in safety and make moral judgements on the basis of that play. Imagination takes on a different force if you have set your heart on something already: then imagination fires your desire, for good or ill. Nancy Friday has published some extremely popular studies on women's sexual fantasies, which have been welcomed by some feminists for giving the lie to the notion that women are not sexual beings and for revealing the diversity of women's desire.[33] Yet they reveal that many women have violent sexual fantasies sometimes involving their own rape. We know too that some people fantasize about having sex with one person whilst having sex with another. Are these types of fantasies which are in the realm of imagination and not 'in our hearts', purely private and beyond the scope of morality? Although acknowledging that the connection between individual sexual desire and collective policies of domination and exploitation or liberation is not obvious, Elaine Graham believes that there must be some connection, for

> Sexual fantasies do not, in one sense, exist: but they draw their potency — if that's the right word — from a *real* world. The meanings which drive fantasies be they images or language, are not in that sense private, because they have been created and invested with meaning by a collective culture.[34]

Our private sexual fantasies therefore give us some indication of how far we are socially conditioned by the construction of desire and sex in our society. They are evidence of our taintedness by the sin of patriarchy. When fantasies involve the objectification and use of another person, when mutuality and equality are absent from them, they are antithetical to the ethos of mutuality and friendship. What we desperately need are writers, artists, filmmakers, teachers who can portray mutuality as sexy, who can eroticize equality. We need prophets, visionaries, who can transcend the mind-set that sex equals domination and submission. Our fantasies need feeding positive images. We also need what Dorothee Sölle calls a *phantasie*, which is more than a mere fantasy.[35] It is a collective vision of what things could be like, not in some far distant and utopian future, but now — a vision that empowers us to work for its realization because it is both enticing and realistic. What has become very clear is that the dualism between public and private which has dishonestly relegated sexuality to the private sphere has to be overcome. The personal is political but the political is also personal. Seeking to change the way people relate to one another 'privately' is not enough, although it is important. Because people are caught in wider social relations and models of relating, change must include cultural, legal and social policy change.

8.5 DESIRE AND THE CHURCHES

Interestingly, the language of desire is notable by its absence from most church reports on sexuality. Whilst the churches are these days generally bending over backwards to be positive about bodies and sexuality in general they are rather coy about talking of desire. Could this be a hangover from Augustinian fear of desire? Perhaps. The Roman Catholic Catechism still bristles with Augustinian distrust of desire and the dualistic pitting of desire against reason:

> Etymologically, 'concupiscence' can refer to any intense form of human desire. Christian theology has given it a particular meaning: the movement of the sensitive appetite contrary to the operation of human reason. The apostle St Paul identifies it with the rebellion of the 'flesh' against the 'spirit'. Concupiscence stems from the disobedience of the first sin. It unsettles man's moral faculties and, without being in itself an offence, inclines man to commit sins.[36]

This is pure Augustinianism and is therefore subject to the same criticisms. Only the Presbyterian (USA) report specifically addresses the subject of desire, arguing that it must be integrated into Christian spirituality.

> For too long Christians have mistakenly viewed eros as a foreign power, outside our true selves. Somehow, eros was seen as beyond rational direction and threatening our personal well-being, as well as all social order. We argue, however, that eros — passionate desire for intimate connection — is a remarkable spiritual resource and a gift fully worthy of its giver.[37]

The report goes on to embrace the concept of the erotic as developed by Heyward and others.

8.6 DESIRE AND GOD

Elaine Graham believes that any attempt to define desire will ultimately fail because it is so complex. 'It may be that we can only experience it, speak of it, theologize about it, as a profoundly complex phenomenon.'[38] Desire is both universal and constantly experienced yet it is also socially constructed. Graham argues that desire is a reflection of human nature: it is physical and mental, it is about satisfaction but also yearning, it is personal but also relational. Desire enables us to hold together transcendental and immanent elements of ourselves, yearning for that which is beyond us whilst always rooting that yearning in the material reality of our lives. Desire is that part of ourselves which 'defies closure and finality' whilst locating us in our bodies. Desire gives us a sense of self but also propels us towards others and makes us realize the extent to which we are fashioned by the culture in which we live. Because it challenges the concept of normality, desire should lead us to compassion and tolerance. Desire in effect makes us human, reminds us what it is to be human and perhaps also serves as a metaphor for the divine. If this is so, then desire has to be placed at the centre of our theological discourse as a central point of **revelation** (albeit an ambiguous and dangerous one). Augustine was right to emphasize the close connection between desire and sin, for desire is easily perverted into lust, but he was wrong to maintain that it is necessarily sinful in a post-fall world. Indeed if our desire is at the root of our humanness and our contact with the divine, then when it is ordered properly it becomes our royal road to God and indeed the location of our most intense experiences of God.

8.7 SUMMARY

In this chapter we have explored the notion of desire as a deeply subversive force. Augustine, Ambrose and other church fathers have been shown to have regarded desire as a force which subverts human nature as God made it and intended it to be and which contaminates it with evil. However we have also seen that there is plenty of material within the mainstream Christian tradition itself which subverts the dualism and fear of desire which has haunted so many Christians for so long. We noted that those who advocate what we have chosen to call passionate **ethics** make desire (ordered within the context of justice and mutuality) our primary source for reflecting upon the nature of a God who is love.

Notes

1 Jonathan Dollimore, *Sexual Dissidence: Augustine to Wilde, Freud to Foucault* (Oxford: Clarendon Press, 1991), p. 131.

2 Richard P. McBrien, *Catholicism*, Vol. 1 (London: Geoffrey Chapman, 1980), p. 164.

3 Augustine, *Confessions*, translated and with an introduction and notes by Henry Chadwick (Oxford: Oxford University Press, 1991), II. iii–iv, p. 29.

4 Dollimore, *Sexual Dissidence*, pp. 133–4.

5 *Ibid.*, p. 40.

6 *Ibid.*, p. 136.

7 *Ibid.*, p. 143.

8 Augustine, *City of God*, edited by David Knowles (Harmondsworth: Penguin Books, 1972), XIV:16, p. 577.

9 *Summa Theologiae* 2–2.153.2 ad. 2.

10 S. D. Goitein, 'The Song of Songs: a female composition', in Athalya Brenner, *A Feminist Companion to the Song of Songs* (Sheffield: Sheffield Academic Press, 1993), pp. 58–66.

11 Mishnah, *Yadayim*, 3:5.

12 Alice L. Laffey, *Wives, Harlots and Concubines: The Old Testament in Feminist Perspective* (London: SPCK, 1990), p. 203.

13 Phyllis Trible, *God and the Rhetoric of Sexuality* (Philadelphia: Fortress Press, 1978), p. 144.

14 Heather Walton, 'Theology of desire', *Theology and Sexuality*, Vol. 1 (September 1994), p. 33.

15 *Ibid.*, pp. 33–4.

16 *Ibid.*

17 Roland E. Murphy, O.Carm., 'Canticle of Canticles' in Raymond E. Brown, SS, Joseph A. Fitzmyer, SJ, and Roland E. Murphy, O.Carm. (eds), *The New Jerome Biblical Commentary* (London: Geoffrey Chapman, 1991), p. 465.

18 David Biale, *Eros and the Jews: From Biblical Israel to Contemporary America* (New York: Basic Books, 1992), p. 17.

19 *Ibid.*, p. 31.

20 Ursula King, *Feminist Theology from the Third World: A Reader* (London and Maryknoll: SPCK and Orbis, 1994), p. 311.

21 Audre Lorde, 'Uses of the erotic: the erotic as power', in James B. Nelson and Sandra P. Longfellow (eds), *Sexuality and the Sacred: Sources for Theological Reflection* (London: Mowbray, 1994), pp. 75–9.

22 *Ibid.*, p. 77.

23 Carter Heyward, *Touching Our Strength: The Erotic as Power and the Love of God* (San Francisco: Harper and Row, 1989).

24 Beverly Wildung Harrison, 'The power of anger in the work of love: Christian ethics for women and other strangers', in Ann Loades, *Feminist Theology: A Reader* (London: SPCK, 1990), p. 206.

25 Mary Daly, *Pure Lust: Elemental Feminist Philosophy* (Boston: Beacon Press, 1984), p. 375.

26 Morton Kelsey and Barbara Kelsey, *Sacrament of Sexuality: The Spirituality and Psychology of Sex* (Warwick: Amity House, 1986), p. 37.

27 *Ibid.*, p. 37.

28 King, *Feminist Theology from the Third World*, p. 73.

29 Rosemary Radford Ruether, 'Homophobia, heterosexism, and pastoral practice', in Nelson and Longfellow, *Sexuality and the Sacred*, p. 393.

30 Sue George, *Women and Bisexuality* (London: Scarlet Press, 1993), p. 12.

31 Gareth Moore, *The Body in Context: Sex and Catholicism* (London: SCM Press, 1992), p. 15.

32 Heyward, *Touching Our Strength*, p. 191.

33 Nancy Friday, *My Secret Garden: Women's Sexual Fantasies* (London: Quartet, 1976), and *Women on Top* (London: Hutchinson, 1991).

34 E. Graham, 'Towards a theology of desire', *Theology and Sexuality*, Vol. 1 (September 1994), p. 20.

35 Dorothee Sölle, *Beyond Mere Obedience: Reflections on a Christian Ethics for the Future* (Minneapolis: Augsburg Publishers, 1970), p. 10.

36 *Catechism of the Catholic Church*, para. 2515, pp. 534–5.

37 *Keeping Body and Soul Together*, paras 646–50, pp. 17–18.

38 Graham, 'Towards a theology of desire', *Theology and Sexuality*, Vol. 1 (September 1994), p. 13.

Suggestions for further reading

Athalya Brenner, *A Feminist Companion to the Song of Songs* (Sheffield: Sheffield Academic Press, 1993).

Elaine Graham, 'Towards a theology of desire', *Theology and Sexuality*, Vol. 1 (September 1994).

Carter Heyward, *Touching Our Strength: The Erotic as Power and Love of God* (San Francisco: Harper and Row, 1989).

Gareth Moore, *The Body in Context: Sex and Catholicism* (London: SCM Press, 1992).

Heather Walton, 'Theology of desire', *Theology and Sexuality*, Vol. 1 (September 1994).

9

SPIRITUALITY

9.1 THREE APPROACHES TO SPIRITUALITY

The term '**spirituality**' has become so over-used that it no longer has a standard meaning. Once there was a straightforward connection between spirituality and the practice of religion. Nowadays the term has been embraced by **New Age** enthusiasts, humanists and secular educationalists, in addition to theologians and religious people. Since the aim of this chapter is to develop a series of connections between spirituality and **sexuality**, it is necessary to restore some sense of order to this term. Assuming that the *use* of the term is the clue to its meaning, a beginning will be made by contrasting anthropological, humanistic and religious uses of it.

An anthropology is a theory or sketch of what human beings essentially are. On this view, people, or a part of them, are designated to be or to have something called 'spirit', and everything that pertains to spirit is 'spiritual'. The spirit is often contrasted with 'body' so that whatever 'spirit' conveys, it becomes the antithesis to body or matter. We have acknowledged (see **4.1**) the growing recognition among the churches of the dangers of this view. The humanistic use of the term is currently widespread in British education. The curriculum of state schools is required to promote the 'spiritual development' of pupils.[1] In the absence of consensus about what this requirement actually entails, a welter of papers, documents, guidance notes and theories has sprung up, almost all of them ignorant of the theological resources and the philosophical traps associated with the topic.[2] Since this material usually seeks a lowest common denominator of agreement, the distinctive teaching of the religions about spirituality is the casualty.

Sometimes this humanistic use is actually counter-productive.

There is a strong temptation in this literature to identify spirituality with something called 'inwardness'.[3] This tendency assumes the truth of inner–outer **dualism**, which turns out only to be the old soul–body dualism in alternative guise. This version of dualism turns out to be anti-religious because it encourages an obsession with individuality and self-identity. It avoids the body and merely reflects the location of religion in the private sphere where late capitalist societies have confined it. This picture of the 'solitary self-communing self'[4] is a distortion.[5] A Christian understanding of spirituality (see below, **9.2**) includes the whole person, his or her relationships with neighbours, and above all, with God. Anything less is a reduction.

A religious understanding of spirituality allows it to be a quality or series of qualities of someone who has made some achievement in a religious life. The philosopher Gilbert Ryle labelled certain words 'achievement words', which he contrasted with 'failure words' or 'missed it words'.[6] Reading a library book is an achievement, while simply borrowing it is not; passing an exam is an achievement, while failing it is not. The designation of a spiritual person implies that she or he has achieved something, has grown or matured in the understanding and practice of religion, even though in fact little may have been achieved. Borrowing again from Ryle, we may say that the achievement of the spiritual life is not just something cerebral or intellectual. Rather it will encompass 'knowing-that' and 'knowing-how'.[7] It will embrace doing as well as being and understanding. In the Christian tradition, achievement in the spiritual life is inseparable from the love of God and the neighbour.

9.2 CHRISTIAN SPIRITUALITY

A simple description (though not an exhaustive one) of the Christian faith is that it is the practice of the love of God, and of the neighbour as oneself. This is the basis of passionate **ethics** (see **2.12**). There is an obvious biblical warrant for this:

> Then one of the scribes, who had been listening to these discussions and had observed how well Jesus answered, came forward and asked him, 'Which is the first of all the commandments?' He answered, 'The first is, "Hear, O Israel: the Lord our God is the one Lord, and you must love the Lord your God with all your heart, with all your soul, with all your mind, and with all your strength." The

second is this: "You must love your neighbour as yourself." No other commandment is greater than these.' (Mark 12.28–31)[8]

Assuming the soundness of the 'achievement-approach' to spirituality, we may say that the 'spiritual' person is someone who has accomplished, or at least begun to accomplish, a little of the love of God and of the neighbour in his or her life. The practice of the love of God and neighbour *is* the spiritual life. This practice is a response to the love of God shown in Christ (1 John 4.9–11). We can assume that achievement in spirituality is never easy, not least because the practice of love, whether of God or of our neighbour, will conflict with our ordinary inclinations. Any success will be partial, honed through many failures. Taking the practice of love as taught by Jesus to be what spirituality is, some of the qualities of spirituality are explored further in **9.4–9.7** below. Since our sexuality is also essential to the practice of spirituality, the meaning of sexuality and its treatment in church reports is discussed first in **9.3**.

9.3 SEXUALITY AND SPIRITUALITY

Several church reports appear at ease with the term 'sexuality' and in handling it, they imbue it with theological assumptions which have a sound basis. The term itself, having as a root meaning 'the condition of being characterized and distinguished by **sex**', has no theological nuances at all. In psychological and psychosexual literature, 'sexuality' comes to mean how one expresses being a woman or a man. The Anglican report from Southern Africa, *The Church and Human Sexuality*, locates a person's sexuality within his or her spirituality.

> Spirituality is not opposed to, but includes, our human sexuality, so that salvation entails the process of recovering sexual wholeness, including growth in bodily selfacceptance and in the capacity for sensuousness. The awakening of the self to its destiny as an embodiment of divine love is intrinsic to the life of the Spirit. Sexuality is therefore to be expressed in ways conforming to the Christian gospel of love, with the recognition of the equal value and dignity of men and women, so that acts of sexual violence within or outside marriage can never be condoned ...
>
> In view of the theological understanding of human sexuality as a gift of God to enable people to attain to a fuller humanity in relationship with others, the parish church has as great a responsibility to teach its members about sexuality frankly and openly as it has to teach other aspects of the faith.[9]

There is much wisdom in this condensed text. It refutes the opposition, so often assumed, between sexuality and spirituality, assuming a person's spirituality embraces his or her sexuality, rather as spirit includes the body in some theories of the person. This is an anthropological view of spirituality (see above, **9.1**) but one which is deeply influenced by theological assumptions. The need to recover sexual wholeness assumes that wholeness has been obscured, not simply by sin but by the division of spirit and body which leads to a bodiless spirituality and the sense of guilt at the knowledge of the body and its **desires**. The Church acknowledges that ignorance and prejudice distort a person's sexuality and spirituality and so it calls for frankness from its pastors in their sexual teaching. Salvation is the overcoming of this division with the help and grace of God, leading to a 'bodily selfacceptance' which enables us to affirm ourselves in spite of the stereotypes we fail to measure up to, our internalization of other people's perceptions of us, our yearnings, our fantasies and our feelings.

The Church and Human Sexuality is a discerning document. It assumes there will be, in the individual's sexual experience, a process of growth and awakening which, if properly interpreted by the church in her teaching ministry, can lead to an understanding of the person as an 'embodiment of divine love'. One is reminded of how the icon is understood in Orthodox Christianity (see **2.6**) and of the closeness of the term 'embodiment' to the term '**incarnation**'. The conviction that divine love makes itself known and expresses itself through human bodies is also an incarnational conviction. It is what God is believed to have done in the body of Christ. Since sexuality is an embodiment of divine love, it cannot be an act of violence or domination, but must be expressed as a mutual giving and receiving. Sexuality is God's way of bringing about fullness of life (see **5.12**) or a 'fuller humanity' by bringing us into intimate relationship with others, and contributing to their fuller humanity also. The document also confirms the view (see above, **9.2**) that the spiritual life, and sexuality as part of it, is the love of God and neighbour.

The Evangelical Lutheran Church in America also allows its definition of sexuality to be shaped by the Christian theological heritage. The first draft of their 'social statement' states:

Our *sexuality* is an intrinsic aspect of who we are and how we live as embodied, sensual, relational human beings. It has physiological,

social, psychological, and spiritual dimensions. Sexuality includes
but is far more than certain biological drives or genital sexual acts.
It is part of our personal identity and of our relationships with one
another, from our birth to our death.[10]

Sexuality is the bridge between personal identity and personal
relationality. The Lutheran Church in the United States is fully aware
of the danger of a narrow individualism, and is careful to insist that
we are just as much persons-in-relation as we are individual subjects
with freedom. With many other Christians who are coming to terms
with the anti-body legacy of much of the tradition, the Lutherans
'confess that through the ages the Church too often has overlooked
the created goodness of sexuality'.[11] Sexuality, as in the Southern
African definition, is an inclusive term. All other dimensions of the
human being are encompassed by it, and since it is a fundamental
characteristic of 'who we are' and 'how we live' it is inevitably
manifested in our relationships with each other. Sexuality is tempor-
ally, not just personally, inclusive. The draft honestly acknowledges
that the smallest children are sexual beings who delight in being
bodies, and that the oldest citizens may have sexual needs.

The Presbyterian Church of the USA, in *Keeping Body and Soul
Together,* also has a comprehensive description of sexuality, which
mirrors many of the emphases of the two documents just discussed.

> Our sexuality — our way of being in the world as embodied selves,
> male and female — involves our whole being and is intrinsic to our
> dignity as persons. Sexuality expresses the wonder of knowing that
> we are created by God with a need and desire for relationship. We
> are created for communion and communication. As sexual per-
> sons, we reach out for the physical and spiritual embrace of others.
> In our capacity to touch and be touched, we experience God's
> intention that we find our authentic humanness, not in isolation,
> but in relatedness.
>
> As an intrinsic component of our humanity, our sexuality mat-
> ters to our dignity as persons. Sexuality is also an indispensable
> element in the divine–human encounter, in our connectedness to
> the source of life and all goodness. Sexuality, our longing and
> embodied passion for communion with others and with God, is
> foundational to Christian spirituality.[12]

The patterned understanding of sexuality and its relationship to
spirituality is now fairly clear. The Presbyterians speak of our 'way of
being' as Lutherans speak of 'how we live'. This is a continuous state
of the person, very far removed from more traditional language

about sexual acts. Sexuality is the basis of spirituality in the Presbyterian document. It is the basis of all human relating, both with other people and with God. In the Lutheran draft, spirituality is the broader term. This is hardly a discrepancy between them, since both of them insist on the inseparability of each from the other. Two of the documents mention dignity in connection with sexuality, perhaps to counter that kind of sexual activity which reduces a partner to an object, or to counter instead the fear of loss of control (indignity) which love-making can bring. All three documents stress that the human person as a whole is involved in sexuality and spirituality. Sexual experience (not necessarily intercourse) is, by the grace of God, a way towards 'authentic humanness' or 'a fuller humanity'.

Sexuality provides a kind of theological proof that human beings cannot exist autonomously and in isolation. God ensures, through their sexuality, that they reach out for relationship and communion. 'Communion' and 'communication' may recall the eucharist and the belief that the divine Word of John 1 is God's 'self-communication' to all humanity. As with the Anglicans of Southern Africa, divine love is manifested in human love. The movement involved in our sexuality, out of ourselves and toward the other, is the movement of the divine love towards the creation. 'Embodied passion' includes more than passion for one's beloved. It is the basis of the pursuit of justice, of our moral intuitions, our hunger for knowledge, our thirst for truth, our desire for companionship.

9.4 THE QUALITIES OF THE SPIRITUAL LIFE: (I) EMBODIED

We have taken our starting-point for a simple, clear understanding of spirituality from the commandments of Jesus to love God and our neighbour (see above, **9.2**), and we have seen that the three church documents just considered link spirituality and sexuality irrevocably, and define sexuality theologically. Several of the characteristics of sexuality in the documents (e.g. embodiment, holism, relation) are already implicit in the love commandments of Jesus. In this and the next few sections these characteristics are located as characteristics of both sexuality and spirituality.

Embodiment and 'body theology' have already received detailed treatment (see **4.4** and Chapter 6). Only the indispensability of the body in Christian spirituality will be mentioned here. We might wonder how the body was ever bypassed in the rush to retreat inwards to the soul or upwards to heaven. The commandment of Jesus summons all one's bodily strength to the practice of the love of God. The bodily senses are fundamental to all our knowledge, including the knowledge of God. Through the sense of sight we appreciate the wonder of the natural world, the beauty of creation, the power and depth of the visual arts, the suffering of victims of hunger, poverty and genocide. Through the sense of hearing we hear the crash of waves, the call of birds, the playing of symphonies, the cry of Tamar (see **5.2**). Through the sense of taste we enjoy a thousand delicacies of food and drink, the bread and wine which is the body and blood of Christ, the kiss of the loved one. Through the sense of touch we delight in the feel of clothes, the coats of pets, the assurance and comfort of hugs, the joy of a friend's embrace. Through the sense of smell herbs, plants and flowers reveal more of their delicacies to us. Smell is the first of the senses to be engaged in the Song of Songs. 'Your love is more fragrant than wine, fragrant is the scent of your anointing oils, and your name is like those oils poured out' (Song of Songs 1.2–3). Our brains, centre of all our sensory experience, give us the power to imagine, to choose, to know, to worship, to love.

Spirituality, understood as the practice of the love of God and neighbour, may begin with the recognition and appreciation of God's grace and bounty in the created world. This recognition has its own expression in worship. Some theologians see Jesus Christ as the fulfilment of the created order, regarding the creation of life as decisive in the long history of creation, the creation of humankind as decisive in the shorter history of life, and the gift of Christ as decisive in the very short history of humankind.[13] But no such claim could be entertained without the conviction, central to traditional Christianity, that God becomes enfleshed, embodied in Christ.

9.5 THE QUALITIES OF THE SPIRITUAL LIFE: (II) HOLISTIC

The church documents have referred to 'components' of our humanity, to 'aspects' of who we are, and to the different 'dimensions' of sexuality. These are **metaphors**, from engineering, surveying and geometry, which convey the sense that the human person has to be considered as a whole or unity. This is what the term '**holism**' means. However, it makes sense to speak of the person as a unity only if there are also 'parts' of the person to be unified. That is why these metaphors are often used. There are many ways of dividing up the study of the person, and many ways of explaining the experiences of the person. 'Spirituality' appears in the documents both as a dimension of a wider whole, and as the unity of the person which embraces all the other parts. This double use of 'spirituality' is common in the literature.

There is a holism in the commandment of Jesus to love God. In what is a primitive anthropology, 'heart', 'soul', 'mind' and 'strength' are the parts; the whole is the person who is the single subject comprising the parts. Just as God is 'the one Lord', so must the person be one in the love of God. The love of God is the integrating factor in bringing the components, aspects or dimensions together. One loves as the totality one is. Love is something that cannot be literally 'half-hearted', because it involves the heart and everything else. There is a love of God which is not holistic because it does not involve the whole person in its expression. A love without soul refuses to involve 'me'. A love without mind is intellectually suicidal (like much religious enthusiasm) or unthinking in its exposure to the other. A love without physical strength is one which does not acknowledge the body and its desires and engage them in loving.

9.6 THE QUALITIES OF THE SPIRITUAL LIFE: (III) RELATIONAL

The relations in the commandments are relations of love. They are relations towards God, towards the neighbour, and also towards the self. In Luke's version of the love commandments, a lawyer asks the question 'But who is my neighbour?' (Luke 10.29) and Jesus replies with the parable of the Good Samaritan. 'Neighbour' has several meanings, from 'lover' (Song of Songs 5.16), to 'friend' or, in the familiar sense, someone living nearby.[14] Neighbour-love was a requirement of Jewish law (Leviticus 19.18), and Jesus deliberately stretches the scope of the term in the Good Samaritan parable. Indeed the **Sermon on the Mount** extends the requirement of love to enemies (Matthew 5.44). There is a strong case for extending 'neighbour' to include all living creatures who are nearby. The deprivation and destruction of the habitats of birds is a spiritual matter, not simply an environmental one. The knowledge that we share our environment with thousands of creatures which God has made, which have lived here for millions of years before we ever arrived to dominate the earth, is essential *for us*, for it punctures the inflated **anthropocentrism** which sees all other creatures as existing for our pleasure and at our disposal.

Christians find in the doctrine of God as Trinity the basis for all personal relations. God's reality is a single communion of Persons, each of whom is in relation to the others. The Persons are co-equal, and each is what he/she is only because of the relation to the others. God is not so much a Person as a communion of Persons who are so perfectly united that it is equally right to say that they are three as to say that they are one.[15] The belief that women and men are made in the image of God entails that relationships are primary at the human level as well, that we are made for relationship, and through relationship we discover our personal identity.

Connections are infrequently made between neighbour-love and spirituality, yet on a biblical view a simple ministry to impoverished and marginalized people is identified with ministry to Christ himself (Matthew 25.31–46, and see **2.12**). This is spirituality, and it stands against what Kenneth Leech calls 'the culture of false inwardness' which 'represents a serious danger to the Church'.[16] Spirituality, like sexuality, drives us out of ourselves. Yet even as the call of Christ through the neighbour summons us to response, the commandment does not require an endless out-pouring of the self which leads to spiritual emptiness, or presses crushing obligations on us, like the doormat theology (see **5.12**) which normalizes suffering and converts it into an imaginary virtue. Rather, self-love is the model for neighbour-love.[17] Self-love is a difficult topic for theology. It is necessary to oppose contemporary constructions of the individual which focus on the self, its presentation, its psychotherapeutic needs, etc. These constructions end in **narcissism** and are pervasive in opulent, capitalist societies. But it is also necessary to insist on self-affirmation and self-worth, especially among people subjected to the misuse of power over them (see Chapter 5). Their difficulty is the expulsion of attitudes towards them as worthless which they have internalized.

The lawyer's question 'But who is my neighbour?' is anxiously asked in every generation, perhaps because Christians may wish to restrict their compassion. 'Compassion-fatigue', the exhaustion and sense of helplessness in the face of exposure to the suffering of others and the appeals of charities in dealing with it, shows our complicity with the lawyer's question. A different version of the same question is a hot topic in contemporary moral and feminist theory, and the answer to it has a direct bearing on Christian spirituality. The issue registers as the influence of two kinds of self–other relations, the 'generalized other' and the 'concrete other'. These terms are ugly. In Christian spirituality the issue stands between the 'generalized' and the 'concrete' neighbour. In a moment they will be replaced by a more suitable pair of terms — 'near neighbour' and 'distant neighbour' will be suggested.

The problem is that the 'other' or the 'neighbour' is capable of becoming an empty concept, an abstraction, a term that defeats us because of the potentially infinite number of obligations it imposes. That is the 'generalized other'. In **Enlightenment** philosophy, formal acknowledgment of the other's independent existence was made, even though in practice it remained largely at the level of words. Seyla Benhabib has written of the generalized other, 'The norms of our interactions are primarily public and institutional ones ... The moral categories that accompany such interactions are those of right, obligation and entitlement, and the corresponding moral feelings are those of respect, duty, worthiness and dignity.'[18] By contrast, the 'concrete other' is a real individual 'with a concrete history, identity, and affective-emotional constitution'. With regard to the concrete other,

> The norms of our interaction are usually, although not exclusively private, non-institutional ones. They are norms of friendship, love and care ... The moral categories that accompany such inter-actions are those of responsibility, bonding and sharing. The corresponding moral feelings are those of love, care and sympathy and solidarity.[19]

This analysis is helpful to Christians. Our neighbours present themselves to us *both* as general *and* as concrete. *Justice* is the over-arching form of relationship to the generalized neighbour; *love* is the overarching form of relationship to the concrete neighbour. Neighbour-love requires enlargement so that the work of justice is seen to be a valid outworking of it. The Samaritan was a 'concrete neighbour' in that he was a particular individual with particular needs. But the parable also teaches that neighbourliness cannot be confined either by class, or race or religion. Its practice is determined by the need to show 'kindness' (Luke 10.37). So the parable moves inexorably from the concrete to the generalized other, from the practice of love to the pursuit of justice.

It may be helpful to speak tentatively of three kinds of neighbour-love. In the first kind our neighbours are our intimate friends. Intimacy need not mean sexual intimacy. The Latin word *intimare* means 'to make known' and comes from *intimus*, which means 'innermost'. Intimacy is a mutual relation which entails sharing our innermost selves.[20] For parents this will involve children. Sally Purvis has argued powerfully that 'mother-love can provide an excellent model for the content of agape'[21] (see **2.4**). Our friends, spouses and sexual partners are among our intimate neighbours. Our 'near neighbours' are people to whom we can reach out. They may be across the street or on the other side of the earth but we must be capable of touching, contacting, or showing kindness in some way (Luke 10.37). 'Near neighbour' is preferable to 'concrete other'. Our 'distant neighbours' are people we do not know personally but with whom we may feel sympathy and solidarity. Ever in danger of becoming 'generalized', they are the hungry, the thirsty, the strangers, the naked and the imprisoned, among whom Jesus Christ waits to receive our love (Matthew 25.31–46). Spirituality is the practice of love among, and toward, such neighbours.

But spirituality is also the practice of the love of God. While the love of God is not the same thing as participating in acts of ritual worship, the love of God is *formally* expressed by Christians in worship, and most significantly, in the eucharist. But such is the depth of the legacy of body–spirit dualism that the God who is encountered in worship may be thought to be removed from the God we encounter in the ordinary things of life, in nature, art and music, and in all the kinds of neighbour-love. Worship may involve, at different times, the practice of prayer, meditation, retreat, confession, praise, listening, reading and being otherwise receptive. Even here it is essential to recognize that worship is an activity of the whole people of God. It is something offered corporately and collectively. As Kenneth Leech has said,

> Spirituality is not a sub-division of Christian discipleship. It is the root, the source, the life. The Spirit gives life and nourishes the whole. Spirituality is a corporate discipline, a corporate experience ... If we are to rescue Christian spirituality from its captivity to **individualism** and the culture of false inwardness, we will need to recover the sense of its social character, indeed the sense of the social character of the gospel itself.

9.7 THE QUALITIES OF THE SPIRITUAL LIFE: (IV) DYNAMIC

The practice of spirituality is a gendered activity. The conclusions of Chapter 6 must be carried forward to the discussion of spirituality, for the difference and diversity among people which gender studies uncovers is a positive aid in this context. The difficulty of arriving at a common, essential, human nature has given rise to the recognition of a multiplicity of differences, not simply between women and men, but between women and women, and between men and men. These differences will inevitably influence our 'way of being in the world as embodied selves'. The diversity which defines us ensures that our spirituality is equally diverse, that we will love God and our neighbour in different ways, in accordance with our physical endowments (our 'strength'?), personal biographies, social histories and much else.

However, human beings grow. They may even become wise. Theories about our moral and spiritual development abound, even faith development,[22] and there is good reason to be critical of them.[23] Nonetheless some theologians claim to be able to discern patterns of spiritual growth among Christians, and the conclusion inevitably follows that, if these patterns of growth are applicable *generally*, then it is right to emphasize similarities as well as differences in the practice of the love of God. Joan Timmerman has put forward just such a pattern of spiritual growth, which has an obvious connection with sexuality.

Spiritual traditions, she thinks, identify five stages of spiritual growth.[24] The first stage is scarcely a stage at all for it consists simply of being 'normal', of learning 'to live in a world of things, effectively linking means to ends, managing nutrition, technology, personal energy'.[25] The 'second rule of the spiritual life' is said to be the imperative 'reach out to others'. This entails 'a real shift of values . . . in which human happiness, relationships, and vitality are assigned priority over the demands of the nonpersonal sphere'. Far from this stage being a preserve of vowed, celibate men and women, it may take parenthood to bring this stage about, as some people 'find the absolute value of human life symbolized in the bodies and lives of their own children'. **Asceticism**, traditionally understood as the practice of extreme self-denial and austerity in the hope that bodily denial releases the soul for union with the divine, is understood here to be release from the preoccupation with material possessions.

The next three stages, purification, illumination and union may also be reclaimed from their monastic form and deployed to inform contemporary understandings of spirituality and sexuality which are available to everyone. Purification becomes the letting-go of *social* as well as individual sins. In this stage, 'social sins, accepted with ordinary socialization, such as misogynism, racism, workaholism, low self-worth, laziness, and half-heartedness are recognized and over-come'.[26] Illumination may take many forms. It may be 'the inner disclosure of what is still lacking in a life which looks very full of spiritual and physical achievements'. It may require 'the surrender of all self-sufficiency' for the light to be 'restored'. In stage five, the stage of union, 'the person lives as one transformed, in authentic connectedness with the Whole, with an awareness of the Mystery in all things'. 'Mystical or semimystical experiences are characteristic of union. These, in some lives, have been extraordinary and dramatic; but there is also a mysticism of everyday things.'

These five stages have been reappropriated from a religious élite and reworked into 'the emergence of the spiritual life among us as a common and expected dynamic'.[27] There may be unfortunate as-sumptions here about the generality of this description, but its importance as a possible model of spiritual growth for everyone should not be underestimated. In Timmerman's hands, however, the model works, not by the repression or exclusion of sexuality, but by the integration of spirituality and sexuality in a 'bodily spirituality'. This is a demanding and adventurous task because 'our religious and cultural memory is so devoid of models of bodily spirituality, we may have to invent them'. Integration takes place by a rediscovery of **sacramentality**.

It comes as no surprise that this account of spiritual growth or formation takes as its theological root the incarnation of God in flesh. This analysis is an unselfconscious example of 'body theology' (see **4.4**), since it derives from the conviction that the God who became flesh in Jesus Christ continues to be made known in the flesh.

> Christian understanding of spiritual formation is incarnational. That means that freedom, ecstasy, openness are performed in the flesh, not by escaping from it. By God's entry into human being, all being, history and nature, is potentially transformed. All reality becomes mediator of Mystery, thus sacramental, to those who can see.[28]

9.8 EMBODIED HOLINESS

In this book we have advocated 'body theology' (see **4.4**), the integration of spirituality and sexuality (see **9.3**), and the abandonment of a body–soul dualism (see **4.1**) which develops the soul by controlling or denigrating the body. Some of the churches, in some of their documents, are moving towards these positions. In this and the next section the question of the continuity of the tradition is taken up. Can these positions be regarded as authentically Christian? Conservative forces in the churches are prone to dismiss any developing understanding of Christian sexual teaching on the grounds (among others) that it capitulates to the secular spirit of the age; or that it accommodates sexual licence of all kinds; or that it robs the Christian life of all its distinctiveness. A convincing answer to these charges must be made.

Richard Price has raised the question of the root of the Church's austere sexual teaching from the second century onwards. There is little doubt that the Church was fierce in its attempt to enforce strict sexual disciplines which included (for the few) complete abstinence. Even sex within marriage was for some orthodox Christians suspect. There was a horror of pre-marital and adulterous sexual intercourse. Some ascetic-minded Christians, still influenced by the belief in the imminent end of the age, advocated even the abandonment of sexual intercourse for the purpose of procreation. Remarriage was generally discouraged, and a penitential system for baptized Christians enforced severe punishments for transgressors. Price identifies the main reason for the Church's cautious restraint. It was because

> Christians saw themselves as constituting a holy people, set apart as a distinct, third race from both Jews and pagans. The boundaries between themselves and surrounding society needed to be variously affirmed, if the Church was not to feel contaminated by its environment. This apartness and **purity** of the Church found expression and reinforcement . . . in her strict penitential discipline, which . . . was more concerned to maintain the holiness of the Church than to deal compassionately with human weakness.[29]

The Church, then as now, needs a 'distinctive Christian sexual ethic'.[30] What is needed is a positive proposal for distinctiveness which does not simply mimic the needs of the Church in the latter days of the Roman empire, but which conveys the gospel to the wider society today. In the second to fourth centuries,

> the dominant factor in the development of a distinctive Christian

sexual ethic was the need to express and preserve the purity of the
Church as the body of Christ through the purity of the bodies of its
members. To maintain her own integrity as a heavenly society that
was only sojourning on earth, the Church needed members whose
own bodies stood apart from the blurring and contamination, the
loss of personal integrity and bodily vigour, brought about by easy
sexual relations. It was this ecclesial concern that gave the sexual
ethic of the early Christians its distinctive edge, its sharp clarity, its
reiterated emphases.[31]

Presumably no Christian alive wishes to see a return to the penitential disciplines which required, say, fifteen years of penance for
adultery. Yet the concern of the Church to be a distinctive people, set
both within and against the wider Roman empire, and seeking to
show also discontinuity between Christians and Jews, was essential to
their mission. In a context of intermittent persecution and martyr-
dom, suspicion and ridicule, the Church rightly wished to distinguish, in the realm of sexual conduct, the practice of her members
from that of surrounding pagans, some of whom were more easy-
going and a few of whom were more strict with regard to complete
renunciation of sexual conduct.

We have already seen both how the Christian gospel abolished
purity laws (see **1.8**) and how in the second century what we called
'body-friendliness' came to be lost (see **4.2**). The context in which the
churches are attempting to maintain their distinctiveness with regard
to sexual behaviour now has markedly changed. The churches within
the continents which were formerly the homes of Christendom do
not witness to a pagan, pre-Christian culture but to one which is in
many respects tired of Christianity. Scholars increasingly call such
countries 'post-Christian'; the problem for the churches here is that
of convincing the wider public that in the area of sexuality it has
anything to say which is positively 'life-giving' (see **1.12**). We have
seen that the churches are not united in their sexual teaching, and
that in some cases that teaching is not supported even by Christians
themselves (see **2.3, 2.11**). Thankfully the churches lack the 'power-
over' their members (see **5.2**) to impose any but token and trivial
penances.

But these discontinuities between an earlier age and our own do
not excuse the Church from the necessity of living and proclaiming
a distinctive life in Christ which is readily capable of being contrasted
with life in the ordinary, **fallen** world. A continuity between our time
and the Roman one is the understanding of the centrality of the

human body as the boundary between the pagan world and the body of Christ, though the boundary will be marked not by the re-imposition of ceremonial purity laws or a return to the petty legalism which seeks to enforce them, but through what is called here 'embodied holiness'. The practice of embodied holiness in the bodies of the members of the body of Christ would, if and to the extent that it was achieved, guarantee a distinctive character and witness to the Christian faith. Embodied holiness would be a sufficient indicator of distinctiveness. But how would we recognize it?

9.9 PASSIONATE SPIRITUALITY AND EMBODIED HOLINESS

The need to envision a genuine contemporary holiness which affirms our sexuality and spirituality together, invites a rereading of our initial approach to sexual **morality** called passionate ethics in the light of this conclusion (see Chapter 2). Passionate ethics, together with the approach to Christian spirituality developed in this chapter, enable us to sketch a possible projection of how holiness might be embodied in the people of God. The dynamic view of spirituality (see above, **9.7**) will be utilized, even though the growth model it advocates can be no more than a single example of how spiritual growth might come about. Embodied holiness is the kind of living Paul may have had in mind when he appealed to the Christians at Rome,

> by the mercies of God, to present your bodies as a living sacrifice, holy and acceptable to God, which is your spiritual worship. Do not be conformed to this world but be transformed by the renewal of your mind, that you may prove what is the will of God, what is good and acceptable and perfect. (Romans 12.1–2[32] RSV)

The first phase of spiritual growth was that of being normal. When the sexual dimension of this phase of spiritual growth is consciously articulated, it may be the time when adolescents, acutely conscious of the changes occurring in their bodies, learn to understand some of these changes and to be comfortable with them. It will involve recognizing desires and learning to deal with them. Sexual arousal is likely to be common at this stage, yet very few adolescents, even those from Christian homes, will be offered the spiritual support they need at this key stage which enables them to see their burgeoning sexuality as a divine gift and the basis of their need for companionship and right relationships.

But this phase need not be confined to adolescence. It also includes the awakening of bodily self-consciousness. It may involve the recognition that some influences on one's life have been negative or oppressive, and that these may have led to complications and contradictions. Some young women and men will learn that their desires do not conform to **heterosexual** expectations of how they should be and what social relationships they should form. **Heterosexism** only prolongs the turmoil that **lesbian**, **gay** and **bisexual** people go through. Being normal at this time means coping with extraordinary developments. It is demanding enough even to grasp what is going on and to begin to accept ourselves among the conflicts and changes. There is a basic gospel intuition here. God accepts us in spite of ourselves and our misgivings about ourselves. In the light of God's acceptance we can begin to relax into a self-affirmation that is deeply grounded in divine grace.

The second phase of spiritual growth was that of reaching out to others. When the sexual dimension of this phase of spiritual growth is consciously articulated, the possibility arises that among many relationships that are entered into, some will involve sexual arousal and contact. The reaching out which is dating and courtship can itself be an essential opening out of the person, an enlargement of personal horizons and experiences. Among the differences between people, a difference yet to be mentioned assumes a critical importance at this stage. The sexual drive or *libido* itself develops at different times, and varies in intensity from person to person. The word 'drive' should probably be banished from theology because it assumes that people are machines and sexual desires are like engines. Desire is more personal, and can be linked with the desire for God, for art, for company, for food, etc., in a way that the mechanical metaphor 'drive' cannot. This phase is an intensely vulnerable time. Too adventurous a reaching out can lead to deep hurt; too timid a reaching out can lead to becoming trapped in a troubled individuality. In the first growth is too rapid; in the second there may be no growth at all.

No assumption is being made that this second phase of reaching out is a preliminary phase leading to the destiny of heterosexual marriage. In this phase some people will discover from their reaching out that they are not ready for close sexual relationships, nor for the commitments they entail. It may be possible at this stage to discern the gift of **celibacy**, perhaps by the self-knowledge disclosed by the possibility of another kind of inclusive loving which is holistic without intimacy expressing itself in sexual contact. This will be the phase where the joy of sexual experience is balanced by a growing sense of sexual responsibility and where fertile heterosexual couples take steps to ensure that they do not conceive children outside of commitments to those children and to each other (see **3.8**). It may be the time when passion comes to be experienced not simply as having a sexual focus but rather as 'the summons to respond to other people' (see **2.12**).

The third phase of spiritual growth was that of purification, of letting-go both individual and social sins. When the sexual dimension of this phase of spiritual growth is consciously articulated, evidence should be available of a refusal to be 'conformed to this world' and to begin to be transformed by the renewal of the mind. The renewal of the mind may underline the conviction that the 'worldly' construction of sexual relationships can lead to overt selfishness, domination and exploitation (see **2.12**). In this phase 'power-over' (assuming one had it) is replaced by 'power-with' (see **5.2**) as control is replaced by mutuality. Awareness of the evil of the commodification of the body, and its **objectification** in pornography (see **5.11**) may be intensified. Letting-go has to include attitudes which, 'in the world', are still pervasive, chiefly those of **patriarchy** and **homophobia**. Embodied holiness in these second and third phases is the practice of neighbour-love with intimate friends, which (as we said of 'passionate ethics' — see **2.12**) 'always affirms the other and never makes him or her a victim of one's own pursuit of pleasure or quest for dominance'.

The fourth phase of spiritual growth was illumination. When the sexual dimension of this phase of spiritual growth is consciously articulated, we may be illumined to link our passion for our intimate neighbours with near and distant neighbours. Illumination may be the exposure of 'the emptiness of one's present life', the 'disclosure of what is still lacking in a life which looks very full of spiritual and physical achievements'.[33] Illumination comes from 'the true light that enlightens everyone' (John 1.3). In accordance with our reconstruction of **natural law** (see **2.3–2.4**) Christ illumines us to discern more of his passionate love among his brothers and sisters who are victims of oppression, and our passionate love towards God and neighbour is rekindled and redirected towards the Christ who calls from the distant neighbours who are victims of social and economic injustice.

The fifth phase of spiritual growth was that of union. When the sexual dimension of this phase of spiritual growth is consciously articulated, union with God may express itself through union with near and distant neighbours who may also include other creatures which God has made. In this stage, illumination and union make possible the affirmation of *Veritatis Splendor* that 'it is *in the Crucified Christ that the Church finds the answer* to the question troubling so many people today ... ' (see **2.3**). At this stage a justice ethic becomes a passionate preoccupation since the demand for the expression of neighbour-love is greater than we are able to supply from our own personal resources (see above, **2.12**). We may also wish to affirm union with all Christians who live in the detritus of the historical denominations of Christendom which are largely discarded and discredited in the eyes of sinners. We may nonetheless want to contribute to 'the community of character' (see above, **2.5**) which is to be found there, thanking God that through it the faith of the first Christians has been handed down to us.

This dynamic view of sexuality and spirituality is tentative. It need not be understood sequentially. Even when it is so understood there will be Christians who do not get very far, and people outside the churches altogether who in their loving appear to be more illumined by 'the true light that enlightens everyone' than their counterparts in the churches. In this sense the redrawing of an ancient boundary between Church and world would be both arrogant and counter-productive. The Spirit is not confined to churches. Nonetheless a people which so lives and understands the love of God and neighbour in a diversity of ways which have something in common with the passionate spirituality indicated in this chapter, may be said to be practising embodied holiness. They will have a good claim to be unconformed to this world (Romans 12.1) and to be united with each other and with Christ.

> For just as in a single human body there are many limbs and organs, all with different functions, so we who are united with Christ, though many, form one body, and belong to one another as its limbs and organs. (Romans 12.4–5)

Embodied holiness is a passionate spirituality which is immune to the charge that it capitulates to secular culture. It represents an attempt both to embody Christ within a secular culture and to 'honour God' in the body (1 Corinthians 6.20).

9.10 SUMMARY

In this chapter Christian spirituality is assumed to be the whole-hearted love of God and neighbour. That spirituality is the practice of love is seen to have profound implications for human loving and for the overlapping relationship between sexuality and spirituality. Several church reports have developed accounts of sexuality which render sexuality inseparable from spirituality. We have examined some of the qualities of the spiritual life as a life flowing outward in the love of God and neighbour. The body is a precondition of all knowledge and love whatsoever. The relatedness of all people to each other and to God is rooted in the Christian doctrine of the Trinity.

As lovers of God and our neighbours, the holistic character of love, already taught by Jesus in the love commandments, is re-emphasized. The expansive character of the term 'neighbour' has been noted, and in order to cope with this, three kinds of neighbour have been suggested, intimate, near and distant, requiring from us both passionate love and passionate justice. Since spiritual growth by definition is a dynamic phenomenon, we have adopted and then expanded a hesitant attempt to sketch a single model of growth which integrates spirituality and sexuality. The phases of this model are normality, reaching out, purification, illumination and union. These phases, applied to an understanding of phases of sexual growth, are found to make sense of the Christian, sexual life. The name 'embodied holiness' describes a corporate way of living in the world as Christians who are also embodied sexual beings. Embodied holiness, like passionate ethics (see Chapter 2) is commended as an authentic Christian way of life which owes more to the way of Christ than to the way of the world.

Notes

1 Education Reform Act (1988), para.1.

2 Some of these are examined in Adrian Thatcher, ' "Policing the sublime": a wholly (holy?) ironic approach to the spiritual development of children', in Jeff Astley and Leslie J. Francis, *Christian Theology and Religious Education: Connections and Contradictions* (London: SPCK, 1996), pp. 117–39.

3 See the influential work by John Hammond, David Hay *et al.*, *New Methods in R.E. Teaching: An Experiential Approach* (Harlow: Oliver & Boyd, 1990). This trend, together with the assumptions on which it rests and the consequences

which follow is criticized in Adrian Thatcher, 'A critique of inwardness in religious education', *British Journal of Religious Education*, 14.1 (Autumn 1991), pp. 22–7.

4 Fergus Kerr's phrase. See his *Theology after Wittgenstein* (Oxford: Blackwell, 1986), p. 72.

5 See Adrian Thatcher, 'Spirituality without inwardness', *Scottish Journal of Theology*, 46.2 (1993), pp. 213–28.

6 Gilbert Ryle, *The Concept of Mind* (Harmondsworth: Peregrine Books, 1963), p. 143 (first published 1949).

7 *Ibid.*, pp. 28–32.

8 See also, Luke 10.25–28.

9 Southern African Anglican Theological Commission, *The Church and Human Sexuality* (Marshalltown, 1995), E4,6, pp. 15–16.

10 Division for Church in Society, Department for Studies of the Evangelical Lutheran Church in America, *The Church and Human Sexuality: A Lutheran Perspective* (Chicago: 1993, first draft), p. 2 (authors' emphasis).

11 *Ibid.*, p. 3.

12 General Assembly Special Committee on Human Sexuality, Presbyterian Church (USA), *Keeping Body and Soul Together: Sexuality, Spirituality and Social Justice* (1991), p. 16.

13 See, e.g., Arthur Peacocke, *Theology for a Scientific Age* (London: SCM, enlarged edition 1993), Part 3; and Ian Barbour, *Religion in an Age of Science* (London: SCM, 1990), Part 3, for two out of many works dealing with this common theme.

14 See Michael D. Coogan, 'Neighbor', in Bruce M. Metzger and Michael D. Coogan, *The Oxford Companion to the Bible* (New York: Oxford University Press, 1993), p. 555.

15 For a more detailed account of the doctrine of the Trinity and its implications for understanding human sexuality, see A. Thatcher, *Liberating Sex: A Christian Sexual Theology* (London: SPCK, 1993), pp. 52–60.

16 Kenneth Leech, *The Eye of the Storm: Spiritual Resources for the Pursuit of Justice* (London: Darton, Longman & Todd, 1992), pp. 14–15.

17 See, e.g., Thatcher, *Liberating Sex*, pp. 65–8.

18 Seyla Benhabib, 'The generalized and the concrete other' in her *Situating the Self: Gender, Community and Postmodernism in Contemporary Ethics* (Cambridge: Polity Press, 1992), p. 159.

19 *Ibid.*

20 For the use of intimacy as a connection between sexuality and spirituality, see Marvin M. Ellison, 'Sexuality and spirituality: an intimate — and intimidating — connection', in Adrian Thatcher and Elizabeth Stuart (eds), *Christian Perspectives on Sexuality and Gender* (Leominster, UK, and Grand Rapids, MI, Gracewing and Eerdmans: 1996), Ch. 5.2.

21 Sally B. Purvis, 'Mothers, neighbors and strangers: another look at agape', in Thatcher and Stuart, *Christian Perspectives*, p. 242.

22 See Jeff Astley and Leslie Francis (eds), *Christian Perspectives on Faith Development* (Leominster: Gracewing/Fowler Wright, 1992).

23 For a criticism of these, and of the language of developmentalism as a whole in relation to children, see Thatcher, ' "Policing the sublime", ch. 8.

24 Joan H. Timmerman, *Sexuality and Spiritual Growth* (New York: Crossroad, 1993), pp. 19–22.

25 *Ibid.*, p. 19.

26 *Ibid.*, p. 20.

27 *Ibid.*, p. 22.

28 *Ibid.*, p. 24.

29 Richard Price, 'The distinctiveness of early Christian sexual ethics', in Thatcher and Stuart, *Christian Perspectives*, p. 28.

30 *Ibid.*, p. 29.

31 *Ibid.*

32 Revised Standard Version. The Revised English Bible has, instead of 'to present your bodies', 'to offer your very selves'. It thus translates the Greek word *soma*, which literally means 'body' in a holistic (see above, **9.5**) way. While this is a welcome translation of *soma*, the older and more familiar translation is retained here because of the obvious link with 'em*bodied* holiness'.

33 Timmerman, *Sexuality and Spiritual Growth*, p. 21.

Suggestions for further reading

Linda Hurcombe (ed.), *Sex and God: Some Varieties of Women's Religious Experience* (New York and London: Routledge & Kegan Paul, 1987).

Kenneth Leech, *The Eye of the Storm: Spiritual Resources for the Pursuit of Justice* (London: Darton, Longman and Todd, 1992).

James Nelson, *The Intimate Connection: Male Sexuality, Masculine Spirituality* (Philadelphia: Westminster Press, 1988; London: SPCK, 1992).

Adrian Thatcher and Elizabeth Stuart (eds), *Christian Perspectives on Sexuality and Gender* (Leominster: Gracewing; Grand Rapids, MI: Eerdmans, 1996), chapters 1, 5–6.

Joan Timmerman, *Sexuality and Spiritual Growth* (New York: Crossroad, 1993).

10

THE BIBLE

A cursory perusal of a handful of church documents on **sexuality** such as *Issues in Human Sexuality* and the Methodist (UK) and Lutheran (USA) reports reveals that the churches do not know quite how to relate the issues of sexuality to the Bible. As we noted in Chapter 7, most of the 'liberal' church reports recognize the difficulties of reading off a particular attitude to **homosexuality** from explicit mentions of same-sex sex in the Bible, but they nevertheless tend to resort to literal readings of Genesis 1–3 in order to establish that marriage is the biblical ideal (see **7.4**). With a couple of exceptions there is a lack of **hermeneutical** sophistication in recent church reports. By this we mean that the reports show insufficient awareness of the multiple and complex issues that are raised by the use of the Bible in debates about sexuality and **gender** and they also demonstrate an inability to be self-aware and critical in the way that they handle scripture. This chapter will explore the hermeneutical issues that surround the use of the Bible in the process of doing theology in the area of sexuality, using the previous nine chapters as a case study.

10.1 STARTING IN THE WRONG PLACE

10.1.1 The 'rule book' approach

For many Christians the matter could not be simpler. The Bible is God's Word inspired by the Holy Spirit and not in any way conditioned by the cultural and historical circumstances in which it was formed. For them all Christian discourse on sexuality must begin (and end) with the Bible. This was the approach adopted by the Evangelical Free Church when responding to the **HIV/AIDS** pandemic (see **4.7**). However, there are huge problems with this approach which many churches in the **Reformed tradition**, and Evangelical and Catholic theologians as well as liberal and radical theologians, recognize. The first and most obvious problem is that Christians do not agree on what the Bible says on some issues. This sometimes leads to one group claiming more authority than another to discern 'the mind of scripture'. Michael Vasey in his study on homosexuality from an Evangelical point of view argues that such an approach ignores the deeply mysterious and heterogeneous nature of the Bible:

> As an exercise in divine communication God's use of scripture is almost as bizarre as his taking flesh at a particular moment in history, or his entrusting a saving message to a corrupt and fallible church. At the same time there is something liberating in his choosing to provide the normative instrument and record of his communication in this form rather than as doctrinal statement or legal and moral code.
>
> There is, in an important sense, no definitive external guide to the scriptures ... But there remains in a certain sense no centre; there is no right place to start, no definitive key to this book ... There is no defining fulcrum outside scripture which gives one person the right to wield this mystery against another.[1]

Vasey goes on to argue that this means that discernment must be a corporate task, as Paul in Romans 12.2 suggests. Different people and types of Christians will bring different perspectives which must be taken into account. The Bible is not a rule book, nor are we Christians, living in the twilight and dawn of two millennia, the people to whom the writings of the Bible were addressed. St Paul may have claimed 'We have the mind of Christ' (1 Corinthians 2.16), but for us to make a similar claim would be arrogant. As Vasey notes, the 'cross over' from the Bible to ourselves will be direct (e.g. the command, 'love your enemies'). But 'often it is not so simple, and principles have to be discerned and reapplied'.[2]

We have already observed (see **7.3.5**) the Bible interpreting itself, as the first generation of Christians attempted to make sense of their liberating experience of the Christ-event in the light of the Hebrew scriptures (see **7.3**). No Christian observes all Old Testament laws, nor do we these days feel any qualms about ignoring Paul's advice about maintaining the institution of slavery. Most Christians would regard the modern slave trades as reprehensible, nor would they believe in unquestioning obedience to civil authority as Paul did. The

Presbyterian (USA) report *Keeping Body and Soul Together* noted: 'If we were to add up all the passages in the New Testament that speak of human sexuality, more would recommend **celibacy** than marriage'[3] (see **3.10**), a view which would not be echoed among conservative Evangelicals today.

Some Christians may believe that others who advocate the acceptance of **lesbian** and **gay** relationships or **cohabitation** (see **3.6–3.7**) have capitulated to the trends of modern secular culture, without realizing that they do the same, unless they believe the slave trade to have been moral or the Christians who supported Hitler to have been correct. We noted (see **2.9**) that biblical literalists were bound to support the practice of **polygamy** and the execution of non-virgin brides, adulterers and some victims of rape. We also noted (see **1.4**) how biblical literalists serve only to bring the Bible into disrepute and prevent it being read as liberating and life-giving.

The Church of England teaches that 'Holy Scripture containeth all things necessary to salvation'.[4] Protestant, Reformed churches have generally claimed that revealed truth is to be found in scripture alone. **Natural law** and tradition have been accepted as necessary alternative sources of knowledge throughout Christian history, especially in the Roman Catholic Church. *Keeping Body and Soul Together* is unique among church reports for combining a conventional acceptance of the scriptures as 'the primary and indispensable resource for theological and ethical reflection',[5] with an honest appreciation of the difficulties involved, and of the need to attend both to the biblical contexts and to the frequent use of scripture 'as a weapon against persons and in defense of moral wrong, including chattel slavery and women's subordination'.[6]

In particular, *Keeping Body and Soul Together* notes that, 'In matters where biblical texts can be found to support alternative concepts or understandings ... it appears that the writers of Scripture were as diverse as present-day Presbyterians.'[7] Indeed, the existence of the many ethical theories formulated by Christians explored in Chapter 2 would not be necessary if we had some kind of *direct* or incontrovertible access to God or the mind of Christ through the Bible. Few Christians would deny that non-Christians have something to teach them about mathematics, motor-car maintenance and gardening skills. Yet when it comes to matters of sexuality many believe that the Bible alone is the source of truth. Vasey argues that 'We are no different from Moses who had something to learn from Jethro, although the latter was a priest of Midian' (Exodus 18.1, 13–27).[8] He goes on to point out that Proverbs 8 portrays God's gift of wisdom as available outside of 'religion'. Wisdom cries out in the street and in the square. What all this demonstrates is that those who claim to follow the Bible and the Bible alone in fact do not do so. They have adopted an unconscious hermeneutic (method of interpretation) which enables them to choose for themselves between authoritative and non-authoritative texts.

10.1.2 The 'relay race'

An interesting similarity between both conservative and liberal Christians is that they both claim to start with the Bible when discussing sexuality. The 'liberal' church documents and reports that have been surveyed in this book almost all begin with a chapter on the Bible. As Stephen Barton has commented,

> Here, the implicit assumption, of course, is that interpretation and application follow the laying of the biblical foundations rather than influencing it from the start! It is as if the answers to this and any question can be 'read off' the text in a relatively straightforward way, either by 'stretching' history (in the case of the fundamentalist) or by asserting historical distance (in the case of the historical critic), with the matter of application following on subsequently.[9]

The process of doing theology then becomes, in liberal circles, a relay race. The biblical scholar establishes the 'original meaning' of certain relevant texts and then passes them on to the theologian who attempts to apply them to his or her historical and cultural context, deciding which teaching has eternal value and which has not. However this process never quite works, because the definitive original meaning of a text is never established. Barton believes that both the fundamentalist and liberal critic treat the Bible unjustly and do violence to it by using it as a source from which useful proof texts can be extracted. He notes the way in which church debate on issues of sexuality tends to circle endlessly around key texts, and believes that this trivializes the Bible and human sexuality. The Bible becomes both a battleground and weapon of different interest groups and issues of human sexuality are reduced to matters of exegesis which only a very few are qualified to carry out. Establishing the original or literal meaning of a text, even if this were possible, does not ultimately help very much.

Barton illustrates this point by referring to the debate over whether Jesus was a feminist. Supposing it were possible to establish that he was,

> What difference does it make to women suffering sexual abuse and political and economic oppression today to know that there happen to be historians who believe that Jesus was a feminist? Unless we have a broader theological and ecclesiological framework of understanding, experience and practice which enables us to see that Jesus' positive regard for the marginalised expresses something truthful about the inclusive nature of human salvation in Christ and about all humankind as made of the image of God, then the supposed attitude of the historical Jesus is hardly more than (so-called) antiquarian interest.[10]

The futility of the relay-race approach is clearly demonstrated by the current deadlock in most churches over the issue of homosexuality. Barton suggests that the issue of sexuality perhaps more than any other forces us to recognize that we have to start somewhere else other than the Bible, that we have first to establish what kind of people we need to be in order to interpret the Bible wisely. In other words, ethical issues actually precede hermeneutical ones: 'It is those who are themselves transformed and being transformed according to the image of Christ who will be best able to perform the scriptures in ways which bring life and Christ-like transformation to human sexuality.'[11] Even though we have some criticisms of Barton (see below, **10.5**) we do believe that he is essentially correct to argue that we cannot begin with the Bible and that the issue is not what the Bible says but how the Bible is read (see **1.4**). We are convinced that the people we have to be in order to interpret the Bible wisely are persons in just and mutual relations with others who are able, through 'empathetic identification' with the oppressed and marginalized, to stand in solidarity with them as Christ did (see **2.12**).

10.2 STARTING WITH OURSELVES: FEMINIST HERMENEUTICS

Studying the debates on sexuality and gender that have emerged in the second half of the twentieth century it becomes clear that two distinct theological methods have emerged. There is the theology of **liberation** model, which begins in an active involvement in a struggle for justice, represented by such theologies as liberation theology, **feminist theology**, **black theology** and gay and lesbian theologies. The experience of this struggle is brought to a reading of scripture. The second theological method is represented by both conservative and liberal theologies which, as we have already noted, begin with the Bible. Liberation, black, feminist and gay theologians claim that what conservative and liberal theologians proclaim are 'neutral' readings of the text are in fact nothing of the kind but are value-laden, laden with the values of white, 'First World', **heterosexual**, middle- and upper-class men. Having defined themselves as the norm, these exegetes are completely unaware of the agenda they bring to the text.

In Margaret Atwood's powerful and disturbing novel, *The Handmaid's Tale*, which imagines life under a governmental regime which bases itself on biblical law, the Bible is in fact only available to be read by the Commanders, the men who hold all the power:

> The Bible is kept locked up, the way people once kept tea locked up, so the servants wouldn't steal it. It is an incendiary device: who knows what we'd make of it, if we ever got our hands on it? We can be read to from it, by him, but we cannot read. Our heads turn towards him, we are expectant, here comes our bedtime story . . . It is the usual story, the usual stories. God to Adam, God to Noah. *Be fruitful and multiply, and replenish the earth.*[12]

Women, gay men, black and Asian people, disabled people, the poor, are among those who have had the Bible locked away from them and who have been made into passive recipients of other people's interpretation of the text. They have been forced to wear the spectacles of those other than themselves, and it is the contention of these groups of oppressed people that they have been read a 'bedtime story', a reading of the text which justifies their oppression. What the Christian churches have witnessed in recent years is whole groups of Christians who, through struggle in 'secular' movements for justice, have gained enough self-confidence and awareness of the dynamics of power and oppression to snatch the key to the Bible away from its previous self-appointed guardians and to read it for themselves through the eyes of their own experience. They do this not in order to produce another 'bedtime story', i.e., to explain away or neutralize passages they experience as oppressive, but to engage with the text honestly and creatively in order that it might become life-giving, enabling all to flourish.

As we stated (see **1.2**), we have chosen to place ourselves in what others may regard as a completely impossible position, namely, a position of loyalty to the Christian tradition and loyalty to those who have been alienated and oppressed by it. We therefore wish to stand in solidarity with all those groups of Christians who, though mindful of how the Bible has been used as a weapon against them, have simply refused to hand it over to their oppressors, but claim at least equal access to it. The theology of access developed by disabled theologians (see **4.6**) can also be applied to the Bible.

10.2.1 Strategies of interpretation

The interpretation of scripture which we have adopted in this study closely resembles feminist hermeneutics, but it is not identical with it. In the remaining sections of this chapter the hermeneutical proposals of an influential feminist theologian are described, and her 'strategies of interpretation' are illustrated with examples from this book. In **10.3** we add 'queer hermeneutics' to feminist hermeneutics, examining some criticisms of both in **10.4**. Finally in **10.5** a comparison with our own practice in this book is attempted.

The feminist biblical scholar Elisabeth Schüssler Fiorenza has identified ten feminist 'strategies of interpretation' with regard to the biblical text. While some of these are more central to sexual **ethics** and theology than others, they are briefly mentioned and illustrated next.

1. Revisionist interpretation. This strategy seeks to highlight the forgotten and ignored women of the biblical and extra-biblical traditions. When the women (often nameless) have been highlighted in the text, then their stories are 'catalogued' into positive and negative ('texts of terror') categories. In this book this method has been evident in drawing attention to the stories of terror built around Tamar and Susanna (see **5.6–5.7**) and the dynamics of power (see **5.1–5.3**) that operate in their stories. They stand in solidarity with the experience of millions of women who have been the victims of unequal power relations between the sexes and they demonstrate the consequences of the **patriarchal**, 'doormat' theology (see **5.12**) that lies behind them.

We highlighted the stories of women who sabotage patriarchy by refusing to play the roles that it assigns to them (see **6.6.2**). We followed lesbian and gay theologians in highlighting stories (see **7.3.4**) which might have more relevance to lesbian and gay existence than the usual proof texts that are trotted out in the homosexuality debate, and that are identified as 'texts of terror'. Our own un-apologetic exposure of the ideologies of 'patriarchy, **purity** and **property**' operating behind the **Holiness Code** and the Household Codes of the New Testament (see **1.6–1.8**) are also examples of revisionist interpretation in action.

Notice that this approach to biblical interpretation also involves going outside of the canon — the collection of writings that make up the Bible. The motivation for drawing up the canon was political, the need to unify the Church (which related to the need to unify the Roman Empire) by creating a class of 'heretics', people who deviated from the 'truth'; but first 'the truth' had to be clearly defined and established. Feminist scholars are suspicious of the powerful 'win-ners' (i.e., those who defined themselves as orthodox), together with their theological judgements and views of history. They also note that many of the writings that were excluded from the canon when it was formalized in the fourth century (although no single canon has ever been accepted by all churches) were focused upon women, e.g. the Gospel of Mary Magdalene which portrays her as the principal apostle. This suggests that part of the agenda behind the formation of the canon may have been to trample on the leadership of women in the early Church. Feminist scholars transgress the walled garden of the Bible[13] for they know that wisdom permeates the whole world (an image which is of course scriptural).

> This image does not allow for an understanding of canonical authority as exclusive and commanding. Rather, it grasps the original Latin meaning of *augere/auctoritas* as nurturing creativity, flowering growth, and enhancing enrichment. Biblical authority should foster such creativity, strength, and freedom.[14]

2. Text and translation. This strategy seeks to expose the way in which **androcentric** translations have obliterated women from the text by either assuming that generic use of the masculine excludes women or opting for a male translation where others are available. For example, in Colossians 4.15 the accusative *Nymphan* can refer to a man (Nymphas) or a woman (Nympha): some manuscripts go on to refer to 'her house', some to 'his'. Most biblical translations have referred to 'his'. In **7.3.4** we exposed the tendency of translators to impose a **homophobic** interpretation on ambiguous words.

3. Imaginative identification. In this strategy women retell biblical stories in such a way that the women in them are not silenced. This retelling is common in the Jewish tradition of midrash and was adopted by black slaves in the USA who were not allowed to read the Bible. Imaginative identification was incorporated in our method for engaging in passionate ethics, claiming that 'being-in-relation' enables 'empathic identification' to take place between ourselves and others. We sought to identify with the 'suffering bodies of abused women and children' and to discern Christ there suffering with them (see **2.12**). Central to the defence of lifelong commitment within Christian marriage was the plight of children who became victims of their parents' promiscuity or lack of commitment to each other.

4. Women as authors and biblical interpreters. This strategy seeks to recover works written by women. Considering the possibility that women might have written the Gospels of Mark or John or the Letter to the Hebrews (possibilities which have all been suggested by respected scholars) expands our theological imagination and also forces us to face the possibility that women have been behind the shaping of some of the biblical material — although we cannot assume that texts will be liberating just because they are authored by women. There is also a long history of women reading and interpreting the Bible which is largely ignored but which could provide a wealth of insight.

5. Historical interpretation. This strategy attempts to restore women to history and to restore history to women by asking such questions as, what would the everyday life of a Palestinian woman have been, could she read and write? Were there women theologians, poets, etc.? What rights did they have? Throughout Chapter 7 we saw that it was necessary to ask what type of same-sex behaviour the Bible authors knew about and in Chapters 4 (see **4.2–4.3**) and 7 we noted how important it was to understand the meaning of the body and bodily action within the world-view of the biblical authors before applying texts to our own time and culture. We noted how Paul's advice about sexual conduct was conditioned by the belief in the **parousia** (see **1.9**).

6. *Sociocultural reconstruction.* Fiorenza, who developed this strategy in her book *In Memory of Her*,[15] recognizes the rhetorical culture of biblical texts. She means by this that most texts are written as part of a struggle for power. Texts about women do not necessarily describe the reality of women's lives. It is necessary to take these texts and seek to discover what reality lies beneath them, to construct the struggle going on, taking care to avoid unconscious anti-Semitism and other xenophobia in this process — assuming biblical texts represent the way all Jews felt about women, etc. This strategy of interpretation seeks to reconstruct history from the perspective of the losers. In Chapter 8 (see **8.2–8.4**) we noted the theme of sexual subversion running throughout the scripture. This may indicate the existence of a debate about the significance of **sex**, **desire** and the body which only surfaces in the fissures between narrative and law in the Hebrew scriptures.

7. *Ideological inscription.* This strategy seeks to expose the gendered nature of all biblical texts, not simply those overtly about women. We found it necessary to devote an entire chapter to gender (see Chapter 6), believing the superficial discussion of it in church documents had impoverished the churches.

8. *Women as subjects of interpretation.* This strategy shifts attention from the text to the reader and to the way in which the reader is already socialized by, and in, patriarchy before reading the text. Sometimes the text itself assumes and demands that the reader take the patriarchal position — e.g., Proverbs 1–9 is constructed as a communication between a father and son (i.e., the reader). We must become resisting readers, resisting the patriarchal grain of the text and reading against it. Much of the use of the Bible in this book has involved reading against the grain of patriarchy. As resisting readers we have refused to 'make excuses' for the 'texts of terror' and we have also pitted parts of the Bible against one another. In **9.2** and **9.6** we took love of God and neighbour as being central to the Christian faith and used this biblical injunction as a basis from which to establish the authority of other passages. In **7.5.1** and **7.5.2** we took

the biblical commandment not to bear false witness and applied it to
the expectation that men should exhibit masculine, and women
feminine, qualities. In **7.5.4** we applied it to the homophobic sentiments of Vatican documents. In **6.4** we considered *men* as subjects of
interpretation, noting how the social construction of masculinity was
likely to impoverish them and lead them in some cases to fear
vulnerability and **mutuality**.

9. Socio-political location.   This strategy draws attention to socio-
political, global-cultural and pluralistic religious locations and contexts of biblical readings. **Womanist** (black feminist) scholars have
argued that racial slavery is the socio-political context of biblical
interpretation. 'Just as the legitimisation of slavery has determined
the biblical readings of white churches, so the experience of slavery
has shaped African-American biblical interpretation.'[16] Latin American feminists have similarly named the oppression of the poor as the
socio-political context of biblical interpretation. These hermeneutics
from the margins demonstrate that there is no such thing as a value-
free interpretation of biblical texts and that 'interested' readings of
the text are no less scholarly than supposed 'disinterested' readings.
Indeed, 'they require a public articulation of scholarly values and
commitments. They draw their intellectual force neither from scientific rationalism nor from academic antidogmatism but rather from
their commitment to the liberation struggle of their people.'[17] The
authenticity of their interpretation does not depend on academic
recognition or agreement but whether it becomes an instrument of
survival and liberation for their communities.

10. A critical model of feminist interpretation.   This is the strategy
which Fiorenza is now trying to develop, drawing on the other nine
methods. It is an interactive and multistrategic model of interpretation which is always focused upon praxis. A critical feminist
rhetoric insists that context is as important as text. What we see
depends on where we stand. Current biblical scholarship claims to be
objective and value-neutral, thereby taking no responsibility for the
political assumptions of the texts or the interpreter. Feminist interpretation takes responsibility for both.

If the Bible has become a classic of Western culture because of its
normativity, then the biblical scholar's responsibility cannot be

restricted to giving contemporary readers clear access to the biblical writers' original intentions. It must also include the elucidation of the ethical consequences and political functions of biblical texts and scholarly discourses in their historical as well as contemporary sociopolitical contexts.[18]

10.2.2 Strategies of reading

Fiorenza then goes on to distinguish four reading strategies or moments in the critical feminist hermeneutical process — a process of conscientization or learning to recognize the socio-political, economic, cultural and religious assumptions involved which lead to cognitive dissonance, i.e., which call into question the common-sense of patriarchy. The first three of these strategies are included in the 'overview' of a feminist hermeneutic.

1. A hermeneutic of suspicion. This strategy turns the searchlight first on the interpreter's own assumptions and then the text's. In feminist terms, it seeks to expose the androcentric and patriarchal assumptions in the horizons of both. In **2.1** we demonstrated the need to be very suspicious of ethical 'theories' and in **7.5.1** we adopted a hermeneutic of suspicion when examining the theory of **complementarity**, exposing the assumptions that are behind that theory and that are then brought to and imposed on biblical texts quite unjustifiably.

2. A hermeneutic of remembrance. This strategy designs models for reconstruction which recover all possible memories of women in the text and stitch them together to form a different and more plausible picture. In **7.3.5** we endeavoured to recover the memories of same-sex lovers in the biblical text, demonstrating how this approach can put a whole different complexion on a fierce but never-ending debate.

3. A hermeneutic of proclamation. This strategy insists that patriarchal texts should not be affirmed but exposed. It therefore judges the texts according to whether they give life or diminish it. This whole book is an example of a hermeneutic of proclamation. We clearly stated in **1.12** that our desire is both to expose texts which diminish and to proclaim those which can be read in a life-giving and liberating way. There is much in the Bible which is anti-ethical for the simple reason that it demands unquestioning obedience to a set of rules. The Holiness Code is a case in point.

We have several times pointed out the disastrous consequences of an ethic of complete obedience. We noted how obedience was used as a defence in the execution of orders carried out by those guilty of war crimes (see **2.3.3**). We have confirmed the claim that churches requiring unquestioning obedience to their teachings behave oppressively (see **5.1**). We also noted that abusers, harassers and rapists were able to use the expectation of obedience in the perpetration of horrendous crimes (see **5.5–5.10**). Philip Davies has pointed out that obedience is a neutrally ethical response because it can lead to ethical and non-ethical action. The 'just obeying orders' explanation for behaviour simply does not convince those of us living in the shadow of the Holocaust. Davies, commenting on Leviticus, argues that it 'represents the values of that least ethical community, the totalitarian state, with its big brother, the all-holy uncompromising sacrifice-consuming despot as the invention of a fascist clique'.[19]

However, in the wisdom tradition it is quite clear that wisdom is not attained as a result of obedience but through *discernment*, in other words, through observation and thought. The prophets added a less individualistic dimension to this by emphasizing the need to stand in solidarity with the poor and oppressed. The Gospels do not portray Jesus as a new law-giver but as someone who stood in active solidarity with the outcast and invited others to do the same. If we are therefore to look for ethical guidance in the Bible, the last place we should look is the law codes, for they are not ethical. We should look to those texts which present us with choices, which allow us to act in freedom, which do not prescribe what we are to do but challenge us to take a life-giving ball and run with it into the midst of our own lives. In **8.2** we sought to draw back the veil of silence and embarrassment which had been placed by the Church over the Song of Songs, which we read as a glorious celebration of desire. It is not in any sense a law book, it does not 'preach' at the reader, but by presenting an example of a relationship almost untainted by patriarchy and **dualism** it takes on a deeply ethical character. It offers the reader an alternative vision of love, passion and desire.

10.3 STARTING WITH OURSELVES: QUEER HERMENEUTICS

10.3.1 Biblical terrorism

Lesbian and gay theologians owe much to feminist hermeneutics in their handling of the Bible. Robert Goss notes that lesbian and gay people have been the victim of 'biblical terrorism': not only has the Bible been used as a weapon to justify discrimination and violence, but churches often exert subtle and not so subtle pressure upon biblical scholars which prevents them from asking appropriate hermeneutical questions which would challenge the use of the Bible against lesbian and gay people.[20] Yet now some Christians are claiming the Bible as a resource in their struggle against injustice:

> The lives of queer Christians become another text from which they interpret the biblical text. Queer Christians refigure the meaning of the text by interpreting and applying it to their lives. They realise that for change in ecclesial biblical discourse to take place, they must start to reject the traditional ecclesial constructions of the text. In fact, they reject all readings that either depoliticise or spiritualise the text. Their commitments to their queer identities, practices, and the struggle for justice become a framework for interpreting a particular biblical text.[21]

Despite its patriarchal bent the Bible does consistently present God as a God of the oppressed, and privileges the non-person as one with whom God stands in solidarity. Queer hermeneutics involve standing in solidarity with the non-persons of the biblical text because lesbian and gay people feel a natural empathy with the marginalized and outcast of the biblical story. As people who are oppressed, queer Christians, like the poor of Latin America, black people, feminists and others, claim the 'epistemological privilege of the oppressed', i.e., as people who correspond to the non-persons of the biblical text they claim a particularly authoritative insight into the text. In this way the texts of scripture are transformed from being weapons of terrorism into narratives of resistance. The Jesus material becomes 'a critical challenge to the "master narratives" of Christian discourse, the homophobic/**heterosexist** reconstructions of biblical texts'.[22] But it also challenges lesbian and gay Christians to ensure that God's justice and compassion undergirds and transforms their political practice.

Goss demonstrates how 'unlikely' texts can become narratives of queer resistance in his analysis of Jesus' exorcisms in Mark's Gospel.

He points out that the demons oppress people, they dominate and enslave them, depriving them of all freedom. Jesus' defeat of the demons 'symbolises the sociopolitical freedom of God's reign'.[23] Demon possession functions symbolically in Mark's Gospel, representing the Roman occupation (the Gerasene demoniac is known as 'Legion') and the divisive Jewish social system. The possessed are suffering from 'oppression sickness'. They manifest in their own bodies the socio-political tensions that rupture their society and they are therefore dangerous parables of reality, which is why they must be marginalized. Lesbian and gay people have a particular type of solidarity with the demoniacs of the Gospel, labelled as they have been as sick and possessed by those whose world-view they challenge, and forced by them to bear the terrible tension caused by compulsory heterosexuality.

> Jesus' exorcisms can be read as public symbolic actions directed against the political and religious order that produced oppressive sickness. The oppression found in these stories can be read in the light of gay/lesbian struggles against homophobia/heterosexism and its damaging effects. Jesus the Queer Christ fights for gay men and lesbians who are dominated by homophobic power relations, and he struggles to liberate them from the effects of homophobic oppression and from antihuman possession of internalised homophobia. He overthrows violent social forces that prevent queer people from experiencing themselves as free and loving human beings. He challenges the religious authority that maintains the social system of violence.[24]

In redeeming such material queer Christians uncover a dangerous memory of God's subversion of human oppression. This dangerous memory of the queer Christ becomes the hermeneutical key to interpreting all other biblical stories. A queer hermeneutic of solidarity will include the memory of all those who have suffered from oppression with whom the queer Christ identifies, such as the hundreds of thousands killed in Nazi concentration camps (see **2.3.3**; **10.2.2**). The solidarity is based upon a commitment to end all oppression.

10.3.2 The Bible as friend

Another gay theologian, Gary David Comstock, has developed a hermeneutic within the wider theology of friendship espoused by lesbian and gay scholars:

Instead of making the Bible into a parental authority, I have begun
to engage it as I would a friend — as one to whom I have made a
commitment and in which I have invested dearly, but with whom I
insist on a mutual exchange of critique, encouragement, support,
and challenge ... Although its homophobic statements sting and
condemn me, I counter that those statements are themselves condemned by its own Exodus and Jesus events. Just as I have said to my
friend, 'How can you express love and be a justice-seeking person
and not work to overcome the oppression of lesbians and gay men?'
In my dialogue with the Bible I ask, 'How can you be based on two
events that are about transforming pain, suffering, and death into
life, liberation, and healing, and yet call for the misery and death of
lesbians and gay men?'[25]

In the writings which make up the Bible we encounter our ancestors in faith struggling to make sense of their experience of God in
their lives. Their experiences and reflection inform, challenge and
inspire our own but cannot replace it. For if God is a God 'not of the
dead but of the living' (Matthew 22.32) then every generation of
Christians has to endeavour to make sense of the presence of this
living, mysterious God in their midst. The image of the Bible as
friend or friends enables us to take it seriously whilst not idolizing it.
It allows it to challenge without controlling. Is it consistent both to
treat the Bible as a friend and yet exercise the suspicious strategies of
interpretation just outlined (see above, **10.2**)? Yes. We can have
confidence in it because it is a record of the faith of the people of
God and because, ultimately, its testimony points to Christ (John
5.39).

10.4 STARTING WITH OURSELVES: PROBLEMS

There are several criticisms which can be made of feminist and queer
hermeneutics. At one extreme there are those such as Frederick W.
Schmidt who accuse feminist and lesbian and gay theologians of an
unnecessary biblicism. If they acknowledge that the Bible is androcentric and patriarchal why do they continue to place such emphasis
upon it?[26] It was originally the creation of the Church and it is the
Church itself, not the biblical text, which has to wrestle with issues of
human sexuality in the present and future. A concept of **revelation**
needs to be developed compatible with the Christian belief that God
continues to be present in our times and circumstances. As Tom
Driver has put it,

The church, broadly speaking, is the author of scriptures and from this their authority proceeds ... This is what we must own up to. Doing so would free us to ask what good the scriptures are for us in the liberating work we are called to share with God in the present-future. It would also free us to see more clearly, and with less rationalisation, the scripture's liabilities. Finally, and most threateningly, such ownership of authorship would make the church clearly political, for its reality would then be understood as the way it acts upon the present scene. As long as scripture is viewed as a purely external authority derived from past time, it circumvents responsibility for present action, no matter if the Bible itself calls to responsibility. But the moment we view the Bible as something we have written, for the purpose of not forgetting the encounters we have had with God, our identity becomes more clear and we may be agents in the new work God performs today.[27]

Schmidt and Driver undoubtedly have a point. Even though queer and feminist theologies may not begin in the Bible they do spend a great deal of time in it. Partly this is because they are responding to the use of the Bible by opponents, but there is also still a reluctance to move from the image of the Bible as parent to that of friend, which may have something to do with learning to trust their own experiences and theological reflection. Ironically, in the examples of Paul and the gospel writers in the Bible itself we have examples of how to be theologically bold and to trust communal experience of the revelation of God even when it appears to rupture the authority of sacred texts.

Anthony Thiselton has written a major study on hermeneutics which includes feminist, but not queer, hermeneutics. In this study he is concerned to distinguish between biblical analysis by a particular group of people which provides genuine insight and which is ultimately liberating for the whole Christian community — what he labels 'socio-critical hermeneutics' — and that which is simply rhetorical and designed to promote a specific cause — 'socio-pragmatic hermeneutics'.[28] He offers three principles to make a judgement upon a particular form of hermeneutics.

1. A hermeneutic of suspicion must work both ways — the Church must be open to the possibility of new truths emerging from new hermeneutics but must also be 'suspicious' of mere self-interest and so must those involved in feminist and (by implication) queer hermeneutics.

2.   An awareness that truth will be revealed — Christianity is at
      heart an eschatological religion which looks towards a final and
      full revelation.

3.   The life, death and resurrection of Jesus must be the pattern by
      which hermeneutics are judged. Any new truth claim must
      exhibit the characteristic of self-sacrifice.

Feminist and queer theologians might respond to Thiselton that a
socio-pragmatic approach may not in fact be confined to the newest
forms of hermeneutics. He also demonstrates the fear of self-love and
confidence that dogs patriarchal theology and has had such a negative effect upon women. The personal cost to women and gay
scholars who dare to step out of the shadows and do theology out of
their own experience is considerable. But Thiselton's main point is
valid, that if the Bible is to be friend, readers and interpreters must be
prepared to allow it to challenge and question them. We have seen in
3.2 and **3.6** that the Bible challenges modern bodily dualism and
ageism and in **8.2** that it challenges ecclesial fear of desire, but
perhaps the greatest challenge the Bible presents to those of us
engaged in the study of sexuality is its remarkable relative lack of
concern for matters sexual. The reign of God certainly impacts upon
sexual relations but it encompasses much, much more than them. It
also reminds us that we are just as much children of our age,
geography and culture as the authors of the biblical material. Our
concerns with matters of sexuality and gender are not only manifestations of our **socialization** but will probably seem quirky and obsessive
to future generations.

10.5 THE BIBLE IN SEXUAL THEOLOGY

Barton believes that the most recent forms of hermeneutics are still
guilty of the 'Little Jack Horner' approach to the Bible. He asks:

> What if the Bible is more like the text of a Shakespearean play or
> the score of a Beethoven symphony, where true interpretation
> involves corporate performance and practical enactment, and
> where the meaning of the text or score will vary to some degree
> from one performance to another depending on the identity of the
> performers and the circumstances of the performance?[29]

Biblical interpretation therefore becomes a communal and practical
activity. We endorse Barton's 'corporate performance' approach but
make two important reservations. First, in order for a biblical performance to be truly communal, all the performers must have a

voice. All 'legitimate voices' must be heard (see **2.6**). Feminist women and lesbian and gay people, along with a host of others, are only just finding their voices, partly through the development of distinctive hermeneutics. Closely related to this is the second point, that performance implies equality and mutuality between performers. The Church has a long way to go before lesbian and gay, women, black people, disabled people, etc., will be able to feel that equality and mutuality. At the moment communal performance would still be a predominantly white, male, 'First World', heterosexual performance.

In truth no hermeneutical key to reading the Bible has yet done justice to the complex relationship Christians have to the Bible. It is not something we come to or can ever come to 'cold' or objectively. Anyone living in the Western Christian world has already been formed by the Bible. Metaphorically we carry it in our genes, as we do our ancestors. It is part of our make up. It is as much behind modern and postmodern liberation movements as it is behind fundamentalism. We do not come to it first or last when we set out to read it, for it is already present. We have yet to learn how to handle this 'incendiary device' so that the explosion creates the right conditions for *communal* flourishing. Ironically it is perhaps the relationship Christians have most trouble managing. All the dangers we have isolated for human sexual relationships: power as domination, faithlessness, lust, etc., are also evident in the way we treat the Bible, and perhaps the greatest challenge we face is to learn how to treat the Bible as we believe we should treat each other, with justice, mutuality and equality.

In **1.12** we noted that the passionate ethics which we were going to develop in this book were fundamentally eclectic, drawing upon the insights of many. We said there that we had 'no quarrel with the Bible ... as long as its testimony is allowed to point to Jesus Christ' (John 5.39). Our own hermeneutical approach reflects this eclecticism and is perhaps best illustrated by our analysis of the Bible and homosexuality in **7.3**. First we sought to expose the common assumption that the Bible only speaks about homosexuality to condemn it and sought to question that assumption. Then we challenged another assumption, namely that the passages condemning homosexuality have more authority than other passages which Christians happily ignore. We exposed the patriarchal bias behind the passages that 'clearly' condemn homosexual behaviour, and pointed out the difficulties of translation. We then suggested a hermeneutical key is needed to deal with scripture with some integrity, a hermeneutical key which will enable us to read scripture in such a way that encourages us to have a deeper love of God and others. Jesus' solidarity with the oppressed, love of neighbour, love and righteousness were all explored as hermeneutical keys.

However, we are clear that our hermeneutic can only be judged by the behaviour it encourages. The fact that many lesbian, gay and bisexual people (and indeed many others) do not feel loved, included, cared for, or supported by many of the churches is the greatest indictment of those churches' hermeneutics. Only by standing in solidarity with those on the margins will those who are responsible for writing church documents on sexuality be able to read the Bible in a way that does help to establish an inclusive, just and justice-seeking Church (which is what they all claim to want). We have attempted to adopt a way of reading the Bible which springs out of our desire to stand in solidarity with all those marginalized on the basis of their sexuality or gender and we believe that our reading of texts is life-giving and liberating, but in the end we cannot be the judge of that.

10.6 SUMMARY

In this chapter we have noted how difficult the churches find it to handle scripture with integrity and consistency. We have explored the problems of beginning with the Bible and suggested that everyone (whether they acknowledge it or not) begins somewhere else. We have examined feminist and queer hermeneutics and noted how the Bible has been used in different parts of this book, including by ourselves. And finally we have suggested that the proper hermeneutical key has yet to be found to the Bible. We have yet to establish what a proper relationship between Christians and their scriptures should be. But we are clear that only a hermeneutic that springs out of an active solidarity with people marginalized on the grounds of sexuality will in the end produce the inclusive, justice-seeking Christian community which everyone involved in the debate around sexuality desires to see realized.

Notes

1 Michael Vasey, *Strangers and Friends: A New Exploration of Homosexuality and the Bible* (London: Hodder & Stoughton, 1995), pp. 12–13.

2 *Ibid.*, p. 52.

3 *Keeping Body and Soul Together*, p. 23.

4 Articles of Religion, 6.

5 *Keeping Body and Soul Together*, p. 22.

6 *Ibid.*, p. 24.

7 *Ibid.*, p. 22.

8 Vasey, *Strangers and Friends*, p. 52.

9 Stephen C. Barton, 'Is the Bible good news for human sexuality? reflections on method in biblical interpretation', in Adrian Thatcher and Elizabeth Stuart (eds), *Christian Perspectives on Sexuality and Gender* (Leominster: Gracewing/ Grand Rapids, MI: Eerdmans, 1996), p. 5.

10 *Ibid.*, p. 50.

11 *Ibid.*, p. 54.

12 Margaret Atwood, *The Handmaid's Tale* (London and New York: Virago and Ballantine Books, 1987), pp. 98–9.

13 Elisabeth Schüssler Fiorenza, *Searching the Scriptures: A Feminist Commentary* (London and New York: SCM and Crossroad, 1994), p. 11.

14 *Ibid.*, p. 11.

15 Elisabeth Schüssler Fiorenza, *In Memory of Her: A Feminist Theological Reconstruction of Christian Origins* (London and New York: SCM and Crossroad, 1983).

16 Elisabeth Schüssler Fiorenza, *But SHE Said: Feminist Practices of Biblical Interpretation* (Boston: Beacon Press, 1992), p. 38.

17 *Ibid.*, p. 39.

18 *Ibid.*, pp. 46–7.

19 Philip R. Davies, 'Ethics and the Old Testament' in John W. Rogerson, Margaret Davies and M. Daniel Carroll (eds), *The Bible in Ethics: The Second Sheffield Colloquium* (Sheffield: Sheffield Academic Press, 1995), p. 170.

20 Robert Goss, *Jesus Acted Up: A Gay and Lesbian Manifesto* (San Francisco: HarperSanFrancisco, 1993), pp. 90–101.

21 *Ibid.*, p. 103.

22 *Ibid.*, p. 105.

23 *Ibid.*, p. 106.

24 *Ibid.*, pp. 108–9.

25 Gary David Comstock, *Gay Theology without Apology* (Cleveland: The Pilgrim Press, 1993), pp. 11–12.

26 Frederick W. Schmidt, 'Beyond a biblicistic feminism: hermeneutics, women and the church', *Feminist Theology*, no. 11 (January 1996), pp. 55–71.

27 T. F. Driver, *Christ in a Changing World: Toward an Ethical Christology* (New York: Crossroad, 1981), pp. 83, 91.

28 A. C. Thiselton, *New Horizons in Hermeneutics* (London: HarperCollins, 1992), pp. 25–9, 331–8, 613–19.

29 Barton, 'Is the Bible good news?', p. 6.

Suggestions for further reading

Stephen C. Barton, 'Is the Bible good news for human sexuality? Reflections on method in biblical interpretation', in Adrian Thatcher and Elizabeth Stuart (eds), *Christian Perspectives on Sexuality and Gender* (Leominster: Gracewing/Grand Rapids, MI: Eerdmans, 1996), p. 5.

Elisabeth Schüssler Fiorenza, *But SHE Said: Feminist Practices of Biblical Interpretation* (Boston: Beacon Press, 1992).

Elisabeth Schüssler Fiorenza, *Searching the Scriptures: A Feminist Commentary* (London and New York: SCM and Crossroad, 1994).

John W. Rogerson, Margaret Davies and M. Daniel Carroll (eds), *The Bible in Ethics: The Second Sheffield Colloquium* (Sheffield: Sheffield Academic Press, 1995).

A. C. Thiselton, *New Horizons in Hermeneutics* (London: HarperCollins, 1992).

GLOSSARY

AGAPE One of the Greek words for love. Usually used in the New Testament for divine love, it has been traditionally interpreted as unconditional, self-giving love, the purest and highest form of love in contrast to **eros**.

AIDS Acquired Immunodeficiency Syndrome. It is a condition which causes the suppression of the body's immune system leaving it vulnerable to a variety of opportunistic infections. AIDS is caused by the Human Immunodeficiency Virus (HIV) which can be present in the body for an indefinite period of time before AIDS emerges. AIDS first came to public attention in the 1980s. HIV can only be passed from person to person through bodily fluids. It cannot be caught through normal interaction. Although early categorized as a 'gay plague' in the West, everyone who engages in unprotected sexual intercourse or shares drug needles is at risk. In places like Africa the disease is ravaging huge swathes of the heterosexual population.

ANALOGY The attempt to explain the meaning of one thing by using another on the basis of their similarities. So Thomas Aquinas argued that by virtue of being made in God's image human beings are able to speak about God in terms derived from human experience. God and humanity are of course not identical but share similarities.

ANDROCENTRISM Male-centredness. It is the claim of **feminist theology** that most biblical thought and Christian reflection since biblical times has been centred upon male experience and self-understanding.

ANDROCENTRIC FALLACY A phrase coined by the feminist writer Gerda Lerner to describe a vast intellectual error which has been built into Western civilization and the mind of those who live in it, namely that the male and his experiences represent the whole of humanity.

ANDROGYNY Androgynous people exhibit what society chooses to define as 'masculine' and 'feminine' characteristics in equal measure. Androgyny must be distinguished from hermaphroditism in which the sexual organs of both sexes are present. The whole concept of androgyny stands or falls on the notion that men and women are fundamentally different and display exclusive characteristics.

ANTHROPOCENTRISM Human-centredness.

ASCETICISM Spiritual discipline focused upon renunciation of the world and of the body.

ASIAN FEMINIST THEOLOGY Theological reflection by women of Asia, part of a wider movement to develop a distinctive Asian theology. Prominent theologians include Kwok Pui-lan and Chung Hyun Kyung.

ATONEMENT The doctrine of the atonement seeks to explain how Christ's life, and particularly his death, leads to at-one-ment between God and humanity. Throughout Christian history many theories have been advanced, including Anselm's satisfaction theory, Abelard's moral theory and the ransom theory. The Church has never adopted one theory. It has simply affirmed that Christ's death was a sacrifice which somehow put humanity back into a right relationship with God.

AUTONOMY Moral autonomy is the freedom of individuals to make authentic moral choices. It is considered in Christian ethics to be a precondition for ethical behaviour and responsibility.

BETROTHAL Historically, the point at which a non-married couple entered publicly into an exclusive social and sometimes sexual relationship and into a solemn commitment to one another with the expectation that they would marry. Some Christian theologians argue that the Church should return to recognizing betrothal and offer liturgies to mark its commencement.

BISEXUALITY A nineteenth-century term to describe those men and women who feel sexual attraction to members of both sexes.

BLACK THEOLOGY Theological reflection from the basis of black experience. Its beginnings are usually dated in the 1960s but in fact its roots are in the slave plantations. There are broadly two centres of black theology, the USA and South Africa. Prominent theologians include Allan Boesak, James Cone, Albert Cleague, John Mbiti and J. R. Washington.

CELIBACY Originally used in the Roman Empire to refer to the unmarried state, in the Christian community it has come to refer to a state of deliberate and freely chosen singleness in which the person is not sexually active.

CHASTITY Often wrongly confused with **celibacy** chastity is a state of sexual wholeness or **purity**. It is essentially about honouring the obligations of one's relationships. So adultery is a sin against chastity because it involves the breaking of the marriage vows.

COHABITATION The term applied to **heterosexual** couples living together outside of marriage, sometimes labelled in popular parlance as 'living in sin'.

COMPLEMENTARITY The theory that men and women are biologically and psychologically created by God to be fundamentally different from one another and yet complement one another, and that only when they come together in heterosexual relationship do they fully image God. This theory has become extremely popular in church documents on sexuality but has been widely criticized for having no biblical basis and for failing to take into account the **social construction** of **gender**.

CONCUPISCENCE According to Augustine the essence of sin. It was for him love of self rather than of God and was therefore a perversion.

CONSCIENCE The experience of ourselves as morally autonomous agents.

CONTINENCE Understood by Thomas Aquinas in two ways. First, abstention from all sexual pleasure, i.e., virginity or **celibacy**. Second, the resisting of evil desires, so it is possible to be married and continent.

COVENANT Refers, first, to the solemn contract between God and ancient Israel and the 'new covenant' made between God and all people through Christ. Second, it refers to solemn agreements between human beings which reflect and embody the nature of God's covenant with humanity.

CREATION-CENTRED SPIRITUALITY Associated with the theologian Matthew Fox this spirituality emerged in the 1980s (although it claims roots in the Bible). It holds that the **fall**/redemption theology upon which Christianity has been based since the time of Augustine has led to the denigration of matter, women and **sexuality**, which has resulted in the near extinction of our planet. Fox argues that we need to recover the ancient biblical teaching of 'original blessing' (as opposed to original sin) and in the process rediscover a love of the earth and our sexuality.

CULTURAL CONDITIONING The process of imbibing cultural norms and values unconsciously and assuming their truth.

DESIRE In post-Augustinian theology desire, particularly sexual desire, is a dangerous and subversive force bending the will away from God and towards the self. In **feminist** and body theology desire, particularly sexual desire, although capable of being distorted by sin and to a large extent **socially constructed**, is identified with **eros** — the drive away from self towards others and God.

DETERMINISM The belief that human freedom is an illusion and that all our actions are determined by a wide variety of factors including family and social background, **gender**, education, economic circumstances.

DOMESTIC CHURCH A Roman Catholic term for the family. It suggests that faith begins and is nurtured first and foremost in the family unit.

DUALISM The division of reality and human nature into opposites, often with the categorization of those opposites as good and evil.

Christian thinking about sexuality has been affected particularly by body–soul dualism and **gender** dualism, but other forms of dualism have also impacted upon it including will–**desire**, culture–nature, public–private and **orientation**–practice dualisms.

ENLIGHTENMENT An intellectual movement of the eighteenth century also known as the 'Age of Reason', which glorified human reason as the sole source and arbiter of all truth including truth about God. The autonomous individual assumed primary importance. The Enlightenment affected Christianity profoundly. One of the most notable areas of influence was in biblical studies. The Enlightenment thinkers questioned the assumption that the Bible was supernaturally inspired and their work led to modern biblical criticism. Although it presented itself as tolerant and optimistic, the Enlightenment has come under the critical scrutiny of **feminists** who have claimed that it simply substituted male reason for the male God.

EROS One of the Greek words for love and in the Christian tradition regarded as a lesser love than **agape** because of its association with **sexuality** and sensuality. Reclaimed by feminists and feminist theologians as deep body knowledge and a longing for **mutuality** expressed in all our relationality including sexual relations.

ESSENTIALISM A term used in feminist and lesbian and gay studies to refer to theories which locate gender or sexual orientation difference in biology and which therefore, in the case of lesbian and gay studies, claim that there always have been lesbian and gay people in every culture. **Social constructionists** challenge this view.

ETHICS Reflection upon matters of **morality** from the perspective of a specific, e.g. Christian, world-view.

FALL The 'fall' of humanity away from God and into sin, represented in Genesis 1 – 3.

FEMINIST THEOLOGY Emerged as a distinct branch of theology in the 1960s and 1970s out of the secular feminist movement. Feminist theology seeks to expose the **androcentric** and **patriarchal** basis of the Bible and Christian tradition and to construct new theologies out of women's experience and reflection. Prominent feminist theologians include Rosemary Radford Ruether, Beverly Wildung Harrison,

Sallie McFague, Phyllis Trible, Mary Grey, Mary Hunt, Grace Jantzen and two post-Christian theologians Mary Daly and Daphne Hampson. Feminist theology has become increasingly multi-faceted as non-white women have reacted against the tendency of early Christian feminists to talk of woman as a **universal** — see **Womanist Theology, Asian Feminist Theology** and **Mujerista Theology**.

GAY A term of self-description adopted by **homosexual** people in the twentieth century as an alternative to the term 'homosexual' which was believed to sound too pathological. Although applied to both women and men, it is more often applied to men.

GENDER Society's interpretation of the biological differences between the **sexes**. Understandings of what it means to be male and female are not read off nature but constructed, as changing understandings of gender and differences in gender understandings across cultures demonstrate.

HELLENISTIC ETHICS Ethical systems which emerged in the ancient Greek-speaking world including **Stoic**, Platonic, Epicurean and Aristotelian **ethics**.

HERMENEUTICS The set of principles which governs a reader's interpretation of a text such as the Bible.

HETEROPATRIARCHY A term used to draw attention to the fact that the **social construction** of **heterosexuality** almost always serves the interests of men over women.

HETEROSEXISM The assumption of the normativity and superiority of **heterosexuality**.

HETEROSEXUALITY The term 'heterosexual' was invented by the same person who invented the term '**homosexual**' in the nineteenth century and was part of the attempt being made at that time to categorize people into quasi-medical categories. A heterosexual person is one who is predominantly sexually and emotionally attracted to members of the opposite sex. Such people are sometimes referred to in common speech as 'straight'.

HIERARCHY The word literally means 'rule by priests' and refers to the ranks of ordained men and women who exercise power and authority in the Church. More commonly it now refers either to an élite body of rulers or to a ranking system in which one person or group of persons exercises authority over another.

HIV Human Immunodeficiency Virus. See **AIDS**.

HOLINESS CODE The name given to the block of teaching in Leviticus 17.1–26.46 which instructs the ancient Israelites on how to remain **pure** and separate, i.e., a holy people. It contains many rules on sexual conduct.

HOLISTIC A term which, when applied to medicine or theology, seeks to convey that the whole person — body and soul/psyche — is being dealt with as a unity and not simply as a body or a mind/soul. Also used to indicate that the whole ecosystem and not simply humanity is under consideration.

HOMOPHOBIA Prejudice against **lesbians** and **gay** men manifested by institutions and individuals. This prejudice is shown in a number of ways, in **heterosexism**, in violence and discrimination. Lesbians and gay men sometimes internalize society's homophobia, which leads to self-hate.

HOMOSEXUALITY A term invented in the nineteenth century to categorize people whose primary sexual and affectional attraction is to members of the same sex. This blanket term has serious deficiencies. Not only does it disguise the multi-faceted nature of same-sex desire, it also carries the questionable assumption that people can be neatly categorized according to their **sexual orientation**.

HOUSEHOLD CODES Found in Colossians 3.18–4.1; Ephesians 5.22–6.9; 1 Peter 2.13–3.7; Titus 2.1–10; 1 Timothy 2.8–16; 6.1–2. Characterized by an exhortation to wives, children and slaves to be submissive to husbands, parents and masters and to the latter to exercise authority with due Christian responsibility. These codes can be found outside the New Testament in works of Greek philosophy and have obviously been adopted and Christianized by New Testament writers. They represent a reaction against the vision of discipleship of equals found elsewhere in the New Testament.

INCARNATION The Christian belief that God became human in the person of Jesus of Nazareth.

LESBIAN A term of self-definition adopted by women whose sexual and affectional orientation is primarily directed towards women.

LESBIAN AND GAY THEOLOGY A branch of theology which began to emerge in the 1980s in which lesbians and gay men engage in theological reflection on their own struggle for liberation. Prominent names in this branch of theology include Carter Heyward, J. Michael Clark, John J. McNeill, Robert Goss, Elizabeth Stuart, Alison Webster, Mary Hunt and Virginia Ramey Mollenkott.

LIBERATION THEOLOGY A term properly applied only to the theology which began emerging in Latin America in the 1960s. It offered a new method of doing theology which begins in active commitment to the struggles of the poor and then moves into critical reflection upon that experience. This is accompanied by a **hermeneutic** of suspicion which interrogates the Christian tradition from the perspective of the poor of Latin America and concludes that most Christian theology reflects white, 'Northern', male, comfortably off clerical experience, and furthermore serves to bolster their power. Liberation theology seeks to do theology out of the experience of the struggling poor. Its influence upon other theologies such as **feminist** and **lesbian and gay theology** has been enormous. Prominent liberation theologians include Leonardo Boff, Enrique Dussel, Gustavo Gutiérrez, Jon Sobrino, María Clara Bingemer and Ivone Gebara.

LUST Disordered **desire** which seeks to possess another person against their will — the antithesis to **mutuality**.

MAGISTERIUM Usually used in a Roman Catholic context to refer to the teaching authority of the Church which belongs to the Pope, bishops and theologians.

MASTURBATION Self-manipulation of the sexual organs for sexual pleasure and satisfaction. Although for a long time condemned by all Churches, it is now accepted as a normal part of sexual development, even to some extent by the Roman Catholic Church.

METAPHOR A word or phrase applied to another object with the intention of drawing out a truth at least partially through the inappropriateness of the comparison. To say that 'God is mother' or the world is 'God's body' are examples of metaphors used in theology. Since no human descriptions of God are going to be adequate we have to adopt metaphorical language to talk about God. The danger lies in forgetting that we are dealing with metaphors and not literal fact.

MONISM The extreme opposite of **dualism**, monism is the belief that the body is of one substance, i.e., matter, and that all human experience can be explained in terms of materiality.

MORALITY Concern with whether actions are right or wrong. Moral reflection is usually based upon a distinctive set of **ethical** principles.

MUJERISTA THEOLOGY Theological reflection by Hispanic women. Prominent Mujerista theologians include Ada María Isasi-Díaz.

MUTUALITY A way of loving in which, through the sharing of power, each person involved is able to flourish. Mutuality is never automatic but has to be worked towards and negotiated. **Feminist theologians** believe that mutuality is right relationship and that in it we experience the nature and love of God most clearly.

NATURAL LAW The theory that there is a moral order existing independently of individuals which is discovered through reason. Problems with natural law theory include a failure amongst its advocates to agree on its contents, the requirement of obedience which denies moral **automomy** and a failure to appreciate the way in which human beings construct concepts of the 'natural'.

NEW AGE A term applied to a loose movement which arose in the 1980s and which is characterized by a focus upon the spiritual, particularly 'old' nature spiritualities, living in harmony with the earth, and a recovery of lost spiritual arts and practices. It is often extremely **dualistic**.

OBJECTIFICATION The reduction of a person to the status of an 'it' or body or part of a body to be used for one's own pleasure or gain. The absence of real relationship and **mutuality**.

OBJECTIVE MORALITY Claims to be based upon a system of morality which exists independently of human beings.

ONTOLOGY Concerned with the nature of being.

PAROUSIA The second coming of Christ.

PATRIARCHY A term used to describe the multiple structures, beliefs and practices which ensure that men exercise power over women.

PHALLOCENTRISM Another word for **androcentrism** but which draws attention to the focus in public discourse upon the male sexual organ.

POLYGAMY The practice of having more than one wife or husband at a time, the opposite of monogamy.

PROPERTY One of the base principles of Old Testament **ethics**. A male head of household was thought to own his wife, children and slaves — any attack upon them was an attack upon his property. Thought by many New Testament scholars to have been a principle overturned by Jesus.

PURITY One of the base principles of Old Testament **ethics** particularly in the priestly tradition. Israel was believed to be called to be a holy people, a people set apart from others, and therefore had to manifest in its internal life and organization a particular purity or wholeness. Cross-dressing and **homosexuality** are among the sexual practices condemned in the **Holiness Code** for violating this purity because they subverted the 'norm'.

REFORMED TRADITION A body of tradition which flows from the churches created by the Reformation.

REVELATION God's unveiling or self-disclosure to humanity through Christ, scripture, creation, events and persons.

SACRAMENT A sacrament is a visible (usually material) sign of the invisible presence of the divine. To say that something is sacramental is to say that it is a sign and bearer of God's loving, saving presence.

SENSUS FIDELIUM The 'sense of the faithful', i.e., the actual belief of the body of the Church which is regarded as having theological authority by the Roman Catholic Church.

SERMON ON THE MOUNT Jesus' teaching in Matthew 5 – 7.

SEX The term refers to two things the biological differences between men and women and sexual activity. What constitutes a sexual 'act' is a matter of some debate once the focus moves off the genitals and on to relationships.

SEXUALITY A term often used to refer to a person's sexual orientation, but which can also be used to describe the source and drive towards bodily relationality.

SEXUAL ORIENTATION A term coined in the 1970s as a value-neutral alternative to 'sexual deviation' or 'perversion' to refer to an individual's sexual and affectional preferences. There are widely believed to be three possible sexual orientations **heterosexual**, **homosexual** and **bisexual**. The term 'orientation' was adopted to acknowledge the fact that the strict binary divide between homo-sexuality and heterosexuality does not in fact correspond to many people's experience of their own **sexuality**.

SITUATION ETHICS Brought to prominence by Joseph Fletcher in the 1960s, situation ethics claims that for a Christian there is only one rule, the rule of love, and love cannot be legislated for in advance, but can only be exercised in a specific context. Although popular in the 1960s, situation ethics has since fallen out of favour because of its individualism.

SOCIAL CONSTRUCTIONISM A theory, particularly associated with lesbian and gay and feminist studies, which claims that gender and sexual difference are not innate but are constructed by society, which reads meaning into biological and behavioural difference. Different societies in different historical periods will invent different meanings. For example, the gay man and lesbian woman are creations of late-nineteenth-century medicine and it is anachronistic to look back in history and claim that men and women who demonstrated erotic attraction to members of the same-sex were 'gay', for that is to impose upon them an understanding of sexuality and sexual orientation which they simply would not have recognized.

SOCIALIZATION The process by which an individual conforms, often unconsciously, to society's values, through a system of rewards and punishments.

SPIRITUALITY The practice of love of God and neighbour in the Christian faith. Therefore intrinsically linked to our **sexuality** although, under the influence of **dualism**, sexuality and spirituality have been perceived to be conflicting opposites.

STOICISM Ancient Greek philosophy which maintained that all branches of learning exist for the purpose of **ethics**, for working out how to live. God, who is immanent in creation, has ordered all things. Human freedom lies in the choice to assent to or dissent from the law of nature which God has created. **Virtue** lies in assent, which does not come naturally but has to be learnt through practice. Stoics were thoroughly suspicious of emotion for it clouded the judgement of the will. The wise person was, therefore, non-emotional.

STRUCTURAL SIN A concept developed to acknowledge the fact that sin is not simply a matter of individual disobedience of God but that sin can be built into the very structures around us, in which we are born and brought up. For example, **patriarchal** and **homophobic** attitudes and assumptions are built into the theology and practices of the Christian Church.

SUBJECTIVE MORALITY Gives value to individual experience and interpretation of it.

SYNOPTIC GOSPELS The gospels of Mark, Matthew and Luke, so-called because they share much material and can be laid out in parallel columns and compared. John's gospel is very different from the other three canonical gospels in its language, imagery, chronology and theology.

TELEOLOGICAL Emphasizes the end or purpose of acts or existence as a whole.

THOMISM A form of theology based upon the teaching of Thomas Aquinas.

TRANSSEXUALITY Transsexual people usually believe that they have been born in the body of the wrong **sex**. The sex that they 'feel' does not correspond to the sex of their body. They may then choose to live as a member of the sex they feel they are and/or to seek a sex-change operation which remodels their bodies according to the pattern of the sex they wish to be.

TRANSVESTISM Also known as 'cross-dressing'. Transvestites are people of all **sexual orientations** who enjoy wearing the clothes which society has decided 'belong' to the opposite **sex** to their own.

UNIVERSALS Concepts such as human nature, the will and free-dom which are used in some branches of **ethics** and which are believed to be shared by all human beings.

VIRTUE A quality of character through the exercise of which moral good results.

WOMANIST THEOLOGY Theological reflection by black feminist women. Prominent womanist theologians include Dolores S. Williams.

BIBLIOGRAPHY

P. Allen, *The Concept of Woman: The Aristotelian Revolution 750 BC–AD 1250* (Montreal: Eden, 1985).

Jeff Astley and Leslie Francis (eds), *Christian Perspectives on Faith Development* (Leominster: Gracewing/Fowler Wright, 1992).

— *Christian Theology and Religious Education: Connections and Contradictions* (London: SPCK, 1996).

Margaret Atwood, *The Handmaid's Tale* (London and New York: Virago and Ballantine Books, 1987).

Augustine, *City of God*, edited by David Knowles (Harmondsworth: Penguin Books, 1972).

— *Confessions*, translated and with an introduction and notes by Henry Chadwick (Oxford: Oxford University Press, 1991).

Derrick Sherwin Bailey, *The Mystery of Love and Marriage: A Study in the Theology of Sexual Relation* (London: SCM Press, 1952).

— *The Man–Woman Relation in Christian Thought* (London: Longmans, 1959).

A. Baker and S. Duncan, 'Child sexual abuse: a study of prevalence in Great Britain', *Child Abuse and Neglect*, **9** (1985).

Ian Barbour, *Religion in an Age of Science* (London: SCM Press, 1990).

Karl Barth, *Church Dogmatics* (Edinburgh: T. & T. Clark, 1961), Part 3, Vol. 4.

Stephen C. Barton, 'Is the Bible good news for human sexuality? reflections on method in biblical interpretation', in Adrian Thatcher and Elizabeth Stuart (eds), *Christian Perspectives on Sexuality and Gender* (Leominster: Gracewing/Grand Rapids, MI: Eerdmans, 1996), p. 5.

Edward Batchelor, Jr, *Homosexuality and Ethics* (New York: Pilgrim Press, 1980).

Zygmunt Bauman, *Postmodern Ethics* (Oxford: Blackwell, 1993).

Seyla Benhabib, *Situating the Self: Gender, Community and Postmodernism in Contemporary Ethics* (Cambridge: Polity Press, 1992).

David Biale, *Eros and the Jews: From Biblical Israel to Contemporary America* (New York: Basic Books, 1992).

Robert Bly, *Iron John* (Longmead: Element, 1991).

Board of Social Responsibility of the Church of England, *An Honourable Estate* [GS 801] (London: Church House Publishing, 1988).

— *Abortion and the Church: What Are the Issues?* [GS Misc 408] (London: Church House Publishing, 1993).

The Board of Social Responsibility of the Church of Scotland, *Report on Human Sexuality* (Edinburgh: Church of Scotland, 1994).

John Boswell, *The Marriage of Likeness* (London: HarperCollins, 1995), also published as *Same-sex Unions in Premodern Europe* (New York: Villiard Books, 1994).

Gerd Bratenberg, *What Comes Naturally* (London: The Women's Press, 1987).

Athalya Brenner, *A Feminist Companion to the Song of Songs* (Sheffield: Sheffield Academic Press, 1993).

Rita Nakashima Brock, *Journeys by Heart: A Christology of Erotic Power* (New York: Crossroad, 1991).

Bernadette J. Brooter, *Love Between Women: Early Christian Responses to Female Homoeroticism* (Chicago: University of Chicago Press, 1996).

Joanne Carlson Brown and Carole R. Bohn (eds), *Christianity, Patriarchy, and Abuse* (Cleveland, Ohio: The Pilgrim Press, 1989).

Peter Brown, *The Body and Society: Men, Women and Sexual Renunciation in Early Christianity* (London and Boston: Faber & Faber and Columbia University Press, 1988).

Raymond E. Brown, SS, Joseph A. Fitzmyer, SJ, and Roland E. Murphy, O.Carm., *The New Jerome Biblical Commentary* (London: Geoffrey Chapman, 1991).

Lisa Sowle Cahill, *Between the Sexes: Foundations for a Christian Ethics of Sexuality* (Philadelphia: Fortress Press, 1985).

— and Dietmar Mieth, *The Family, Concilium* (1995/4).

Hilary Cashman, *Christianity and Child Sexual Abuse* (London: SPCK, 1993).

Catechism of the Catholic Church (London: Geoffrey Chapman, 1994).

Henry Chadwick, *Augustine* (Oxford: Oxford University Press, 1986).

Church of Scotland Panel on Doctrine, *Report on the Theology of Marriage* (1994).

Gillian Cloke, *This Female Man of God: Women and Spiritual Power in the Patristic Age AD 350–450* (London: Routledge, 1995).

Gary David Comstock, *Gay Theology without Apology* (Cleveland: The Pilgrim Press, 1993).

Congregation for the Doctrine of the Faith, *Letter to the Bishops of the Catholic Church on the Pastoral Care of Homosexual Persons* (London: Catholic Truth Society, 1986).

Pamela Cooper-White, *The Cry of Tamar: Violence against Women and the Church's Response* (Minneapolis: Fortress Press, 1995).

William Countryman, *Dirt, Greed and Sex: Sexual Ethics in the New Testament and Their Implications for Today* (London: SCM Press, 1989).

Mary Daly, *Gyn/Ecology* (London: The Women's Press, 1979).

— *Pure Lust: Elemental Feminist Philosophy* (Boston: Beacon Press; 1984).

Philip R. Davies, 'Ethics and the Old Testament' in John W. Rogerson, Margaret Davies and M. Daniel Carroll, *The Bible in Ethics: The Second Sheffield Colloquium* (Sheffield: Sheffield Academic Press, 1995).

Norman Dennis and George Erdos, *Families without Fatherhood* (London: IEA Health and Welfare Unit, 1993).

Division for Church in Society, Department of Studies of the Evangelical Lutheran Church in America, *The Church and Human Sexuality: A Lutheran Perspective* (Minneapolis: ELCA Distribution Service, 1993), first draft.

The Doctrine Commission of the Church of England, *The Mystery of Salvation* (London: Church House Publishing, 1995).

Jonathan Dollimore, *Sexual Dissidence: Augustine to Wilde, Freud to Foucault* (Oxford: Clarendon Press, 1991).

Jack Dominian, *Passionate and Compassionate Love: A Vision for Christian Marriage* (London: Darton, Longman & Todd, 1991).

Mary Douglas, *Purity and Danger: An Analysis of Concepts of Pollution and Taboo* (London: Routledge and Kegan Paul, 1966).

Susan Dowell, *They Two Shall Be One: Monogamy in History and Religion* (London: Collins Flame, 1990).

F. Driver, *Christ in a Changing World: Toward an Ethical Christology* (New York: Crossroad, 1981).

Susan Durber, *As Man and Woman Made: Theological Reflections on Marriage* (London: United Reformed Church, 1994).

Nancy L. Eiesland, *The Disabled God: Toward a Liberatory Theology of Disability* (Nashville: Abingdon Press, 1994).

Encyclical Letter Veritatis Splendor Addressed by the Supreme Pontiff Pope John Paul II to All the Bishops of the Catholic Church Regarding Certain Fundamental Questions of the Church's Moral Teaching (London: Catholic Truth Society, 1993).

Jacqueline Field-Bibb, *Women towards Priesthood: Ministerial Politics and Feminist Praxis* (Cambridge: Cambridge University Press, 1991).

Elisabeth Schüssler Fiorenza, *In Memory of Her: A Feminist Theological Reconstruction of Christian Origins* (London and New York: SCM and Crossroad, 1983).

— *But SHE Said: Feminist Practices of Biblical Interpretation* (Boston: Beacon Press, 1992).

— *Searching the Scriptures: A Feminist Commentary* (London and New York: SCM and Crossroad, 1994).

Joseph Fletcher, *Situation Ethics: The New Morality* (London: SCM Press, 1966).

— *Moral Responsibility* (London: SCM Press, 1967).

Marie Fortune, *Is Nothing Sacred? When Sex Invades the Pastoral Relationship* (San Francisco: Harper & Row, 1989).

Michel Foucault, *The History of Sexuality: Volume 1, An Introduction* (Harmondsworth: Penguin Books, 1981).

Nancy Friday, *My Secret Garden: Women's Sexual Fantasies* (London: Quartet, 1976).

— *Women on Top* (London: Hutchinson, 1991).

Sue George, *Women and Bisexuality* (London: Scarlet Press, 1993).

Anthony Giddens, *The Transformation of Intimacy: Sexuality, Love and Eroticism in Modern Societies* (Cambridge: Polity Press, 1992).

Sean Gill, 'Odd but not queer: English liberal Protestant theologies of human sexuality and the gay paradigm', *Theology and Sexuality*, no. 3 (September 1995).

Carol Gilligan, *In a Different Voice? Psychological Theory and Women's Development* (Cambridge, MA: Harvard University Press, 1982).

John R. Gillis, *For Better, for Worse: British Marriages, 1600 to the Present* (New York: Oxford University Press, 1985).

Philip Goodchild, 'Christian ethics in the postmodern condition', *Studies in Christian Ethics*, 8(1) (1995).

Robert Goss, *Jesus Acted Up: A Gay and Lesbian Manifesto* (San Francisco: Harper, 1993).

Elaine Graham, 'Towards a theology of desire', *Theology and Sexuality*, 1 (September 1994).

— *Making the Difference: Gender, Personhood and Theology* (London: Mowbray, 1995).

Vigen Guroian, *Ethics after Christendom: Toward an Ecclesial Christian Ethic* (Grand Rapids, Michigan: Eerdmans, 1994).

James M. Gustafson, 'Nature: its status in theological ethics', *Logos*, **3** (1982).

Julian Hafner, *The End of Marriage: Why Monogamy Isn't Working* (London: Century, 1993).

John Hammond, David Hay *et al.*, *New Methods in R.E. Teaching: An Experiential Approach* (Harlow: Oliver & Boyd, 1990).

Tracy Hansen, 'My name is Tamar', *Theology*, **95** (767) (Sept./Oct. 1992).

Bernard Häring, *My Witness for the Church* (New York, 1992).

A. E. Harvey, *Promise or Pretence? A Christian's Guide to Sexual Morals* (London: SCM Press, 1994).

Stanley Hauerwas, *A Community of Character: Toward a Constructive Christian Social Ethic* (Notre Dame: University of Notre Dame Press, 1981).

— *The Peaceable Kingdom: A Primer in Christian Ethics* (Notre Dame: University of Notre Dame Press, 1983; London: SCM Press, 1984).

Carter Heyward, *Touching Our Strength: The Erotic as Power and the Love of God* (San Francisco: Harper and Row, 1989).

Homosexuality Working Party, *Homosexuality: A Christian View* (London: United Reformed Church, n.d.).

House of Bishops of the General Synod of the Church of England, *Issues in Human Sexuality* (London: Church House Publishing, 1991).

W. D. Hudson, *Modern Moral Philosophy* (London and Basingstoke: Macmillan, 2nd edition 1983).

Mary Hunt, *Fierce Tenderness: A Feminist Theology of Friendship* (New York: Crossroad, 1991).

Linda Hurcombe (ed.), *Sex and God: Some Varieties of Women's Religious Experience* (New York and London: Routledge & Kegan Paul, 1987).

Luce Irigaray, *Marine Lover of Friedrich Nietzsche* (New York: Columbia University Press, 1991).

Lisa Isherwood and Dorothea McEwan, *Introducing Feminist Theology* (Sheffield: Sheffield Academic Press, 1993).

Catherine Itzin, *Pornography: Women, Violence and Civil Liberties* (Oxford: Oxford University Press, 1993).

Grace M. Jantzen, 'Feminism and flourishing: gender and metaphor in feminist theology', *Feminist Theology*, **10** (September 1995).

Elizabeth A. Johnson, *She Who Is: The Mystery of God in Feminist Theological Discourse* (New York: Crossroad, 1993).

Michael Keeling, *The Mandate of Heaven: The Divine Command and the Natural Order* (Edinburgh: T. & T. Clark, 1996).

Morton Kelsey and Barbara Kelsey, *Sacrament of Sexuality: The Spirituality and Psychology of Sex* (Warwick: Amity House, 1986).

Margaret Kennedy, 'Christianity: help or hindrance for the abused child or adult?', *Child Abuse Review*, **5**(3) (Winter 1991–2).

Fergus Kerr, *Theology after Wittgenstein* (Oxford: Blackwell, 1986).

Ursula King, *Feminist Theology from the Third World: A Reader* (London and Maryknoll: SPCK and Orbis, 1994).

Alfred Kinsey *et al.*, *Sexual Behaviour in the Human Male* (Philadelphia: W. B. Saunders, 1948).

Alice L. Laffey, *Wives, Harlots and Concubines: The Old Testament in Feminist Perspective* (London: SPCK, 1990).

Michael G. Lawler, *Marriage and Sacrament: A Theology of Christian Marriage* (Collegeville, Minnesota: Liturgical Press, 1993).

Kenneth Leech, *The Eye of the Storm: Spiritual Resources for the Pursuit of Justice* (London: Darton, Longman & Todd, 1992).

Graham Leonard, Ian MacKenzie and Peter Toon, *Let God Be God* (London: Darton, Longman Todd, 1989).

Gerda Lerner, *The Creation of Patriarchy* (Oxford: Oxford University Press, 1987).

Letter of Pope John Paul II to Women (London: Catholic Truth Society, 1995).

C. S. Lewis, *The Four Loves* (London: Collins, 1960).

Ann Loades, *Feminist Theology: A Reader* (London: SPCK, 1990).

Richard McBrien, *Catholicism* (London: Geoffrey Chapman, 3rd edn, 1994).

Timothy McDermott, *Summa Theologiae: A Concise Translation* (London: Methuen, 1991).

J. I. H. McDonald, *Biblical Interpretation and Christian Ethics* (Cambridge: Cambridge University Press, 1993).

Sallie McFague, *Models of God: Theology for an Ecological, Nuclear Age* (London: SCM Press, 1987).

Alasdair McIntyre, *After Virtue: A Study in Moral Theory* (London: Duckworth, 1981).

James P. Mackey, *Power and Christian Ethics* (Cambridge: Cambridge University Press, 1994).

Marriage and the Church's Task (The Lichfield Report) (London: Church Information Office, 1978).

Emily Martin, *The Woman in the Body* (Milton Keynes: Open University Press, 1989).

J. Gordon Melton, *The Churches Speak on AIDS* (Detroit: Gale Research Inc., 1989).

The Methodist Church, *Report of Commission on Human Sexuality* (Peterborough: Methodist Publishing House, 1990).

Bruce M. Metzger and Michael D. Coogan (eds), *The Oxford Companion to the Bible* (New York: Oxford University Press, 1993).

John Milbank, *Theology and Social Theory: Beyond Secular Reason* (Oxford: Blackwell, 1990).

Giles Milhaven, 'A medieval lesson on bodily knowing: women's experience and men's thought', *Journal of the American Academy of Religion*, **57** (2) (Summer 1989).

Elizabeth Moberly, *Homosexuality: A New Christian Ethic* (Cambridge: James Clarke, 1983).

Virginia Ramey Mollenkott, *Sensuous Spirituality: Out from Fundamentalism* (New York: Crossroad, 1993).

Elisabeth Moltmann-Wendel, *I Am My Body: New Ways of Embodiment* (London: SCM Press, 1994).

Gareth Moore, *The Body in Context: Sex and Catholicism* (London: SCM Press, 1992).

Richard Mouw, *The God Who Commands* (Notre Dame: University of Notre Dame Press, 1990).

James A. Nash, *Loving Nature: Ecological Integrity and Christian Responsibility* (Nashville: Abingdon Press/Churches' Center for Theology and Public Policy, 1991).

National Conference of Catholic Bishops (USA), *To Live in Christ Jesus* (Washington, DC: United States Catholic Conference, 1976).

James B. Nelson, *Embodiment: An Approach to Sexuality and Christian Theology* (Minneapolis: Augsburg Publishing House, 1978).

— *The Intimate Connection: Male Sexuality, Masculine Spirituality* (London: SPCK, 1992).

— *Body Theology* (Louisville: Westminster/John Knox Press, 1992).

— 'On doing body theology', *Theology and Sexuality*, no. 2 (March 1995).

— and Sandra P. Longfellow, *Sexuality and the Sacred: Sources for Theological Reflection* (London: Mowbray, 1994).

Ronald Nicholson, *God in AIDS: A Theological Enquiry* (London: SCM Press, 1996).

Friedrich Nietzsche, *Twilight of the Idols* (Baltimore: Penguin Books, 1968).

The Office of the General Assembly, The Presbyterian Church (USA), *Pornography: Far from the Song of Songs* (Louisville, Kentucky, 1988).

Helen Oppenheimer, *Marriage* (London: Mowbray, 1990).

Susan Parsons, 'Feminist reflections on embodiment and sexuality', *Studies in Christian Ethics*, **4**(2) (1991).

— 'Feminist ethics after modernity', *Studies in Christian Ethics* **8**(1) (1995).

Arthur Peacocke, *Theology for a Scientific Age* (London: SCM Press, 1993).

D. Z. Phillips, *Religion without Explanation* (Oxford: Blackwell, 1976).

Ken Plummer, *Modern Homosexualities: Fragments of Lesbian and Gay Experience* (London: Routledge, 1992).

Jean Porter, *The Recovery of Virtue: The Relevance of Aquinas for Christian Ethics* (London: SPCK, 1994).

— *Moral Action and Christian Ethics* (Cambridge: Cambridge University Press, 1995).

Rosemary Radford Ruether, *Gaia and God: An Ecofeminist Theology of Earth Healing* (London: SCM Press, 1993).

Uta Ranke-Heinemann, *Eunuchs for the Kingdom of Heaven: The Catholic Church and Sexuality* (Harmondsworth: Penguin Books, 1991).

D. L. Rhode, *Theoretical Perspectives on Sexual Difference* (New Haven: Yale University Press, 1990).

Alan Richardson and John Bowden (eds), *A New Dictionary of Christian Theology* (London: SCM Press, 1983).

John A. T. Robinson, *The Body: A Study in Pauline Theology* (London: SCM, 1952).

— *Honest to God* (London: SCM Press, 1963).

— *Christian Freedom in a Permissive Society* (London: SCM Press, 1970).

Kathy Rudy, ' "Where two or more are gathered": using gay communities as a model for Christian sexual ethics', *Theology and Sexuality*, **4** (March 1996).

Peter Rutter, *Sex in the Forbidden Zone: When Men in Power – Therapists, Doctors, Clergy, Teachers, and Others – Betray Women's Trust* (Los Angeles: Jeremy Tarcher, 1989).

Gilbert Ryle, *The Concept of Mind* (Harmondsworth: Peregrine Books, 1963; 1st edn, 1949).

Frederick W. Schmidt, 'Beyond a biblicistic feminism: hermeneutics, women and the Church', *Feminist Theology*, 11 (January 1996).

Steven Seidman, *Embattled Eros: Sexual Politics and Ethics in Contemporary America* (New York and London: Routledge, 1992).

Jeffrey S. Siker, *Homosexuality in the Church: Both Sides of the Debate* (Louisville: Westminster/John Knox Press, 1994).

Ninian Smart and Steven Konstantine, *Christian Systematic Theology in a World Context* (London: Marshall Pickering, 1991).

D. Moody Smith, *The Theology of the Gospel of St John* (Cambridge: Cambridge University Press, 1995).

Robin Smith, *Living in Covenant with God and One Another* (Geneva: World Council of Churches, 1990).

Social Welfare Commission of the Catholic Bishops of England and Wales, *An Introduction to the Pastoral Care of Homosexual People* (London, 1979).

Society of Friends, *This We Can Say: Talking Honestly about Sex* (Reading: Nine Friends Press, 1995).

Dorothee Sölle, *Beyond Mere Obedience: Reflections on a Christian Ethics for the Future* (Minneapolis: Augsburg Publishers, 1970).

Susan Sontag, *AIDS and Its Metaphors* (New York: Farrar, Strauss and Giroux, 1989).

John Shelby Spong, *Living in Sin: A Bishop Rethinks Human Sexuality* (San Francisco: Harper & Row, 1988).

Edward Stein, *Forms of Desire: Sexual Orientation and the Social Constructionist Controversy* (Routledge: New York and London, 1990).

Elizabeth Stuart, *Just Good Friends: Towards a Lesbian and Gay Theology of Relationships* (London: Mowbray, 1995).

Cristina Sumner, *Reconsider: A Response to Issues in Human Sexuality and a Plea to the Church to Deal Boldly with Sexual Ethics* (London: Lesbian and Gay Christian Movement, 1995).

Adrian Thatcher, 'A critique of inwardness in religious education', *British Journal of Religious Education* 14(1) (Autumn 1991).

— 'Spirituality without inwardness', *Scottish Journal of Theology* 46(2) (1993).

— *Liberating Sex: A Christian Sexual Theology* (London: SPCK, 1993).

— and Elizabeth Stuart, *Christian Perspectives on Sexuality and Gender* (Leominster: Gracewing/Fowler Wright, 1996).

— 'Singles and families', *Theology and Sexuality*, 3 (March 1996).

A. Thiselton, *New Horizons in Hermeneutics* (London: HarperCollins, 1992).

Joan H. Timmerman, *Sexuality and Spiritual Growth* (New York: Crossroad, 1993).

Phillip Tovey, 'Matrimony: an excellent mystery', *Theology* **97** (777) (May/June 1994).

Phyllis Trible, *God and the Rhetoric of Sexuality* (Philadelphia: Fortress Press, 1978).

Michael Vasey, *Strangers and Friends: A New Exploration of Homosexuality and the Bible* (London: Hodder and Stoughton, 1995).

Lenore Walker, *The Battered Woman* (New York: Harper Colophon, 1979).

Michael J. Walsh, *Commentary on the Catechism of the Catholic Church* (London: Geoffrey Chapman, 1994).

Heather Walton, 'Theology of desire', *Theology and Sexuality* **1** (September 1994).

Alison Webster, *Found Wanting: Women, Christianity and Sexuality* (London: Cassell, 1995).

Kay Wellings *et al.*, *Sexual Behaviour in Britain* (Harmondsworth: Penguin Books, 1994).

Evelyn Eaton Whitehead and James D. Whitehead, *A Sense of Sexuality: Christian Love and Intimacy* (New York: Crossroad, 1994).

John Wilkins, *Understanding Veritatis Splendor* (London: SPCK, 1994).

Working Party of the Board of Social Responsibility of the Church of England, *Something to Celebrate: Valuing Families in Church and Society* (London: Church House Publishing, 1995).

James Woodward, *Embracing the Chaos: Theological Responses to AIDS* (London: SPCK, 1990).

Charles Yeats, *Veritatis Splendor: A Response* (Norwich: Canterbury Press, 1994.

INDEX

INDEX OF BIBLICAL CITATIONS